The Craft of Psychodynamic Psychotherapy

The Craft of Psychodynamic Psychotherapy

ANGELICA KANER AND ERNST PRELINGER

JASON ARONSON
Lanham • Boulder • New York • Toronto • Plymouth, UK

Published in the United States of America
by Jason Aronson
An imprint of Rowman & Littlefield Publishers, Inc.

A wholly owned subsidiary of
The Rowman & Littlefield Publishing Group, Inc.
4501 Forbes Boulevard, Suite 200, Lanham, Maryland 20706
www.rowmanlittlefield.com

Estover Road
Plymouth PL6 7PY
United Kingdom

British Library Cataloguing in Publication Information Available

The hardback edition of this book was previously catalogued by the Library of Congress
as follows:

Kaner, Angelica
    The craft of psychodynamic pyschotherapy / by Angelica Kaner and Ernst Prelinger.
    p. cm.
    Includes bibliographical references and index.
    1. Pyschodynamic psychotherapy—Philosophy. 2. Pyschodynamic psychotherapy—
Methodology.   I. Prelinger, Ernst. II. Title.
RC489.P72K6 2003
616.89'14—dc21   2006005308

    ISBN-13: 978-0-7657-0372-9 (cloth : alk. paper)
    ISBN-10: 0-7657-0372-6 (cloth : alk. paper)
    ISBN-13: 978-0-7657-0582-2 (pbk. : alk. paper)
    ISBN-10: 0-7657-0582-6 (pbk. : alk. paper)

Printed in the United States of America

Contents

Preface

The Spirit of This Book

Loren Eiseley's essay, "The Snout," is a meditation upon the evolution of man. An anthropologist and naturalist, Eiseley writes of nature still busy with experiments, still dynamic, and not through or satisfied because a Devonian fish, what he calls the Snout, managed to survive oxygen-starved pools "to end as a two-legged character with a straw hat." He goes on to say that there are things still brewing in the oceanic vat. There in the ooze, unnoticed in swamps and along the tide flats, fish climb trees and "ogle uneasy naturalists who try unsuccessfully to chase them back to the water." He says that it pays to know this.

From a different tradition Shunryu Suzuki speaks of beginner's mind. The mind that is free of learned, perhaps overlearned, routines: open, vast, capable of seeing things afresh and new. It is an attitude of doubt, of receptivity, of possibility, "always ready for anything." Suzuki says that with beginner's mind we look out over limitless meaning and "can really learn something." Our challenge is not to lose beginner's mind.

As with the evolution of the struggling fish there are no preset paths or guarantees in the psychotherapeutic journey. We may have a well-reasoned hypothesis or just a hunch, but we really don't know what will come ashore. The influences on human psychological development and adaptation are as manifold and wide ranging as those on the physical. What happens along the way is often better grasped in retrospect, in case conferences, individual supervision, or unexpectedly as one walks alone in the woods or down the produce aisle. As much as we are taught, as much as we employ theory, any theory, we must be sure to remain gracious hosts to mystery, our inevitable companion.

It is with this spirit of openness so eloquently expressed by Suzuki and Eiseley that we present this book. In attempting to put forth a somewhat coherent view of psychotherapy we have been mindful not to coerce parts into place, thereby falling into the seductive arms of intellectual closure. The process of writing has asked us to reckon with pieces that don't fit together quite as neatly as we would like, with questions for which we don't have easy answers. And, of course, what we have left out, by design or ignorance, is far greater than what we have included. But if the joints of this work are not seamlessly linked, neither, we like to think, are they arthritic or fixed. After all, the survival of psychotherapy, both the practice and the writing of it, requires of the psychotherapist a flexibility of thought and feeling. It requires an openness to experience, as well as a willingness to face the uneasy challenges of puzzlement and uncertainty without having to chase them back to the water.

—A. K. and E. P., New Haven, Connecticut

Acknowledgments

First of all we would like to express our gratitude to the Division of University Mental Hygiene at the Yale University Health Services, and especially to Lorraine Siggins, its director. We learned a great deal there from our colleagues, students, and patients and had the good luck to teach in the seminar Theory of Psychotherapy. We also derived much benefit from the reading and helpful suggestions of Rosemary Balsam, Michael Groner, Naomi Kaner, Sidney Phillips, Stanley Possick, Jane Prelinger, Rosemarie Prelinger, and Joan Wexler. Finally, we wish to extend our heartfelt appreciation to Olga Kaner and the late Nathan Kaner for their unwavering encouragement and support.

Introduction

One-to-one psychotherapy. Essentially two people come together in a room and talk. One of them has come to the other because of troubles in his life, has come because he hopes that the other may help him ease his conflicts, confusion, and suffering. In some instances they talk for but an hour or two, perhaps more; in other instances the hours extend over many years. They agree to talk because one of them has reached an impasse and cannot continue as he has been doing. The ways in which he has dealt with the various challenges life has presented him are no longer useful. He must find other ways to go on.

It is the *way* they talk that is key. Generally speaking, the manner of this conversation will depend on the type of psychotherapy being practiced. And there are many. Indeed, the word *psychotherapy* is now a fairly generic term covering a wide range of activities. Interpersonal, cognitive, rational-emotive, memory recovering, short-term, psychodynamic, and other therapies, as well as classical psychoanalysis, compete for membership in this category. Professionals from varied backgrounds and courses of training who seriously practice these different disciplines all have a common and honorable purpose: to help people who are hampered by difficulties in their lives and to assist them in finding better ways. Psychotherapy is fundamentally about helping a person go on.

1

We intend this work to be an introduction to the practice of psychodynamic psychotherapy and hope to provide students an orientation to a craft of great richness and interest. It is a craft that offers a kind of adventure in intimacy the like of which many may never have had. It presents a means to help people address mysteries in their inner lives and ways of being with others and the world at large. We approach psychotherapy as a very special event in the life of a person, an irreplicable journey through the variegated landscape of an *inner world*, the heights of its emotional peaks, the depths of its valleys, the meandering and branching of its thematic rivers.

In this book we try to describe in a quite basic manner the defining elements of the accumulated working knowledge of psychodynamic psychotherapy. We do not, however, aim to offer a new model or doctrine for it. We think that the elements presented distinguish the "talking cure" from other kinds of conversations and create for it the potential to affect people's lives for the better.

This book was born of many kinds of interactions. It is the product of experiences with our own patients and from conferences and discussions with colleagues as well as with trainees at Yale. The opportunity to work with trainees both in individual supervision and in a seminar, Theory of Psychotherapy, at the Yale University Health Services has been our special good fortune. A multidisciplinary student group, including practicum students, pre- and postdoctoral psychology fellows, graduate social work fellows, and psychiatry residents, offers varying perspectives from different kinds and levels of training. Particularly, it provided us a chance to listen and talk to those who are still close to the beginning of their learning, for whom psychotherapeutic practice is still new and confusing, scary, at times disappointing, but also, at times, beginning to be satisfying and enjoyable.

Any new book about psychotherapy ought to contribute something useful to the already available and still growing literature, be it observations, therapeutic experiences, discoveries, or understandings of the psychotherapeutic enterprise, new clinical tips, or further ways of organizing and presenting existing knowledge. Our classroom and supervisory contacts gave us something of a feel for what, we hope, might help our students to find their bearings. The trainees would struggle with concepts and raise questions over and again. Their varied expressions, progress, "aha" experiences, criticisms, continued confusions, and frustrations highlighted for us what was or was not experienced as clinically useful.

While this book is intended to orient beginning students, it may also be helpful to practitioners with some experience in psychotherapeutic work. Increasing mastery or competence in practicing the therapeutic craft is not accomplished in a linear or formulaic way. It cannot be learned by simply reading a straight sequence of books or attending a series of lectures. Each patient and therapist pair creates a singular interpersonal universe, requiring the therapist to apply her accumulated experience in ever original ways. Every course of therapy is different from every other even though some events (marriage, divorce, birth, death, newly found wealth, bankruptcy, migration, promotion, and so on) and themes (trauma, abandonment, rejection, and the like) may make their appearance in each one. These are common to all people's lives including the therapist's. Her way of developing her practice, like that of shaping her own mode of living, is influenced by all kinds of life experiences in an unforeseeable order, for which there is no ready map. They shift her priorities and interests, ask her to revisit the raw pointedness of old questions that, in the thick of life's ongoing demands, may have been left behind too soon. Some of them concern her work: What is psychotherapy? What makes it meaningful to me? What do I say when a patient asks me how therapy works? How long will it take? How does change happen?

At whatever stage you, our reader, may be in your professional development, we hope that this book will stimulate you to identify and formulate your own questions and rework them again and again in the varying lights of time and experience.

Alice . . . peeped into the book her sister was reading, but it had no pictures or conversations in it, "and what is the use of a book," thought Alice, "without pictures or conversations?"

—Lewis Carroll, *Alice's Adventures in Wonderland*

Perhaps the greatest challenge facing us in this endeavor involved bringing to life the happenings encountered in the course of the psychotherapeutic process. Conveying what happens in a clinical hour or series of hours is difficult. The power of psychotherapy lies in the *experience* of psychotherapy: its highly personal meaning; the context shared between two people and built up over time; the relationship, articulated or otherwise; the immediacy of the feelings involved. How often have we tried to tell others of a meaningful moment in our work only to have its importance fall heavily on the floor? Its hot essence turn cold? Evaporate in the telling? Describing psychotherapy, then, whether to a friend or to a larger audience, can be as frustrating as describing a good book or a film or a funny moment. How often have we all, in benign resignation, delivered the line, "I guess you had to have been there"?

So how are we, as writers, to bring you there? Into the clinical hour, into the experience? We hope to do this through storytelling, a genre that seems particularly suited to our task because we conceive of what we are doing as, for one thing, telling a story and as, for another, telling a story of stories.

Stories embed experience within a context. They provide it a setting without which it would remain disconnected and meaningless. Such a setting fuels the told experience with the energy of relevance, something like the way a warm sea fuels a tropical depression. An experience, or as Breuer and Freud put it, an idea "torn from its context and without being led up to" remains incomprehensible. And we might add without narrative or emotional power. It remains but a moment stranded.

So, first, we are telling a story. About psychotherapy. More specifically, it is a story of a process, a *journey*, in which we accompany the psychotherapist from beginning to end. The complexity of the psychotherapeutic process, however, makes it hard to describe. It requires to be looked at simultaneously from two perspectives. From one perspective we recognize that many therapies show certain similarities in their overall pattern of events. Phases appear in a rough sequence, each with its dominant meanings and emphases, although they are not necessarily sharply distinguished from one another. Being aware of such sequences can serve as a general means of orientation to the progress of therapeutic work.

Looking at the psychotherapeutic process in terms of general sequences of events suggests that its nature is linear in some way. But this is not true. From another perspective we appreciate that psychotherapeutic progress is also highly individual, can show itself as a continuous flow of waxing and waning themes, all occurring in various rhythms, a process reminiscent of poetry and certain forms of prose. Themes appear, disappear, some return. Different phenomena, connections, and types of interplay between therapist and patient emerge or recede amidst such flow at different times. Consequently you will recognize the prominence of the nonlinear throughout this book. In fact you will find that, similar to the psychotherapeutic process itself, various ideas or themes recur in different contexts throughout the book, each time adding further to their meaning.

By saying that we are telling a story of stories we are, second, referring to psychodynamic psychotherapy as a process of helping patients tell the stories that make up various versions of their lives. This takes much of the skill and effort we as psychotherapists bring to the clinical hour. We learn to listen carefully to all the different kinds of tales the patient brings and comment on them now and then or more frequently as the situations call. To give examples we have provided a heap of stories in the form of clinical accounts. They are illustrations all drawn from our actual practices. Virtually every session began to bring up useful instances of something or other once we started writing this book. To protect patient privacy we have taken care to omit or disguise identifying information. Also, in the interest of making a point, some of the accounts reflect condensed versions of what patients had in fact said. We elected to use actual case material because while illustrating the text, it can also elicit resonances to our readers' own practical experience and may contribute to an enhanced understanding of their own work.

It is a sentiment common among writers, and rightly intuited by Alice, that effective storytelling is in fact story showing, showing by means of the stimulation of pictures and conversations. Good stories are made of them. They make vivid the context. They breathe life into words and ideas. They stir imagination and feeling and bring one into the experience—the now *felt* and *visualized* experience which, in turn, can pave a connection, build a bridge, or resonate with the world of unconscious processes, themselves imagistic.

So, to this end, we have followed Alice's implicit recommendation that every book include conversations and pictures: conversations by way of clinical dialogue as expressed in clinical accounts; pictures in large part by referring to and quoting various writers who are not themselves clinicians but whose work seems to touch upon important aspects of dynamic psychotherapy. Of these works, C. S. Lewis's children's story, *The Lion, the Witch, and the Wardrobe*, appears particularly relevant and, therefore, requires a brief description. It is a tale of four children, Lucy, Edmund, Susan, and Peter, who are sent to the country house of an old professor in order to escape air raids in London. One dreary morning they come upon an old wardrobe, which leads them into a fantasy world, called Narnia, where their adventures begin. In Narnia they meet up with many characters, prominent among them the majestic Lion called Aslan, and the wicked White Witch. To our reading, Narnia can be understood to be the expression of the robust unconscious dramas alive and well in these children, indeed, in many of us. Besides Lewis, we also quote Loren Eiseley and Virginia Woolf and others because their ideas equally resonate with what we have to say.

Theirs are stories that take us into the realm of fantasy and are allegories of events in the internal world of the writer; they touch upon and move the reader's imagination as well. They also remind us of our humanity, without which, ultimately, the therapist and the craft have no worthwhile foundation.

All types of psychotherapy imply theories of "mind." A person's inner life is "mind." There are many kinds of inner events, experiences, and activities. While such inner events are private and not immediately or easily perceptible to others, we tend to take for granted that "mental" processes are happening "within" all of us all the time whether or not we are aware of them. Inner life also includes psychological work a person does for himself. We will discuss psychological work at some length.

On grounds of different training and experience therapists may have various conceptions of mind, of its importance, of how it develops and changes, of how it "works," and how it may at times "break down." Psychodynamic psychotherapy places particular emphasis on exploring and understanding a person's inner world. Some of this emphasis is also shared by the cognitive and psychoeducational therapies and hypnosis. Still other therapies focus on surface phenomena, that is, on what is immediately and manifestly observable, namely behavior.

Psychodynamic therapy differs from other models, including other mind-oriented models, in several important ways. First of all it relies on *an elaborate and detailed conceptualization of mind.* Mind is not thought of as motivated by any single predominant thought or belief, although at any given time one or another may become particularly relevant and emphasized. It is viewed as full of all kinds of internal contents; these include our images or representations of other people and ourselves, our desires, urges, fears, fantasies, wishes, dislikes, beliefs, hopes, expectations, and more—all in complex relation. Further, mind is seen as *full of activity.* These contents of which we speak can be thought of as currents and *forces that motivate* or push us along. Like wind or ocean currents, these are in *constant motion and interplay,* often in harmony and settled patterns, often also *conflicting,* shifting, and unstable.

The earth doesn't stop spinning; neither, as it were, do we. Ours is a *dynamic* psychology: movement predominates; things change. We also look at any inner happening in context. What preceded it? Led up to it? What is its connection to other internal happenings? Of some of these internal processes a person may be consciously aware. Others take place *unconsciously* but, nonetheless, exert significant sway upon the person's adaptation in general, especially upon his relations with other people. Throughout this book you will notice the recurrence of themes pertaining to movement and change: widening, deepening, unfolding, working through, reworking.

Psychodynamic therapy especially emphasizes the importance of a person's history, of his psychological development over time, and of his understanding of critical events and their consequences in his life. Experience is not thought of as lost as time goes by; mind accumulates, organizes, and continues to exert its influence. The past has clout.

For good reason then psychodynamic therapy pays close attention to the form and quality of the unfolding relationship between patient and therapist. The patient's internal dynamics will affect that relationship, and the therapy itself will reflect particular patterns recurring in his interactions with others. This is what is referred to as the *transference*, and we will have much more to say about it later. The exploration of such emerging patterns and of their history in the patient's life is one of the hallmarks of psychodynamic psychotherapy because the shape taken by that relationship conveys important parts of the patient's psychological story.

Not surprisingly, the way one thinks about mind will influence how a given therapist will approach her work. Those therapies that put the spotlight on overt behavior will concentrate on examining and challenging the patient's current ways of managing his relations with other people and circumstances. Theirs will be an external focus. Psychopharmacological treatment methods aim at palliating disturbing thoughts and emotional reactions by chemical means. Other approaches, such as those based on learning and behavior theory, aim at modifying the patient's conduct by encouraging or discouraging some of his action patterns. Real or symbolic reward or punishment are their essential ingredient. Therapies which focus on conscious mental content such as the psychoeducational and cognitive therapies provide the individual with new, sometimes expanded, perhaps more reasoned, perspectives on and formulations of their experiences and circumstances, and of their meanings. And in the case of hypnosis we find primary emphasis on suggestion. Common to these techniques, which in practice sometimes overlap, is the therapist's manifest activity. That means the therapist's provision and pursuit of some kind of planned agenda of directive influence. Whether as a hypnotist, a behaviorist, or cognitive or psychoeducational therapist, she tries to provide some direction, be it in the form of encouragement, alternate views, information, constraint, or control.

Psychodynamic psychotherapy, in contrast, is designed to encourage the patient's own activity in observing and telling about himself. Conscious of her own ideas and preconceptions and of not unduly imposing them, the dynamic therapist tries to help him give voice to his internal world, to his thinking and feeling and imagination. The therapist strives to stimulate the patient's curiosity, even puzzlement, about himself and asks that he second-guess himself, read between his own lines. She tries to encourage his explorations and his keeping an open mind to where they might lead. In principle nothing is done to or for a patient; rather something is evoked in him; a situation is created which sets in motion a process to be jointly examined and understood. It is assumed that in time by means of such a process the individual can reshape a troublesome internal geography, leading to greater inner comfort and less disruptive, damaging, and painful ways of living. The patient becomes an active participant in the therapy and will be assisted in finding his own unique way by recognizing and pursuing his own intents and purposes instead of feeling driven or compelled.

The importance that psychodynamic psychotherapy attaches to the patient's own internal world, to telling his own story, directs us to yet another fundamental departure from other therapeutic approaches. And this has to do with the idea, to which we alluded earlier, of creating context. As a person begins to tell about himself he can become active in remembering, assembling, and reviewing the various experiences that make up the stories of his life, and, if the therapy is developed and lengthy enough, the various stories that make up the epic of his life. Invariably, however, there are those bits, pieces, and chunks of experience, adrift in conscious and unconscious forms, torn, as Breuer and Freud put it, from their context. The vital links, submerged in one's unawareness, are not recognized. Psychodynamic psychotherapy sets up conditions, which give such links a chance of becoming conscious to the patient, a chance of coming ashore. Because these links emerge from within the patient's own internal waters they have emotional nearness, which innervates, so to speak, the disconnected bits of experience with personal significance and meaning. As his internal activity becomes more animated the patient can in this experiential way come to understand more clearly what drives him in what he does as well as the conflicted and harmonious interplay of forces within. In this manner, in the therapy, in vivo, he is helped to grapple with how they operate and how the situations in which he finds himself come to be. At its most piercing and powerful, psychodynamic therapy is really not intellectual, although intellectual forces are rallied to make sense out of what occurs. As more connections are made a network of linkages, that is a larger context, is created, likely to hold experiences together with even greater coherence. The tropical depression has become something stronger, more organized, a cyclone perhaps. And with this the patient is, at least in principle, further stimulated to curiosity and puzzlement about his ways. The experiential quality of the patient's knowing together with the wider context in which this knowing rests is thought to contribute to deeper and more lasting change. All of this has to be "led up to." All of this takes time. None of this is easy. Neither for the patient nor the therapist.

Of the mind-oriented group of therapies psychoanalysis, in the strict and technical definition of the term, is the most developed and ambitious. It has cultivated most extensively the practice of listening at deeper levels. In the course of the last several decades a number of variations on "classical psychoanalysis," that method worked out and articulated largely by Sigmund Freud, have sprung from it. They are characterized by special emphases on particular aspects of human development and of the therapeutic method. Examples of these include *object relations theory, attachment theory, self psychology, control-mastery theory,* and *interpersonal theory.* Being psychoanalytic, however, they all assume the importance of exploring the person's intrapsychic processes with the least amount of influence by the analyst, of developing an understanding of unconscious processes operating in a person's past and present development, of the forces involved in internal conflict, and of the centrality of the therapeutic relationship. The psychoanalyst's contribution consists of communicating considered observations of the underlying issues emerging in the patient's wide ranging stories and pointing to their possible as yet unrecognized meanings. Psychodynamic psychotherapy has many roots in psychoanalysis and shares its basic understandings. What is different about psychodynamic psychotherapy is the scope of exploration, which tends to be less wide than that sought in analytic work. Consequently it does not in practice require or entail the same kind of major exploration of the driving issues that dominate the patient's life. Nor does it depend on the same kind of strict adherence to specific technique.

It is important to add here that stressing the prominence of the inner world does not preclude consideration of external influences affecting the patient. On the contrary, a psychodynamic perspective acknowledges the impact that both present and previous, even very early, experiences have on the characteristic ways in which people cope with life and its challenges. It appreciates their continuing influence, so intricately linked to human adaptation, as it maintains a steadfast commitment to exploring and widening a patient's views of his past and present circumstances. They would include events in his life, his relations with others, and his actual efforts and actions in the world.

Nor does emphasis and focus on internal processes imply that the psychodynamic therapist ignores immediate and acute distress when it comes to be overwhelming. Practical measures may have to be taken to restore conditions in which psychotherapeutic work can be resumed. Stabilizing the patient's situation, internal or external, or both, may become the most important, immediate obligation. Psychodynamic work can begin and proceed best when serious external demands are addressed either by the therapist or by others in a treatment team, once the atmosphere is reasonably settled, and the sense of urgency is calmed.

It is helpful and important to keep in mind that no model is ever entirely exclusionary, nothing is ever that "pure." Suggestion will find its way into every dynamically oriented therapy and the idea that a patient should increase self-awareness and do his own psychological work will influence even the most directive of treatments. We merely try to point out some of the central ideas that orient different therapists, especially psychodynamic therapists, and shape how they go about their work. With growing experience, therapists settle on an approach of their own. Still, consciously or otherwise, they will resort to a variety of therapeutic interventions from time to time as particular situations demand.

Fundamental to our view of psychotherapy is that it is the exercise of a *craft*. This view also shapes the organization of our book. Perhaps we are using the word *craft* in a somewhat unusual way. Generally, the word *craft* brings to mind the production or manipulation of *physical* things such as clay for making pottery, fabric for clothes, leather for shoes, or wood for cabinetry. Psychotherapy, on the other hand, deals with much less tangible matters. But quite like its more material cousins, it does consist of applying special and complex skills. These skills must be studied and read about, but they are really developed only in actual practice. The training of psychotherapists, therefore, rests heavily on the guidance, supervision, and example provided by experienced practitioners. We would like to note here that the word *craft* holds an additional meaning relevent to our subject. It also means *vessel.* Given our conception of the story of psychotherapy as involving a journey, the term *craft* seems ever more apt. Psychotherapy imagined as a vessel in which a journey of self-discovery is made. This significance came to us with unexpected delight. Now back to where we left off. All forms of craft similarly depend on the following fundamentals: (1) familiarity with the materials to be used and handled, (2) knowledge and assimilation of a body of work rules and of particular techniques and devices that experience has proved useful and productive, (3) a concept of what defines a successfully completed product, and (4) the arousal of a creative element.

In the context of dynamic psychotherapy we might think of "materials" as referring to the patient's internal processes and to his communications, which include expectations of the assistance he hopes to receive. Materials also include the therapist's experience of the patient's actual and implicit communications, the exploration of her own responses as well as the interactions between them. Psychodynamic psychology is the discipline necessary to an understanding of these materials. It comprises knowledge of human motivation, development, and maturation, of the structure of personality and the processes involved in adaptation. It provides a framework for the therapist's thinking and understanding of patients' internal conflicts and for finding ways of assisting in their useful, adaptive resolution.

Theoretical grounding is also requisite to mastering the considerable body of "work rules" that the craft has acquired and developed over roughly one hundred years of development. Essential are the understandings that guide the therapist's "technical" activities such as listening, communicating with a patient, and developing a sense of timing. Under work rules we also include ways of constructively handling the patient's emotional relationship with the therapist, as well as the therapist's own responses to the patient and to the work. Some work rules concern the conditions of the setting, known as "the frame," within which the work is supposed to be done. One can think of these conditions as defining the workshop. Managing them constitutes a most important part of the therapist's expertise, of what makes up her professional offering.

A craft also requires some notion of what is an acceptable "product," and so a set of ideas about a successful outcome of psychotherapeutic work is a must. These ideas include a mix of both general and person-specific criteria given the individuality of each particular patient. Very general criteria of a successful psychotherapy can include relief from suffering, greater personal confidence, increased capacity to cope, and a sense of purpose in living, as well as better relations with other people, increased joy, and perhaps most of all improved ability to do his own individual psychological work. Somewhat more specific criteria may include the ability to get angry without self-recrimination, grieve without despair, succeed without guilt, love without fear, and feel safe in the presence of another. Although it need not always be articulated at the outset, it is very important for the therapist throughout the work to keep in mind the basic aim of creating a product. Without such a notion therapies can go on endlessly, unproductively, round and round in circles.

When the craftsperson goes beyond the mere production of an object, when it reflects a special individuality and newness, her work can be said to have reached a level of artistic creation. One may, of course, debate whether and how the work of psychotherapy can assume artistic qualities. It is probably safe to say that, done well, psychotherapy can reach beyond learned routines and show something of an artist's touch. A therapist's creativity may, for instance, appear in her imagination, her openness to new and unexpected resonances to the patient's material. She may perceive new patterns in the material and find just the right way of communicating her observations in her own style. She may even develop new theories and techniques. In the same way, the patient's creativity, too, may appear as a new openness to heretofore uncharted aspects of the self, in finding new and individualistic meanings or just the right word. Both parties may stimulate new development in the other. Therapeutic work has the potential to be deeply creative for both parties and to leave them profoundly transformed. Yet, because of the subtle and private nature of this work, a psychotherapist's creative efforts go largely unnoticed, at times even by the patient himself and certainly by the public world.

This book is divided into six parts. In part I, "Inner Life and Adaptation," we review our understanding of psychotherapy as an event that fits into the continuity of the person's ongoing internal psychological work. We believe that people in the normal course of their lives do psychological work in their own individual ways. They become puzzled by themselves, their feelings, their relations with others, and question who they are and how they should be. They may develop vague intimations about what goes on within themselves or they may form perceptions or conclusions. As new issues come up, a person tries to put them into perspective and settle them as best he can. We describe such processes of individual psychological work and how they can fail, for it is at these times that a person is likely to look for help and may approach a psychotherapist. Our view then is that a psychotherapist essentially comes in as an assistant to someone who, for the moment, has become unable to do his own psychological work successfully enough; we see the therapist's role primarily in terms of helping the patient restore his ability to do his own psychological work. We go on to orient this discussion by considering it in terms of the concept of adaptation. The interplay of the various internal forces that operate in the process of adaptation is the subject of *psychodynamic theory*. Further, those adaptive processes that shape an individual's life also help form what we call his "character."

In part II, "Creating a Room of One's Own," we draw upon Virginia Woolf's ideas to talk about the making of a therapist and the setting within which she and the patient find themselves together. This setting provides the special environment in which the therapeutic process can develop and flourish and surrounds it by the *frame*.

In subsequent parts we describe how the developing therapeutic process quite consistently shows the previously mentioned rough thematic sequence of events. Based on this we propose an empirical, slightly schematized, longitudinal model, the essentials of which experienced therapists may easily recognize. They include the ways in which patients first present their initial situation and how they think and feel about it. Then there may follow characteristic periods in which therapist and patient seem to cooperate in developing a greater freedom and flexibility of conversing. Often, then, patients may reach a point where their story has the potential of widening beyond their previously accustomed way of viewing it. Motivated by unease and anxiety, they may shy from further explorations for a while. Sooner or later, as the therapy continues, patients may show preoccupation with the very relationship they find themselves developing with the therapist. Exploring what the patient brings from his own present and past life experience to how he shapes that relationship may become a prominent aspect of the work. In this and many other important respects the therapist becomes able to show the patient how aspects of the way he lives have remained outside his awareness. The joint scrutiny and evaluation of the patient's ongoing ways and purposes continues until he begins to apply his new understandings to making changes in how he lives including his relations with other people. If he increasingly succeeds in doing so, the therapy's ending comes into view. Beginning therapists may at times be puzzled and confused by the complexities they encounter and the many subtle and not always very visible issues. Any type of orientation would be good to have as a kind of rough compass to guide their difficult voyage. Later we enumerate what are to us some of the frequently encountered events in as well as the active processes leading to productive psychological work.

A word or two about a few other things. First, this book is the product of two voices. And you will hear them both throughout. At times you may hear one over the other; at times you may, for who knows what reason, hear something more unified. Initially we thought that this fluctuation could be a problem, but after some pondering we decided it wasn't. We would not edit our different personalities and energies out of the text but let them be in whatever concentration each was at at any particular time. Second, we do not make a systematic effort to relate our observations to the body of theoretical and professional literature because we wanted to continue a steady flow in telling the story of psychodynamic psychotherapy. And in the course of doing so we wanted to think through for ourselves, once again, those concepts that in our view seem to have become part of the broader body of accepted work rules in our craft. We do, however, provide a bibliography of important and relevant further readings. Third, we do not limit ourselves by following strictly the vocabulary or set of concepts of any particular "school" of psychodynamic psychotherapy. Instead we try to implement a broad dynamically and developmentally informed view by expressing it in a current common language widely resorted to by those in our field.

Fourth, individual psychotherapy is based on the joint work and cooperation of two people, often referred to as "patient" and "therapist." These terms, rather specifically, reflect a piece of medical tradition as does the term *psychotherapy*. Indirectly they invoke an image of the patient's situation as a form of sickness, and of treatment as leading to a "cure." Alternative terms such as *consumer* and *client* have been proposed. They, again, have other connotations; they sound commercial and legal. The issue of how to call the players in this dyad runs deeply into how psychotherapeutic work is conceptualized.

Despite the foregoing considerations, we did not succeed in finding and thus suggesting alternate terms. Therefore, we decided to return, throughout the book, to the term *patient* for a person who is conflicted, suffers, seeks assistance, and actively participates in a piece of joint psychological work. And we shall use the term *therapist* to refer to all persons providing such assistance to the patient. Further, in the course of general discussion throughout this book, we refer to the patient as male and the therapist as female.

You will also surely notice the extravagant frequency with which the words "may," "might," and their kin have been used in the text. This is not necessarily due to bad writing. Rather it expresses the consistent precariousness of psychotherapeutic work. While we may (here we go!) feel that we have a general grasp of what goes on in the inner lives of human beings, there is *never* any certainty that a particular detail is properly understood or responded to. There are times when doubt overcomes us.

Virginia Woolf writes of "the world's notorious indifference." "It will not pay," she says, "for what it does not want." Our current cultural climate does not favor bothering with a person's inner life. Social, economic, and political conditions during the last two decades have imposed significant limitations on investigating the mind's ways, particularly in the area of health care and its financing. They reflect a bias against the practice of psychodynamic therapies, which take mind most seriously, are rooted in the scrutiny of mental processes, and rely on the private exploration of interpersonal relatedness.

It is, of course, a reality that psychodynamic therapy exacts demands, sometimes considerable, on time and money. But this is not the whole story. The "invisible" nature of psychological processes for one thing, and the privacy and complexity of therapeutic work, tend to conflict with current emphases on accountability within the economic contexts of health care. Behavioral, neurological, biochemical, and genetic explanations of human functioning and pathology, which rest on physically measurable data, are much preferred.

Being forced to make practical compromises in the more intensive study of internal processes has led therapists themselves to develop abbreviated and modified treatment methods. These range from the behavioral and suggestive methods to the use of psychotropic medication, which, as we have mentioned, influence mind from the outside. Our rapid-fire and trendy culture does not prepare people who seek psychological help for a process that may be quite lengthy. Thus an expectation prevails that the fix will be quick, perhaps surreptitious, the intervention swift, the return to "normalcy" expeditious, as if we were taking out an appendix or casting a broken arm. Short-term efforts indeed have their rightful place in the spectrum of psychotherapeutic interventions and can be enormously helpful in circumstances in which suffering is acute. Undeniable, for instance, is the capacity of psychotropic drugs to reduce painful or paralyzing affective states or to organize disrupted thought to some extent. By no means do we wish to say that measures to relieve acute suffering should be avoided. We do, however, mean to distinguish between acute, perhaps intolerable, stress or trauma and the more protracted, less defined, perhaps more chronic pain that persists beneath it, before it, after it. If exploratory psychotherapy is undertaken to approach such pain it seriously requires the time appropriate to the individual's case. And the premium placed on very time-limited techniques that aim to affect mental processes by means of external management makes it difficult to practice a craft that is not sympathetic to shortcuts.

Useful therapeutic results can at times be attained even in very short-term treatment. Generally, though, the work can't be rushed. Each human being is governed by his own pace, his own rhythm, his own capacity to know and not know things about himself. Development can be stimulated, catalyzed if you will, but it cannot be hurried, even though we might wish it could be and that we had the power to bring this about. As dynamic therapists we try to set up a space in which the patient-to-be can begin to feel safe and attended to and begin to learn speaking about and to himself. We then can listen carefully, wait patiently, and speak when we have something to say. Experienced practitioners of this craft know this and know it deeply. It is a profound and humbling recognition. They know that what they can hope to do is provide an opportunity for self-knowledge with their steadiness, commitment, skill—and humanity—and pay attention to what happens. And that, by the way, can turn out to be a great deal.

Psychodynamic psychotherapies have managed to endure in the face of changing configurations of the social and economic environment. In our experience dynamic psychotherapy is able to offer much that is sound and useful in creating psychological change. Given the challenges and disregard facing our craft we feel it is all the more important that its effectiveness and the conditions that make it possible be reemphasized. Also a thorough understanding of the psychotherapeutic craft itself—of its requirements and its implications—is necessary to maintain its integrity and help it weather the rough seas surrounding it. Although in practice many therapies have to stop and be satisfied with the alleviation of urgent and immediate concerns, not in itself any small achievement to be sure, this book tries to convey a perspective that shows where an enriching, individually tailored psychotherapy might go. We hold on to the hope and the belief that the subtle and studied craft of psychotherapy can withstand the prevailing inclement atmosphere.

In this regard we encounter a sort of historical irony. Only a little more than one hundred years ago a number of investigators, Freud prominently among them, began to identify and unravel the importance of psychological processes in people's pathological efforts at adaptation. They had to confront much opposition and resistance to their work. As the result of an elaborate interplay of factors, sociological and political on one side and the special nature and complexity of "internal" psychological processes on the other, we again find a disregard for psychological dynamics and must, like Freud, struggle to reassert them.

I

INNER LIFE AND ADAPTATION

1

Individual Psychological Work

"You might find anything in a place like this. Did you see those mountains as we came along? [said Peter]. And the woods? There might be eagles. There might be stags. There'll be hawks."

"Badgers!" said Lucy.

"Foxes!" said Edmund.

"Rabbits!" said Susan.

But when next morning came there was a steady rain falling, so thick that when you looked out of the window you could see neither the mountains nor the woods nor even the stream in the garden.

"Of course it *would* be raining!" said Edmund. . . .

"Do stop grumbling, Ed," said Susan. "Ten to one it'll clear up in an hour or so. And in the meantime we're pretty well off. There's a wireless and lots of books."

"Not for me," said Peter; "I'm going to explore *in* the house." [Italics ours]

Everyone agreed to this and that was how the adventures began.

—C. S. Lewis, *The Lion, the Witch, and the Wardrobe*

People come into psychotherapy for a variety of reasons, all characterized to varying degrees by a subjective sense of distress. Distress by itself, however, does not enable the person to do good psychotherapeutic work or to profit from it. A degree of interest in and respect for his own "inner world" is also required. Such interest in one's own inner processes varies a good deal from one person to another. It may also vary notably within the same person during different times in his life or under the influence of life events of different sorts.

Exploration of a person's inner world is at the center of the psychotherapeutic enterprise, but it does not take place only in the consulting room. Indeed we assume that *individual psychological work* is something that most people do, at least occasionally, throughout their development. When this work runs aground we think of a person as being "stuck." We conceptualize individual psychological work as a decision to look inward rather than outward, to go, as Peter declared, exploring *in* the house rather than outside. For some people, perhaps even many, this inward shift can happen when the impulse to focus outward is challenged. How often have we said to ourselves or heard comments such as "I think I need some time to think this over," "I couldn't go on," "I need to take stock of my life," "I needed to be quiet, to look inside," or "It was no longer business as usual." For the children sent to the Professor's house it happened by way of a rainy day that thwarted plans to go outdoors. They could, of course, have distracted themselves with the wireless and books but chose not to. Thus while entering therapy might be a new experience in the prospective patient's life, he does not come to it totally unprepared. Like most other people he has done some sort of psychological work on himself in his life up to the present.

When we speak of individual psychological work we also refer to a person's effort at organizing what he knows about himself in order to understand himself better, deal with new experiences, with confusion, puzzlement, and inner contradiction, as well as change things within himself and in his relationships. Doing such work may lead the person to form at least temporary insights and conclusions about himself, some of which could become the basis for new resolutions, decisions, plans, objectives, and changes in his adaptational state.

Individual psychological work involves intentional self-reflection, an ability to stand back, to take distance from the experience at hand, and to look at oneself in a somewhat objective, albeit sometimes puzzled or skeptical, way. In other words individual psychological work is an internally active process by means of which a person strives to make his *own* way in his relationship with

himself and with the people and objects around him. However dimly formulated, temporary, or ambitious it may be, a person engaged in psychological
work thinks about, evaluates, and questions his inner states and behavior. He
may examine himself in conversation with others, in letters or journals, check
and reason out his feelings. He does, of course, do this work with various degrees of intention, consciousness, intensity, and success at different points in
his life.

There are many organizing processes in the psychological repertoire of human beings. Not all of them, however, are recruited in the service of individual psychological work. Many predominate unconsciously, such as in
unreflectively performed behavior, the use of psychological defenses, dreaming, even some fantasizing. Although things sometimes get worked out by
these means, in dreaming for instance, we would not in a strict sense consider
them part of a person's individual psychological work if they were not motivated by conscious intent, curiosity, and a need to look inward.

Psychological work revolves around the many tasks that confront the majority of people as they go through life. Central among these is the development of a coherent sense of one's body. Knowing one's physical needs, wants,
comforts, pains, limitations, satisfactions, and desires and how to master deprivation and frustration are all important tools for managing well-being and
security. People contemplate their relations with the external world as well.
They strive to achieve some capacity to trust, to love and be loved, to negotiate the vicissitudes of intimacy with partners, family, and friends. How one relates to others also has consequences for how one manages being alone. People
aim to find success and satisfaction at work, to develop their creativity, as well
as to attend to needs for regeneration and play. They must cope with the multiple changes that accompany growth, aging, disease, and the inevitability of
loss and death. And life asks that a person construct an identity for himself:
establish a set of beliefs and values, perhaps give and leave something of himself for the present and future good of others.

Navigating these common human waters requires that a person apply certain
further tasks or skills. Depending on the specific circumstances of any person's
life these may be more or less well developed. They involve the ability to distinguish between reality and fantasy, to evaluate decisions and make choices, to
scrutinize one's morality, select role models, take internal positions vis-à-vis offers, demands, and opposition from others. One needs to clarify and express

feelings, to cope with and manage contradictions and conflicts. When in difficulty a person must be able to find and accept help from others.

But the course of development is not always smooth. Often it is interfered
with by efforts to avoid conflict, anxiety, or pain, or by attempting to limit the
experience of unpleasant, confusing, or frightening realities.

Psychological work may be stimulated in different ways. A person responds
to observations, appreciation, or criticisms given to him by others and tries to
absorb them. He may spontaneously notice things about himself or make surprising discoveries. He becomes aware of certain weaknesses and liabilities
and tries to correct them. He finds that he cannot get over a loss, that he cannot refuse a drink. Noticing how one has been gripped by something that just
happened or that is happening at the moment might set individual psychological work into action. Such work itself can turn into a major life project
such as "becoming a better person." In pursuit of self-understanding people
may ask themselves all sorts of questions:

"What is it that I feel? Is it jealousy? Is it telling me that I am in love?"

"Why do I insist on wearing these blasted sausage-casing jeans that make
me feel so fat?"

"Why was I so afraid of my boss in the meeting today? I hardly dared open
my mouth."

"Why am I so lonely? I've got to do something about it, and soon. If I spend
another weekend by myself I'll go nuts. But where do I turn?"

"Is it normal to love one's cat so much?"

They may observe things about themselves:

"Perhaps I was too outspoken just now."

"Wow, I really see myself in my mother."

"I can't help looking at myself in the mirror."

"I keep on getting dumped by guys."

Certain puzzling feelings or behavior that show up frequently may also
stimulate psychological work:

"I guess I really do avoid women."

"I have to do something about my anxiety going on interviews."

"This procrastinating is for the birds. It has *got* to stop. I'll flunk everything."

"I don't know what I'm feeling. I don't think I can trust myself."

A person may also be curious why he remembers or forgets certain things, why a thought seems to always cross his mind, or why he feels compelled to perform senseless actions. And the list goes on.

Individual psychological work is never done. And what comes of it is often quite unpredictable.

It was the sort of house that you never seem to come to the end of, and it was full of unexpected places.—C. S. Lewis, *The Lion, the Witch, and the Wardrobe*

2

Impediments to Individual Psychological Work

"I'm in the pay of the White Witch." (said the Faun) . . . "It's she that makes it always winter. Always winter and never Christmas; think of that!"
    "How awful!" said Lucy.

—C.S. Lewis, *The Lion, the Witch, and the Wardrobe*

Feeling incapacitated in doing one's psychological work can be a painful experience. A person might feel that he is going around in circles that lead to no change. As a consequence he feels paralyzed or "stuck," less effective in his life, not pleased with his present existence, at times desperate. In some people confidence suffers; ease in being with people diminishes. Timidity and discouragement destroy a sense of competence. Doubt and finding fault with themselves prevail. Anxieties appear or grow more intense, optimism gives way to pessimism and an attitude of defeat. Depressive feelings arise together with a sense of being physically and mentally sluggish and burdened. For yet others, emotional control is impaired; they experience unaccustomed fits of panic or rage, confusion, and emotional pain.

Impediments to successful individual psychological work can derive from internal as well as external sources. In the first case lack of relative maturity may be a factor: a person's sense and experience of an inner world of his own (and of others) may not be well-enough established. This might be due to a dearth of empathic relationships in his early life, perhaps a lack of reflection about himself given by others, especially early caretakers. In persons with an already developed ability to do psychological work different barriers may arise, stemming, for instance, from certain personality traits such as overriding dependency needs. They pressure the person to regressively abandon all efforts to do his own work; instead he tries to turn to others to somehow do it for him. In other cases troublesome and upsetting emotional reactions arise when they approach difficult issues. These kinds of stirrings may reflect particularly intense, and for the moment irresolvable, inner conflict between temptation and conscience, for example. Such conflict may block and preoccupy a person to such an extent that individual psychological work becomes impossible.

External circumstances can equally render the person unable to carry out his psychological work. Interfering preoccupations resulting from too many reality demands can be overwhelming and make it difficult for the person to "stand back" from his own internal experience and from giving it psychological consideration. In the course of their lives people are beset by many desperately frustrating, frightening, or intrusive external pressures, some boiling over into crises. Family catastrophes, death, personal illness, poverty, credit card debt, a consuming legal matter or academic schedule are examples. Psychological paralysis can also result from struggles with irreconcilable and confusing external demands. Such may be especially true for people living in troubled families or other organizational systems. Double-bind, catch-22 situations, in which the person feels "damned if he does and damned if he doesn't," can powerfully block a person's efforts at internal work. External demands can conflict with the individual's internal needs and positions as well. Imagine a situation in which a married CEO of a large corporation with impressive philanthropic commitments is having an affair. His lover satisfies his many important, pressing, as yet unresolved developmental needs for sexual expression and satisfaction. So he agonizes. On the one hand he wants to continue the relationship with this compelling and lovely woman. On the other he wants to honor his responsibilities to his loyal wife, children, business, and community.

In more extreme instances, inability to cope and loss of emotional control can produce a state commonly referred to as "nervous breakdown."

3

Adaptation

It takes a swamp-and-tide-flat zoologist to tell you about life; it is in this domain that the living suffer great extremes, it is here that the water-failures, driven to desperation, make starts in a new element. It is here that strange compromises are made and new senses are born. The Snout was no exception. Though he breathed and walked primarily in order to stay in the water, he was coming ashore.

—Loren Eiseley, "The Snout," from *The Immense Journey*

Another way of looking at a person's individual psychological work is to consider its role in serving the person's efforts at *adaptation*. This is a central concept guiding psychodynamic thinking. Adaptation applies to all living things. It is not simply "adjustment." It refers to the processes and activities by means of which an individual being strives to fit its needs and capacities with the opportunities and restrictions in its surroundings. These surroundings may in turn be transformed in the process. In the case of human beings these processes are highly complex. From birth on we are motivated or driven to fill a variety of needs. Some are biological and part of our mammalian nature, some are psychological and social and less tied to physiology. These needs unfold during the growth and development of a human being and shape his dealings with his surroundings. However individually they may be patterned in any one person they are recognizable in the course of psychotherapeutic work and require the attention of both therapist and patient.

Individual psychological work plays a significant role in a person's adaptive efforts. It is implicitly steered by his striving toward a degree of stability and consistency within himself and predictability in relating to people and circumstances around him. As the person grows and develops he continually works and reworks a flexible balance both within himself and between himself and his human and nonhuman surroundings. Speaking about adaptation is really a way of speaking about living. Consciously or unconsciously we are all involved in developing, expanding, and safeguarding adaptations most of the time, sometimes in hardly discernible, sometimes in intense, dramatic, and conflicted ways. People who look for psychotherapeutic assistance are usually driven by the sense that something is not right within themselves, in their relationships, with the circumstances of their surroundings, or, perhaps, in more or less all of these contexts. Their state of adaptation is impaired and they wish to improve it.

We can speak of certain bundles of needs. There is first of all the *body*, with its requirements for nourishment, protection, care, physical, and later, sexual, contact. It requires stimulation, reasonably consistent surroundings, and safety. Throughout life the body is the most immediate source of inner experience, the source of a sense of presence. This has implications as well in the therapeutic situation in which two bodies find themselves present, and relating to each other, in the consulting room.

Out of the context of the infant's early and pressing needs for care and safety, needs for *attachment* develop. These needs are always active in a person's life and take different forms, being directed toward other persons, perhaps to a task. Powerful motivations arise from needs for *closeness* and *affection*, for satisfying sexual relations, for friendship, sensory pleasure, play, entertainment, and for the satisfaction of curiosity.

There are also needs for a *living*, for the acquisition of sufficient material supplies. These needs motivate much of a person's efforts at work and are, thus, a very large part of his adaptation.

Essential for a person's development is being *recognized* by others: to know he exists in the minds of others, to find self-esteem and self-respect, to establish a position in the community, to form an identity, to have and maintain "face." Related here is the need for a sense of *agency* and *effectiveness*, of being able to affect and influence things, to make changes in one's situation, to produce results.

These, among others, are important needs that come into play as a person strives to live, to shape his relations with the world that surrounds him, and to find coherence, sense, and comfort within himself. Much internal personal and psychological work is required here. Failure of such work, disappointment with existing adaptation, and a pressing desire for change are major reasons people look for psychotherapeutic assistance.

In the normal course of things resources for an individual's adaptation are supplied from the beginning by the biological equipment with which he is born: his reflexes, the progressive maturation of his sense organs, his motility, memory, and capacity to think. But early on in life an individual is also very much dependent on his parents and other caretakers. Thus the adaptive capacities of the child are greatly influenced by the quality of his relationship to caring adults and their adaptive strengths. By observing his parents and gradually identifying with them in certain ways the child may eventually take in some of their adaptive modes.

In time the child himself learns to coordinate his desires, needs, and wishes with what he learns the world can provide. When tense or lonely he comes to console himself by imaginative fantasies and daydreams but can increasingly distinguish them from reality. More and more the child becomes able to weigh the intensity of his demands against the danger of being responded to angrily or with a momentary withdrawal or loss of love by parents. He develops patience and can to some extent protect himself from the pains of frustration. And later he will balance some of his desires against the requirements and pangs of conscience. The growing person lives in a flux of constant efforts, partly conscious, partly not, to regain the best possible balance within himself and between himself and his surroundings.

When things go "well enough" reasonably secure and consistent conditions may prevail in a person's social and material existence. In such a more or less peaceful context a generally coherent, flexible adaptation can result with consequent comfort and sense of safety as well as a potential for further development and change. Sudden, massive, and unexpected changes such as the death of a loved one, betrayal, divorce, migration, war, bankruptcy, or catastrophic illness, injury, or accident, however, may overwhelm him and result in an adaptational crisis or trauma. The experience of being traumatized is, in and of itself, hard to cope with, but especially if it occurs on top of ongoing adaptive stressors, such as chronically destabilizing family dynamics, or in people who had always thought of themselves as being fully in control.

Slow, sometimes long-term changes within himself or in his surroundings can also disrupt an individual's adaptation. These may include aging, a family member's painful terminal illness, slowly increasing addiction to alcohol or other substances, or the threats of a worsening economy on a person's life. Gradually the person becomes aware of increasing discrepancies, discomfort, disappointment, or conflict, and the effectiveness of his own psychological work begins to suffer.

If an existing state of adaptation becomes less gratifying, less secure, and more stressful, some *action* on the person's part is called for. New impressions, understandings, emotional reactions, moral dilemmas, and painfully altered expectations have to be *worked into* existing attitudes, assumptions, and feelings. This can lead to changes in aspects of the person's behavior, possibly even in some alterations of his character. Decisions have to be made and evaluated; practical steps need to be taken. His actions, in turn, may affect how people relate to him, requiring that he make further changes.

Adaptation is a wide-ranging concept. Although most forms of adaptation depend on *psychological activity* we can also speak of adaptations that have become routinized and thus involve minimal current psychological work. They may include habitual performances such as the sequence of things a person goes through in the morning to get ready for work. We can also speak of *compliances,* behaviors that are superficially adjusted in order to manage an inconvenience or threat with the least amount of trouble. Once these forms of relatively passive, seemingly "automated" adaptations are established they require little reflective psychological work. There is no inner "standing back"; there is little gain in self-awareness, insight, or understanding. Such limitations are sometimes found in people who come to therapy, not out of their own desire, but who are, for example, legally or by some other authority (even that of parents) mandated to do so. Treatment is hard with people who are living or are forced to live in passive modes of adaptation.

Of course there are times when optimal adaptation suggests that compliance and conformity are the best strategy, but these are still chosen on the basis of internal psychological work and considered self-scrutiny. They are flexibly adopted, with the person's retaining the ability to make modifications and changes in his adaptive stance when doing so becomes possible. The chance of successful adaptation requires the mobilization of individual psychological work.

LENNY

Lenny is a young man of twenty-four who came to therapy after a brief hospitalization, his first. During his stay Lenny was diagnosed with major depression with psychotic features and put on a neuroleptic and an antidepressant. Much of Lenny's childhood and adolescence was spent moving from town to town as his father pursued various jobs. Both parents had professional degrees. Lenny came to therapy not having washed himself in what appeared to be a number of days. His hair was matted and his clothes were creased and stained. He smelt of cigarettes and body odor. Lacking the initiative to buy or cook food for himself he would take his meals at a soup kitchen. Let us consider Lenny's situation from the perspective of his psychotherapist, Dr. L:

Dr. L was not at all sure how to proceed with Lenny. Foremost on her mind was his smell, which she found very difficult to bear. She also worried about it lingering on and affecting her next patient. She thought about scheduling him at the end of the day. Then she thought that perhaps a private office was not the place to see such an individual. Then she wondered whether maybe it was "just her." Another therapist might not be so sensitive.

As the day wore on Dr. L wondered about the idea of pointing Lenny's presentation out to him. She wanted to be tactful and respectful. Something like "You look as though you didn't have time to get ready today." No. She didn't like the sound of that. Sort of beating around the bush. Even a little passive-aggressive. What about just being direct and, in a nice and civil way, making his cleaning up a condition for psychotherapy? What might this mean to him? That would be hard to know. Lenny might simply comply without much inner work. Actually, given his terrible odor, that really wouldn't be so bad, she thought. She could, of course, all the while encourage him to talk about this requirement. And in the meantime people might begin to relate to him differently. So it could be that stating conditions for therapy would result initially in some compliance but might come to stimulate more psychological work. She could then support this more active kind of adaptation. In time Lenny might be able to verbalize something about his manner of existing. Dr. L would then be on the look-out for signs that Lenny was grappling with the meanings of his unclean state, some recognition of conflict. He might, for example, say that he has become dependent on the soup kitchen, or that he identifies with the indigent people that show up there, that he doesn't want to be anything like his parents. Eventually he could indicate a desire to find another way of being in the world. He might begin to experience problems with his identity or express a fear of the obligations and expectations that come with cleanliness.

As Dr. L continued to ponder the situation she smiled to herself. What an absurd thought she had just then! What if Lenny took a very different action, electing to round up all soup kitchen patrons to protest the cleanliness requirements of mental health professionals? Her smile broadened as she thought of Lenny mobilized in this way. Such an action was not in keeping with his depressive style. It certainly wasn't what she had in mind for him. But it would undoubtedly constitute some form of adaptation, a way of changing his environment if not himself. And how self-reflective it would be she couldn't know. Dr. L was glad she could find some humor in the situation. She often got way too serious. What Dr. L really didn't want was to run the risk of Lenny's leaving therapy, as much as she was offended by his smell. There was after all something sympathetic about this young man. She liked him. She may just have to wait this out a bit more because she simply did not have enough information to size him up with any real accuracy.

Lenny was definitely on Dr. L's mind. As she cleaned up after dinner that night she began to think more about how being dirty itself could be adaptive for Lenny. It might function as a barrier for him, protecting him from moving on in the world, facing the responsibilities and self-awareness this entails, from possibly scary feelings connected to getting close to others. Or it may be even more primitive. The layer of dirt could be functioning as a "second skin," providing Lenny with a needed sense of body boundary. To strip him of this layer prematurely would be too much for him. This was not going to be a simple treatment. Working with processes of this sort, if indeed this was something going on, can take years. And their relationship was so new. Dr. L was anxious and in a quandary. Thinking about these things she knew herself to be already engaged in the work. As she dried off the last dish she decided to sleep on it and if necessary to seek consultation. Maybe there was another approach that she had not considered.

When a person's repeated efforts at coping with a problem in his inner world or in dealing with his surroundings lead to no resolve or relief, we view this as failing adaptation and an impasse in his capacity to do his own psychological work. Such an impasse may reflect itself in increasing uneasiness. Symptoms may appear such as general anxiety, depression, impulsive behaviors, mood swings, obsessions, compulsions, phobias, panic attacks, problems with eating or sleeping, body image issues, or various other physical complaints such as headaches, fatigue, and pains. Uneasiness can also express itself through deeply entrenched, troublesome, sometimes self-destructive ways of dealing with life that have become a distinguishing feature of the patient's *character*. For a therapist to be of assistance she must, therefore, have some sense for the interplay between psychological development and individual life experiences, especially those deriving from relationships with other people. From the perspective of this book, she must understand *psychodynamics*.

4

Psychodynamics

Shadowy thoughts are brought into the light of reason; echoes are traced to their sources.

It is like following a branch to find the trembling leaves, like following a stream to find the spring.

—Lu Chi (261 A.D.), *Wen Fu: The Art of Writing*

A thorough grasp of psychodynamic psychology is essential to understanding the patient's internal processes and communications, what we have conceptualized as comprising in large part the materials of our craft.

WHY DYNAMICS? WHAT'S MOVING? OR, BETTER YET, WHAT'S MOVING US?

Psychodynamics first of all tries to understand the forces that operate in a person's psychological world—that is, his *motivations*. As stated earlier, "dynamic" implies activity and refers to the *constant interplay* of these motivating forces, to how they combine, mingle, or conflict with each other. We encounter them in many forms such as feelings, desires, needs, impulses, interests, intentions, and continued pursuits. Some are parts of our mammalian nature with its corresponding bodily requirements. Others reflect the requirements, opportunities, and restraints of modern civilization. Dynamic motivations direct a person's inner mental activity, propel his actions, and influence how he experiences himself and the surrounding world. They may also serve

35

such important internal purposes as coordinating and reshaping or some-times opposing the person's more primitive, powerful, and self-centered de-mands and interests. Thus they contribute to safeguarding the coherence and integrity of his functioning.

There is good reason to think that many of these motivations operate un-consciously (therapeutic encounters provide many examples of this); of oth-ers one might be perfectly aware. Still others seem barely conscious or "preconscious." In this case we are talking about things that are near to being known, near awareness, but not quite. When stimulated by the relevant con-text they may be recognized.

Therapists, by training or personal inclination, orient themselves by plac-ing special emphasis on the developmental or clinical importance of one or another source of motivation (for example, sex, attachment, competition, identity, relatedness, spirituality). While this may be of interest theoretically in practice we must remain open-minded to whatever a patient brings and stay aware of the highly individual thematic motivational patterns that emerge in his particular case.

DEVELOPMENT AND REGRESSION

Psychodynamic theory assumes that all these motivating forces have emerged and become organized in an ongoing way from birth onward, qualifying it as a psychology of *development*. That we have a past is taken for granted in dynamic thinking, a past that is linked to the present by memory. (Note that this longitu-dinal perspective is always accompanied by a cross-sectional frame of reference concerned with the multiplicity of internal processes interacting simultaneously in a person's mind.) Human beings possess a nervous system capable of storing and processing enormous amounts of experience, and there is reason to believe that even seemingly forgotten experiences, in fact, do not disappear from mind. Rather they are overlaid by new experiences much as the Grand Canyon demon-strates layers of sediment one on top of the other. Thus certain motivations and adaptational themes show *continuity*, some persisting throughout the lifetime. As this huge body of experience grows it is continually reorganized in different ways and with different intensities. All this takes place unconsciously. In practice, then, it is important to be aware that as patient and therapist sit together two very complex developments come to bear on the occasion. Their interaction will re-quire recognition during the course of the therapy.

When a person is under very demanding and stressful circumstances that inundate his capacity to cope he may experience a *regression* to an earlier stage of developmental organization.

Let us consider the plight of a college freshman, Clyde, forced to adapt to being away from home. On the one hand he is excited to begin a new phase of his life: learn new things, meet new people, even date. On the other hand he feels overwhelmed by what is asked of him living apart from his family for the first time. Entering the dining halls is especially difficult for Clyde because he is confused and frightened by the multiple social demands. At times he finds himself having difficulty sleeping and resorting to buying food outside. He calls home every day and stays for long periods in his dorm room. At times he considers taking the next plane home.

Clyde is having great difficulty adapting to his new environment. Besieged by compelling and stressful circumstances he seems to be experiencing here a return or regression to avoidant, dependent behavior typical of a level of development in which conflicts around separation and dependence were prominent. Depending on the individual, reactivations of earlier developmental stages can be short-lived episodes that pass as he gets used to the new experience. Or they can be prolonged, indicating that he is dealing with problems that are more deep-seated.

CONFLICT AND ANXIETY

Inasmuch as forces such as the ones considered become organized over time they may also become involved in internal *conflict*. Indeed dynamic clinicians take the phenomenological and philosophical position that we are all conflicted, that this is what it is to be alive. Recognition of conflicts, as well as their resolutions, can contribute favorably to one's development, resilience, and outlook on life. Unrecognized conflict can interfere with development and become a cause of emotional or behavioral difficulties. Clyde, our freshman, is ostensibly conflicted about college, wanting to be there, yet extremely frightened of social demands. With the opportunity to look a little deeper this conflict may become better defined. Perhaps unconsciously he is feeling guilty for leaving his parents, outshining them, even wanting to outshine them, or maybe something else altogether. While exploration of our conflicts may help us to resolve or come to terms with them there may often be no easy or immediately apparent answers.

Related to the idea of conflict is the concept of *anxiety,* an unpleasant emotional tension signaling danger of some sort. Again we see this in Clyde's experience of college, namely, entering the dining halls. Generally speaking this danger can be many, often unconscious, things such as sexual or aggressive impulses of one's own, or the voice of one's conscience for falling short of some inner standard or ideal, or anticipated rejection. The degree of anxiety experienced by a person often reflects the intensity of internal conflicts. Sometimes people go on tolerating such a situation, at other times they may be forced to feel that some kind of action or resolution has to be accomplished. In such instances anxiety may play a very important motivational role. Much of a person's inner life and manifest actions are driven by needs to reduce anxiety. We certainly see this in Clyde, so anxious about socializing in the dining halls that he buys his own food and contemplates returning home.

Let us look at another example.

Jenny is a twenty-eight-year-old graduate student forever busy grading, writing, and teaching. She is single, having had several short-term relationships. She shares an apartment near campus with another graduate student, Liz, three years her junior. Jenny is slightly overweight by today's standards, and she feels this like an albatross around her neck. She cannot remember a time when she felt comfortable with her body, always trying to cover up this or that part, a chronic downer. Periodically she will get very angry and curse her thighs and pout. Once or twice she has thrown her clothes on the floor in frustration. This usually happens before her period, but not always, so she is never quite sure what the pattern is, if there is any. It just gets all too confusing. Over the years her M.O. has been to focus on her work and wait out these episodes.

Recently Liz began dating Greg. Greg is cute. And smart. He will come over, and the two will cook, watch TV, talk. Increasingly Greg has been staying over, not excessively, usually once, maybe twice a week. Jenny, however, begins to get irritated. After all this is a small apartment, and it is hard to work with "all the noise." Jenny begins to feel worse about her body and will periodically stop to look at her running shoes. She will snap at Liz, and the household becomes tense and unpleasant.

Several weeks of this have gone by, and Jenny notices that she is feeling minor fatigue; she will catch herself yawning at odd times. Soon thereafter she starts to experience a floaty feeling together with a pounding heart. This usually happens at night when she is in bed, after she turns out the light. Lying there in the dark she finds herself imagining Liz and Greg kissing, cuddling, having sex. She tries to turn off the thoughts only to have them return. Jenny's difficulty getting to sleep contributes to her increasing fatigue during the day and inability to concentrate on her work. She keeps thinking of those running shoes in the back of her closet. Eventually Liz approaches her. She is concerned about the changes in Jenny and in their good friendship and suggests that Jenny speak to someone.

UNCONSCIOUS PROCESSES

Initially Jenny did not feel anxious. Rather she felt angry that Liz and Greg were so inconsiderate. Only later does her anxiety become conscious or felt, experienced in her body, coming to her as fatigue, then this "floaty feeling" together with heart palpitations. Perhaps not to Jenny, it is, nonetheless, clear to the observer that her anxiety has something to do with Liz and Greg's relationship. Jenny's awareness of what is guiding her reactions is limited.

A dynamic therapist will typically approach Jenny's dilemma by wondering about what this anxiety might be referring to, or *signaling*. She will think about possible internal conflicts, assuming that these are not necessarily available to Jenny, that is, they are *unconscious*, and that as long as they remain so she will likely continue to feel as she does to her own and her friend's puzzlement and frustration. The therapist begins to wonder about the possible nature of the conflict or conflicts. She will ask herself why Jenny is single with a sparse relationship history, why she looks at her running shoes. She will likely form some preliminary hypothesis such as that Jenny struggles with her sexuality, wanting a sexual relationship similar to the one Liz has with Greg but fearing it at the same time and avoiding the struggle by focusing on her academics. She may go on to speculate that Jenny's weight and body image concerns may have to do with fear of sexual involvement. She will wonder about Jenny's connection with her parents. Liz's new relationship seems to have brought all this into prominence, unleashing significant anxiety in the process. *Unconscious conflict* is an issue always in the therapist's mind. Let us consider yet another example.

Donald, a married, middle-aged man with three children, is beset by obsessive thoughts of potentially deadly weather—floods, tornadoes, lightning—wreaking havoc, conceivably death, upon his family. He is unable to rid himself of these terrible images and thinks he is going insane. He has resorted to medication, which has been helpful in reducing the intensity of the images and the attendant anxiety, but not eliminating them. He is concerned, however, about the disheartening sexual side effects. He also worries that if he stops the medication he will be back where he started. Donald wonders if talk therapy might help, so he sets up an appointment with a psychotherapist. He likes the therapist and decides to give therapy a try. At first Donald talks almost entirely about his fear of going crazy. He wonders if the therapist thinks he is so and brings in a number of books and articles that describe experiences similar to his. He wants the therapist to help him match his symptoms with those he is reading about and to discuss theories of mental illness with him. It is quite a while before Donald is able to talk about other things. When he does it becomes apparent that he and his wife resent each other and bicker and argue constantly. Further Donald is enraged at having married when he was only in his early twenties and having taken on the responsibility of raising three children whom he loves "mind you," but whose care derailed him from the single life some of his friends enjoyed for much longer. It also emerged that he married as young as he did because he was very dependent on his wife. As much as he loved the idea of the single life it too frightened him. Slowly he began to see that such angry dependency characterized other aspects of his life, such as his relationship to his boss. Donald was initially conscious of his frightening images and feelings of anxiety; he was unconscious of his conflict over his anger and dependence on his wife and others.

Therapists often encounter multiple instances of a person creating and recreating similar situations, circumstances, and events, repeatedly sometimes, with little or no awareness that they are doing so or *why* they do so. The person seems motivated, even driven, compelled to do so, sometimes to his disadvantage. Donald's inability to reconcile unsatisfying relationships and Jenny's jealousy and angry avoidance of her sexuality were not new to them and are cases in point. Such phenomena have been characterized as manifestations of a *repetition compulsion.* To cite other instances a woman, for example, continues to appeal to her mother for love even after years of rejection and disappointment. A man, angry at his overly dependent friends, continues to offer them assistance even though they show no indication of trying to become more self-sufficient. Another person successfully starts and pursues new career efforts but in the end always unwittingly destroys them only to repeat the same sequence over again. Someone else goes through a series of disastrous marriages and still does not understand why.

Such repetitions should not be seen as mechanical routines. It is more promising to think of them as repeated efforts motivated to finally reach certain, perhaps irrational, goals or to accomplish a particular purpose that still has never met with success. Such goals are typically unconscious. To identify them may be an important aim in a given psychotherapy. They may be such things as appeals for care; recognition and enhanced self-esteem; respect; a convincing experience of being loved or desired; a need to demonstrate one's own power and effectiveness; a search for confirmation and acceptance of an idea; a longing for safety.

Much of our internal functioning goes on unconsciously. As we deal with the various issues of life over time we never really abandon past ways of coping and understanding. They are always alive and operate as unconscious efforts that underlie adaptation. Our unconscious activities are influenced by demands from many sources (by our body's needs and sensations, by the whole range of our experiences of other people and their qualities) in a simultaneous interplay from the earliest experiences to the most recent ones. In therapy we have the chance to become aware of such internal workings and, perhaps, with courage and newfound insight, to modify our adaptive efforts.

A few important words about unconscious activity: first, the term *unconscious* (or *preconscious* or *conscious* for that matter, even the term *ego*, which we will get to) does not refer to an actual place in the brain or elsewhere. It is a term that denotes a theoretical concept, not something concrete. Note, however, that for convenience we do use this and other such terms as nouns complete with the article *the*. Second, when we speak of unconscious activity we refer to a mode of processing characterized by often unusual organization, which lacks conventional realism and logic, time and space. Unconscious processes depend on fantasies in which images, memories, and desires of any time or circumstance can be combined and recombined in all sorts of order and with great fluidity. Hours, even years, can be experienced in moments. Seemingly unrelated images may appear contiguously, united by themes that may not be immediately obvious. This is most evident in dreams, which we will talk about later on. Unconscious activity can only be *inferred* from a person's thinking and acting. Nonetheless, it must be understood by the psychodynamic therapist as a set of underlying forces with their own validity and reality.

One could interpret C. S. Lewis's story *The Lion, the Witch and the Wardrobe* as a foray into the unconscious activities of its characters. In the following excerpt the two eldest children, Susan and Peter, are distressed by Lucy's stories of the fantastic world called Narnia. Is she mad? A liar? They decide to bring their worries to the Professor.

So they went and knocked at the study door, and the Professor said "Come in," and got up and found chairs for them and said he was quite at their disposal. Then he sat listening to them with the tips of his fingers pressed together and never interrupting, till they had finished the whole story. After that he said nothing for quite a long time. Then he cleared his throat and said the last thing either of them expected:

"How do you know?" he asked, "that your sister's story is not true?" . . . Susan looked at him very hard and was quite sure from the expression on his face that he was not making fun of them.

"But how could it be true, sir?" said Peter.

"Why do you say that?" asked the Professor.

"Well, for one thing," said Peter, "if it was real why doesn't everyone find this country every time they go to the wardrobe? I mean, there was nothing there when we looked; even Lucy didn't pretend there was."

"What has that to do with it?" said the Professor.

"Well, sir, if things are real, they're there all the time."

"Are they?" said the Professor; and Peter did not know quite what to say.

"But there was no time," said Susan, "Lucy had had no time to have gone anywhere, even if there was such a place. She came running after us the very moment we were out of the room. It was less than a minute, and she pretended to have been away for hours."

"That is the very thing that makes her story so likely to be true," said the Professor. "If there really is a door in this house that leads to some other world (and I should warn you that this is a very strange house, and even I know very little about it)—if, I say, she had got into another world, I should not be at all surprised to find that that other world had a separate time of its own; so that however long you stayed there it would never take up any of our time. On the other hand, I don't think many girls of her age would invent that idea for themselves. If she had been pretending, she would have hidden for a reasonable time before coming out and telling her story."

"But do you really mean, sir," said Peter, "that there could be other worlds— all over the place, just round the corner—like that?"

"Nothing is more probable," said the Professor, taking off his spectacles and beginning to polish them, while he muttered to himself, "I wonder what they do teach them at these schools."
— C. S. Lewis, *The Lion, the Witch, and the Wardrobe*

FANTASY

We will now turn more fully to the notion of *fantasy*. Fantasizing means imagining things. By imagination we mean an appearance, although perhaps at times muted or disjointed, of visual pictures, sounds, and other sensory experiences sometimes related to memory, and often related to pleasurable wishes, possibly their fulfillment. Fantasies happen when we play, daydream, and dream. They combine thought and memory, even some emotional stirrings, and altogether are set in motion by desires or hopes, all more or less unencumbered by the requirements and restrictions of reality. The demands of reality give way to make us free to entertain all sorts of things that are impossible in real life or to create situations in which we have no reason ever to find ourselves. We see a movie star, for example, and imagine what it must be like to be with that person. We flirt with an unavailable person, "lusting in our hearts," in the words of one American president. We daydream about making all sorts of money, beating our competitors, and being beautiful, smart, witty, sexually alluring, and satisfied. Fantasies serve us in several ways. They can provide gratification and tension release without harming anyone. They can provide creative images to be realized later on or comfort us when we are alone. Much fantasizing can go on unconsciously and contribute in unrecognized ways to how a person may shape his adaptations and life plans. Fantasizing should be seen in the context of a person's actively playing with adaptational possibilities. In other words they represent a healthful activity. There are situations, though, in which fantasizing may be less so. This can occur when a person is so overwhelmed by intense conflict that his fantasies go beyond anything that can be real, and their sights and sounds and storylines turn into hallucinations and delusions. In this case we are looking at kinds of pathology that, in the clinical situation, may need evaluation of possible organic impairments in addition to psychodynamic assessment.

People vary in the degree to which they engage in fantasy. On one extreme are those who spend a great deal of their time in fantastic reverie, perhaps as a way of escaping dull or frightening realities; on the other are the very constricted. Anxieties may arise when fantasies become too intense or tempt too much toward action; a person then may put such fantasies out of his mind, repress them. *Unconscious fantasies* result, fantasies that must remain beneath awareness because of their "unspeakable," even their "unthinkable" quality. In Donald's case, for example, one could hypothesize that his conscious fears of disaster befalling his family signaled an unconscious wish to have them disappear, to be single and carefree. But as we have seen Donald is also very dependent upon his wife and frightened of independence. Pleasurable as they can be fantasies can also cause much anxiety and unconscious conflict.

RESISTANCE AND DEFENSE

As conflictual material begins to knock on the door of consciousness, anxieties will typically increase together with a growing opposition to awareness of such material. This opposition manifests itself as *resistance*. It appears in therapy in the patient's inability or refusal to notice or think, speak, hear about, or act upon anything that nears a particular conflictual issue. Resistances encountered in the therapeutic hours are overt expressions of *unconscious processes of defense*. In other words, resistances are observable phenomena; defenses are inferred underlying processes. Both are driven by anxiety.

Defensive processes, in principle, serve to hold anxiety at bay by keeping conflicting aspects of inner experience apart. They also strive to prevent threatening unconscious material from entering the person's awareness. Defenses appear in a variety of forms. For example people may pretend that something is not so. They will deny certain realities, such as a fast approaching deadline for a project, the health consequences of smoking or drinking, or the impact of a loss. We see this in Jenny's denying her sexual and relational needs by throwing herself into her work. Others may adopt an emotionally distant and overly academic view of their symptoms. This is what Donald has done. He intellectualized his symptoms and invited his therapist to do the same. *Denial* and *intellectualization* are but two of a number of defenses. *Repression* defines another kind of defensive operation by means of which people unconsciously prevent themselves from recognizing some of their needs, wishes, and conflicts, or don't allow certain ideas or memories to be known. People can also alleviate anxiety about troubling personal attributes by believing that they belong to someone else. For instance "I'm competitive" becomes "You're competitive"; "I hate you" becomes "You hate me"; or "I'm angry at you" becomes "You're angry at me." This is a defense known as *projection*. *Projective identification* is another phenomenon. Here the recipient of the person's projection, for psychological reasons of his own, begins to feel and act in terms of the role attributed to him in the projection. His ability to stand back and examine what is happening is impaired. *Regression* refers to the person's returning to an earlier level of functioning that allows him to hide from difficult realities in the here and now. By avoiding the dining halls and contemplating returning home our college freshman, Clyde, seems to have done just that. *Reaction formation* serves to deal with difficult feelings by turning them into their opposite. Angry feelings toward another, for example, give way to excessive niceness. Someone unable to bear the tension of understanding the complexity of positive and negative features in another human being deals with this by *splitting*. He assigns the perceived positive and negative traits, and his feelings about them, separately to different people.

Returning to Donald we see that by intellectualizing he seals off his rage and disconnects his longing to be on his own from his dependence on his wife and fear of living alone. He avoids confronting this conflict. Jenny, by contrast, denies the reality of her sexual and relational needs in order to avoid awareness of some unknown unconscious threat. Perhaps she feels guilty for having such needs or perhaps she is afraid that no one could or will ever love her. As long as conflictual material is kept from consciousness we can feel *relatively* safe, but as we see from these cases, at a cost: it is hard to move on. Some defensive configurations, in fact, may turn into lifelong features of a person's character.

Defensive processes can be very effective, but like all things human, they are imperfect, and unconscious material occasionally slips through. When this happens it tends to do so in disguised form. Disguises serve as another layer of protection. Such masked content forms much of what we deal with in psychotherapy. People often talk about important issues indirectly. Unconscious material can, for example, show itself as *slips of the tongue*. An amusing example comes to mind. On a midsummer day, stiflingly hot and humid, one very high-class, arrogant woman, let us call her Francesca, was obviously feeling the heat. As Francesca weakly "fanned" herself with one hand she remarked, "It is so hot here I can't breathe. I'm *sophisticating*." Unconscious material also reveals itself in *dreams, symptoms,* and *associations,* which at first blush seem unimportant, even irrelevant. We will discuss dreams and associations later; for now let us consider Jenny and Donald's symptom picture.

Some of Jenny's presenting symptoms included her increasing insomnia and inability to focus at work. Donald's symptoms included his obsessive rumination concerning family tragedy. Symptoms reflect a person's attempts at coping with paralyzing conflict; they amount to an impasse in his capacity to do adaptively successful psychological work. Dynamically speaking symptoms are attempts at adaptation by means of *compromise.* That is to say they at once express but also hide threatening, conflictual material. In Jenny's case we might speculate that her insomnia expresses a preoccupation with Liz and Greg's sexual relationship while preventing distressing images from emerging in her dreams. In Donald's case obsessive thoughts might indirectly express enormous rage at his family. They also serve to confine or contain this inner turmoil. Symptoms often vary in their intensity depending on the extent to which events in the patient's life situation stimulate one side or another of his unconscious conflicts.

The ability to recognize unconscious material as it reveals itself in the therapeutic conversation requires learning how to listen, how to keep an eye and an ear out for clues to a person's inner life.

EGO

Defensive operations such as those described here are said to represent the efforts of *ego.* When we refer to ego we are not using it in the sense of "self-esteem," as is popularly done, such as by describing someone full of himself as having "a big ego"! Ego rather denotes the pattern of a person's psychological organizing processes, both conscious and unconscious, that drive and shape his adaptive efforts. Ego is viewed as an "organ" of adaptation, regulating the relation between the person's inner world with its needs, desires, and anxieties, and the circumstances, conditions, and demands of his surroundings. Individual psychological work can be thought of as one of the important activities of the ego. In the clinical situation the therapist will try to monitor the patient's *ego strength,* meaning the flexibility, reliability, and efficiency with which the ego does its work. Sufficient ego strength is thought to develop primarily from early experiences of stable and dependable care, affection, and security. It also thrives from further experiences of being respectfully regarded as a person growing in his own right and by the availability throughout development of possibilities for identifying with constructive aspects of important people in the person's life.

SYNTHETIC FUNCTION

The initially scattered and seemingly incidental pieces of experience, learning about the world, and identifying with others gradually become increasingly related to one another in the course of development. Such relating is described as the ego's *synthetic functioning*. Many of the ego's mediation efforts aim to safeguard its coherence under the disruptive pressure of unrealistic, potentially disturbing, uncontrolled, selfish, sexual, and aggressive impulses and from actual or imagined threats from without.

Creativity is a manifestation of the ego's synthetic function. One sees this when connections between seemingly unrelated thoughts, feelings, and experiences are forged, when fragments of experience are brought together and reconfigured into something new. Psychotherapy gets its power from its capacity to create conditions that allow a widening of consciousness, that allow heretofore disavowed material to enter awareness and become reorganized into more flexible and adaptable patterns. When Edwidge Danticat mused about the process of writing in her book of stories *Krik? Krak!* she spoke ever so poetically of something akin to the synthetic function:

> It's like braiding your hair. Taking a handful of coarse unruly strands and attempting to bring them unity. Your fingers have still not perfected the task. Some of the braids are long, others are short. Some are thick, others are thin. Some are heavy. Others are light. Like the diverse women in your family. Those whose fables and metaphors, whose similes, and soliloquies, whose diction and *je ne sais quoi* daily slip into your survival soup, by way of their fingers.
> —Edwidge Danticat, *Krik? Krak!*

As in most creative endeavors the outcomes or reconfigurations taking place during therapy can happen on different levels of consciousness and are seldom known in advance. Psychodynamic psychotherapy, therefore, cannot and does not claim to know a priori what these syntheses will look like for any given person. If, for example, Donald can tolerate the pain of bringing into awareness his early decisions that set the course for much of his life, if he can expand his understanding of why he felt compelled to marry when he did, he may be able to internally reorganize his experiences and create something new. Whether that means developing a more meaningful relationship with his wife and children or a decision to try life on his own or something else we cannot know at the outset. We would have to wait and see. Similarly with Jenny. If she can bring into awareness her conflicts around her body and sexuality then perhaps she can find a way to go about her life differently, with more groundedness and gratification.

INTERNALIZATION

Much of the ego's contents, its integrity, and the quality of its character derive from what it takes in from the person's experiences with the world at large. Such "taking in" is broadly referred to as *internalization*. A specific form of internalization, *identification*, consists of an individual taking into himself significant aspects of a "model person," thus becoming in some ways similar to him. A central task of living and growing is to organize differing identifications into something coherent and stable, an inner "identity."

Identifying begins in early childhood and may well continue throughout a person's lifetime. It originates in the close encounter between an infant and its caregivers; it first manifests itself in small instances of imitation. In cooing to one another mother and child become attuned to each other, form similar sounds or imitate each other's playful movements. As the child comes to perceive the important people in his surroundings in more focused and defined detail he begins to sense himself as a being similar in certain ways to some of those around him even though they are so much bigger. He tries to "be like" particular grown-ups. As the child himself develops and becomes an adult he encounters new demands and requirements for adaptation (becoming a parent for example). He will draw on his memories of, perhaps fantasies about, how important model persons had handled similar challenges. Identification then gradually comes to be a complex internal process in which various perceptions relating to emotionally important others become part of an individual's self and contribute to giving it its particular shape. They all contribute to forming a person's style of thinking, his goals and intentions, attitudes, convictions, and conscience. Depending on the qualities of available and influential model persons identifications of all sorts may develop, from the socially acceptable and constructive to the disordered or criminal.

Significantly, identifications tend to be stirred by *object loss*, meaning the discontinuation of a significant relationship with another either as a whole or with particular aspects of that person. Such loss may be caused by tangible events such as being separated or abandoned by someone or by a death. In a sense a person continues an internally living relationship with someone who is lost in the "real" world. Influential losses may also be of a more subtle sort as caused, for example, by another person's change of attitude or interest. Identifications may vary greatly in degree of complexity. Examples of such identifications include graduating students who find that they have adopted some of the characteristics of important teachers. Also, near the end of a psychotherapeutic relationship patients can be observed trying to "take into themselves" certain pieces of the therapist's manner or personality. Small temporary identifications occasionally appear even within therapy sessions when patients unconsciously assume certain of the therapist's characteristics in ways of moving, sitting, speaking, or remaining silent.

Identifying essentially occurs unconsciously. A person, however, may come to notice its results. In the course of therapeutic exploration patients are sometimes surprised by how much some of their feelings, attitudes, or values resemble certain aspects of parents and other influential figures. Now they may even find themselves in conflict because certain recognized elements of identification turn out to be incompatible with other internal positions they have come to accept. The person may then experience *identity conflict* and temporary or lasting difficulties in trying to sort out what is "me" from what is "not me."

A special situation results in the case of "identification with the aggressor," a defensive measure adopted in the interest of attaining a sense of safety and connection ("If you can't beat 'em, join 'em"). It involves a person's unconscious attempt to disarm a dangerous aggressor by modeling himself after him and has been observed in people's adaptation to violent external circumstances. On a small everyday scale it may also appear in one's agreeing, against one's normal standards, with opposing ideas held by another person. Identifications result not only from benevolent and loving relations; powerful identifications can also derive from hatred.

"Taking in" aspects of other people does not necessarily result in identification in the sense of a modification of the person's self. We speak of *introjection* when images of another person dominate in an individual's mind and exert influence but are not sensed by that individual as part of his own self. In extreme cases this may be reflected in someone's saying "I don't know what made me do it" or "This isn't me" or in his feeling "possessed" by a strange force. People often tend to evaluate themselves by comparing what they feel they are like with an introjected ideal image of a "good" person.

OVERDETERMINATION AND MULTIPLE FUNCTION

Under the pressure of complicated and multiple adaptational demands the ego frequently can be understood as forced into serving several aims at once. The ego's synthetic efforts then appear as *overdetermined,* that is, a particular piece of a person's behavior can be read as having been shaped by more than one influence. The ego's simultaneous mode of dealing with them is conceived of as its *multiple function.* Remember Lenny who came to therapy without having washed? His uncleanliness could mean a number of things—a way of avoiding relationships and responsibility, an expression of hostility, a way of identifying with homeless people—none of which need be mutually exclusive. Development and adaptation always involve the continuous and simultaneous management of many disparate influences, pressures, and discoveries. When colleagues discuss a case, one not rarely finds that each stresses a different aspect of the story. Someone will mention aggressive impulses in the patient, another will stress an uninhibited sexuality, and still another will say something about identification with a parent. All of the issues raised may be significant. The patient's ego may be working on them all. The skill involved in psychotherapy, however, is deciding what of this range of meanings to address at the moment. The question is: Which issue is the most salient or accessible one for a person at a particular time?

In speaking about the ego's multiple and synthetic functions we point to the interplay of the patient's needs, desires, and aims with his life experiences, and with efforts to shape minimally conflicted and sufficiently realistic adaptations. Reasonably coherent inner experience and modes of external adaptation may in time result from such efforts. Because human beings share a common biological nature and often similar environments, their individual ways of coping may loosely fall into a number of recognizable groups or patterns. Such patterns may appear as character structures, personality types, and kinds of emotional difficulty and disorder. A well-trained and experienced therapist may get a first orientation to a patient's difficulties by referring to her own mental library of such patterns. This may assist her in widening the exploration and the comprehension of the patient's story as it develops in the course of therapeutic work. The aim is gradually to empower the patient to review, test, and alter some of his ways of coming to terms with his life.

MEANING

Psychodynamic psychotherapy, then, is in major part a process that strives to loosen defenses and bring warded-off, threatening material into consciousness. It depends on the ego's synthetic capacity to work out disparities, contradictions, and inconsistencies. Of course the way life is it is impossible to bring all things into harmonious integration. Not everything will always fit together perfectly. There will always be wayward strands of hair. There will always be conflict, and conflict can never be fully reconciled, and this is part of the human package. But the idea is that a person's life can become more livable if at least some of its disparities are made conscious and woven together somehow. There is something wonderful and wholesome about creating even a modicum of order out of the experience of chaos, about understanding the forces that motivate our puzzling, distressing feelings and behavior and their repetition. It is hard to live a painful, discordant, and incomprehensible existence. So we can see how dynamic psychotherapy is in large part an endeavor to *make meaning*. Thus it can be a decidedly *creative* part of the person's life and development. While reducing or managing anxiety, depression, or other forms of distress may be initially the primary therapeutic goal, the actual nature and quality of the outcome of the therapeutic work are not easily foreseen.

5

Character

Science seeks essentially to naturalize man in the structure of
predictable law and conformity, whereas the artist is interested in man
the individual.

—Loren Eiseley, "Strangeness in the Proportion," from *The Night Country*

When the therapist encounters the patient for the first time she will collect
her impressions and try to form a picture of what kind of person he might
be. She finds herself encountering expressions of the prospective patient's
"character." We are not speaking here of *character* in popular terms, where it
is most often used in a moral context. In that sense one speaks of excellent,
bad, or peculiar characters, even of people who lack character altogether. In
the psychodynamic context, on the other hand, character stands for a person's *individual style*, which develops as he goes through life, the particular
manner in which things about him hang together. It refers to a kind of broad
pattern and summarizes a person in more or less consistent ways, successful
or unsuccessful, good or bad, by which we can recognize this person at any
time as being the same as the one we have known before. (An observer, however, may also find that sometimes people act in ways that appear "out of
character," even "out of their minds.") Character, though, is not merely a matter of overt appearance. It refers as well to ways of shaping and dealing with

inner life, which depending on the person can be more or less harmonious or conflicted.

From a psychodynamic perspective character is understood as an ego phenomenon, a product of development. It arises from the interaction between the pressure and pursuit of a person's major motivations and interests (satisfying needs and desires, going after goals); endowments from birth (sensitivity to stimulation, liveliness, frustration tolerance); influences exerted upon him by the human (caretakers, siblings, friends, mentors), social, and material conditions that surround him; from understanding of opportunities and limitations and ways of absorbing internal conflict. Character incorporates, among other things, a person's defensive organization and identifications. Just as we have seen in investigating the nature of symptoms the same processes operate in the way a person's character forms. That is to say character represents a kind of compromise, a complex tool and result of adaptation.

The psychodynamic psychotherapist finds a great deal of leverage in the concept of character. It helps her in understanding the kind of trouble that brings the patient to therapy and in forming a possible therapeutic approach.

Clyde Kluckhohn and Henry Murray, an anthropologist and a psychologist, respectively, wrote that

Every man is in certain respects
   like all other men,
   like some other men, and
   like no other man.

When we think of our patients we do so in all of these terms. We understand that as human beings we are akin to *all other people* through common biology and life experiences such as birth, aging, and death. As members of groups we also have certain characteristics that connect us to *some other people* while distinguishing us from the rest. And as individuals we will possess characteristics that make us idiosyncratic and unique, like *no other person.*

From a psychodynamic view a person is like all other people in that he needs to survive the vagaries of life. This need posits that we share certain basic mental resources that facilitate adaptation. We described them in the previous chapter. Here we call attention to how our patients are like some other people in terms of character types and how, as individuals, each is like no other person. All these perspectives help orient us to what we are seeing and experiencing in the session.

When a prospective patient walks into our office we don't know him at all but may be helped in organizing our perceptions of him by reference to a *typology* of character. Such a typology is composed of standard sets of parameters, which define different personality patterns. The general psychological literature is replete with types too numerous to present here. One particularly ambitious attempt to encompass the variation in pathological, human characteristics can be seen in the system proposed by the *Diagnostic and Statistical Manual-IV*. For us as clinicians some knowledge of types can come in handy.

Although it may be an economical way of talking about people it must be remembered that as categories typologies are not geared to the individual per se, and ultimately they do not do justice to the varieties of human adaptation and their expression. A person's character is ultimately more than a type; it has individual qualities as well, some more nuanced, some mysterious. Working as we do in the context of the individual we are asked to sharpen our perceptions and further develop our knowledge of people.

Here then we arrive at the outlook which emphasizes how a person is unlike any other. We recognize the highly specific manner in which any given person's character features combine over the course of his development. Such attention to individual detail will connect us to our patients, will help them feel truly seen and known as no other person, and will tailor our interventions. Assessing character in this way is descriptively or phenomenologically based. The clinician must rely on herself more than on already established typology, must rely more on reading living people than on studying theory: the glint in the eye; the tilt of the head at a puzzling thought; that heart-melting grin; the punch of contempt; the heave of great sorrow. It requires a skill that in German is called *menschenkenntnis*, knowledge of people. Serious and abiding interest in people, family members, friends, public figures—all will develop it. Such knowledge of the individual is decidedly more fluid and complex than that mediated by statistical research, "objective" personality tests, and diagnostic handbooks. It is more akin to what is found in art, literature, theater, and the movies. Take, for example, this description of a person from Thomas Mann's *Death in Venice*:

> He was of medium height, thin, beardless, and strikingly snub-nosed; ... He was
> obviously not Bavarian; and the broad, straight-brimmed straw hat he had on

even made him look distinctly exotic. . . . His chin was up, so that the Adam's apple looked very bald in the lean neck rising from the loose shirt; and he stood there sharply peering up into space out of colourless, red-lashed eyes, while two pronounced perpendicular furrows showed up on his forehead in curious contrast to his little turned-up nose. . . . At any rate, standing there as though at survey, the man had a bold and domineering, even a ruthless air, and his lips completed the picture by seeming to curl back, either by reason of some deformity or else because he grimaced, being blinded by the sun in his face; they laid bare the long, white, glistening teeth to the gums.

And this from James Joyce's "The Dead":

His aunts were two small, plainly dressed old women. Aunt Julia was an inch or so the taller. Her hair, drawn low over the tops of her ears, was grey; and grey also, with darker shadows, was her large flaccid face. Though she was stout in build and stood erect, her slow eyes and parted lips gave her the appearance of a woman who did not know where she was or where she was going. Aunt Kate was more vivacious. Her face, healthier than her sister's, was all puckers and creases, like a shrivelled red apple, and her hair, braided in the same old-fashioned way, had not lost its ripe nut colour.

And this vivid portrait of Anna O. from Josef Breuer and Sigmund Freud's *Studies on Hysteria*:

One of her essential character traits was sympathetic kindness. Even during her illness she herself was greatly assisted by being able to look after a number of poor, sick people, for she was thus able to satisfy a powerful instinct. Her states of feeling always tended to slight exaggeration, alike of cheerfulness and gloom; hence she was sometimes subject to moods. The element of sexuality was astonishingly undeveloped in her. The patient, whose life became known to me to an extent to which one person's life is seldom known to another, had never been in love; . . .

This girl, who was bubbling over with intellectual vitality, led an extremely monotonous existence in her puritanically-minded family.

Portrayals of this kind are textured, evocative, and unique, and they rarely if ever fit perfectly over a typology. The originality of the individual, therapist as well as patient, always asserts itself.

Having said all this let us now shift back to the general and describe five of the character types that help us organize and group our perceptions of our patients: depressive, narcissistic, hysterical, obsessive, and paranoid. These are frequently encountered types and much has been written about them in the clinical literature. They do not necessarily correspond to diagnostic types provided in current manuals primarily for use in research, statistics, accounting, and financial management. A short description of each is followed by a clinical example in which, we hope, something of the patient's uniqueness will come through as well.

DEPRESSIVE

Most people can become depressed at times in response to certain situations or events, such as disappointments or losses bound to occur in anybody's life. We speak of *depressive character features*, however, in people with impaired self-confidence, who continually sense themselves as being of little value, little respected, undeserving, or are plagued by chronic, unrealistic feelings of guilt. Some of these individuals may despise themselves, tend to be pessimists, and expect only further disappointments, failures, and humiliations. People with depressive character features seem on the whole more dissatisfied and unhappy with themselves than sad about an external event. The depressive person does not usually respond to encouragement; he may manifest a sense of hopelessness, become quite dependent on the therapist, and yet reject help. Depressive character features can reflect a regressive level of functioning adding some childlike qualities to the patient's ways. Patients sometimes obtain subjective relief by the characteristic defense of *denial*, which can result in an ill-founded, shallow sense of well-being or by exaggerated activity and compensatory grandiosity. A profound and conflicted desire for attachment often plagues them. Aggressive feelings may rarely be expressed directly tending, instead, in the form of criticism and devaluation, to be turned upon the person's own self.

Doreen, a twenty-nine-year-old woman and salesperson for a jewelry manufacturer, has been in therapy a little over a year. Doreen's divorce from her husband, Jonathan, was finalized two months ago. Their relationship had been "on the rocks" for much of its six years, reaching an irreconcilable impasse after Jonathan's confessing to loving another woman. Doreen was enraged at Jonathan. She had helped him through law school both financially and emotionally and felt deeply betrayed but could not allow herself to truly give voice and heart to these intense feelings. This session finds Doreen having just resumed therapy after a two-week Christmas break from her therapist who was on vacation.

Pt: The break was awful. I'm so depressed. I've been having awful thoughts about death. Not suiciding. That's not what I mean, but I don't know what's in it all for me. In life I mean. I want antidepressants I think.

Th: Well, why don't we wait on that? You know you've just gone through your first Christmas without Jonathan. Let's see how January shakes out. Tell me more about what you are experiencing.

Pt: I'm tired of not feeling better. (*Silence*) And I'm tired of telling you that. (*Silence*) And I'm tired of therapy. (*Silence*) And you.

Th: Go on.

(*Silence*)

Pt: I'm angry at you for having been away. (*Silence*)

Th: What about that?

Pt: I wanted to speak to you. I know. I know. I know. *I know.* You have someone covering for you. I know. I could have called.

Th: Something kept you.

(*Silence*)

Pt: I don't know. I was very busy. Rushing around from client to client. Christmas is a very busy time for us, and Amy, my assistant, was sick with the flu.

Th: You have two assistants, don't you?

Pt: I couldn't impose on Greg. He's busy enough as it is. And he has his own family to attend to. And I don't want people to think I'm unfairly imposing on them. I pride myself in being fair-minded and treating people as I wish to be treated. I also want to be responsible and get my work done.

Th: You really struggle with asking for help.

Pt: I don't want to be too needy. Jonathan would always say I was too needy. I honestly don't know what he meant. I put him through law school for god's sake. What more did he want? Did he want me to ask for nothing? I do a lot for people. Now I cover my bases so that when I ask for something it can't be taken for me being "too needy."

Th: You needed me. You were angry at me for being away.

Pt: And I was angry at me for needing you.

(*Silence*)

Th: You stopped talking.

Pt: Yes, I did. And I don't know why. (*Silence*) How was I supposed to call your stupid backup? How was I supposed to tell her I was angry at you for having fun when I wasn't? Jonathan was with someone. You were probably with someone. (*Silence*) Listen, I'm sorry. I have no business spouting off like that. You're a decent person and you deserve time off. I lost myself for a moment.

Th: I wonder why you took back your anger.

Pt: Because you might leave me like Jonathan if I make any demands.

Th: So it's very dangerous for you to need me *and* to be angry with me.

(*Silence*)

Pt: I'm so afraid of living life alone. Growing old alone. No one to give Christmas presents to. No husband. No children. No future. Christmas brought so much up.

Th: No one to give Christmas presents to *you.*

Outstanding in this vignette is Doreen's feeling abandoned and deprived and bitterly resentful. She is not only angry at her circumstances and at people she feels have neglected her, she is also—and this is very important—angry at herself for feeling needy. Feeling critical about herself is not very helpful to her self-esteem and contributes to her depression.

NARCISSISTIC

A high degree of self-absorption characterizes narcissistic people. They are themselves their most important object, often consider themselves exceptional persons entitled to special considerations from other people. Others are often not worth the pronounced narcissist's while. A notable inability or refusal to "give" emotionally or to empathize with others prevents them from considering seriously anybody else's inner world, needs, individual qualities, or interests. They sometimes give an overt show of interest, social responsiveness, or affective involvement in others, particularly, perhaps, in order to solicit services or support; nevertheless, they may still seem distant, cold, uninterested, and unapproachable. Their high, perhaps exaggerated, apparent self-regard often reaches the grandiose but is basically a strained defensive effort to compensate for an underlying sense of profound loneliness, emptiness, and lack of self-esteem. The *narcissistic organization* in general represents an anxiety-driven reaction against the anticipated danger of being dependent, helpless, or having to accommodate to others. A deep unarticulated sense of having been deprived of essential care, perhaps early in their lives, dominates them. They have come to believe that in the end they can really only rely on themselves. Narcissistic persons can thrive on flattery and are often vulnerable to, and resentful of, any exposure of imperfection. Anticipating such possible exposures in the therapeutic situation can create considerable anxiety, shame, defensiveness, and sometimes rage.

Neil, a good looking, immaculately dressed thirty-five-year-old man, came to therapy after he ended a six-month relationship with his fiancée. When his therapist returned his initial call quickly his first words on the telephone were, "Boy that was fast. I just called." Neil was quite verbose on the telephone. Despite having been given clear directions on the phone he walked into the therapist's office five minutes early expecting it to be the waiting room. During the session he said of his former fiancée, "I realized that I didn't have feelings for her. She was devastated. Now I feel lonely. It's not like I want to go back to her. I just don't want to end up a lonely old man." Neil had difficulty making connections. He made sure that he was never in one place very long. Indeed he never stayed on one topic very long, which gave the impression of a scattered person. After the fee was set Neil said, "Well, I'm a challenge. I think I'm worth the money. I hope you think you are." Upon leaving at the end of the hour he stopped for a moment, turned to the therapist and asked, "What can I expect from you?" The therapist soon came to see that Neil habitually dealt with his anxiety by throwing people off balance, forcefully intruding upon them, then rejecting and abandoning them. Subsequent sessions revealed his intense rage and contempt for his parents and fears of rejection. He also spoke of his idealization and rapid devaluation of women, and his disgust at what he felt to be the masculine aspects of their bodies, like body hair. The material emerged in an emotionally vapid way, however. He seemed emotionally distant from it. At one point he asked if the therapist would read his lengthy autobiography because he wanted her to really understand him. After four months Neil announced unexpectedly that he decided to take a job in a Nordic country. The following is excerpted from the final session.

Th: You do everything you can to run from the ordinary life.

Pt: That's what my ex-fiancée used to say. I run from the normal. So what's so bad about going away? This is kind of an adventure. Life is short. I want to live it.

Th: I'm not thinking in terms of good or bad. I'm thinking of your abrupt leaving in light of your not wanting to end up a lonely old man. I wonder if this move has been thought through. (Silence) What are you thinking?

Pt: Are we wrapping up now?

Th: Wrapping up? No. We have more time. But why do you ask?

Pt: Well, I wish there was something divine you could say to me to tie it all together.

Th: Well, I can't do that you know.

Pt: Do you have anything to say to me?

Th: I've been saying things all along. What do you recall?

Pt: I really don't recall much.

Th: What do you make of that?

Pt: I have a bad memory. (Pauses, then smiles broadly.) Or may be you haven't said much that is memorable.

Th: That's certainly a possibility. (*Smiles.*) But I will say what I have all along. That you do all you can to avoid ordinary life. And therapy is not all pithy phrases. It is plodding through the ordinary mush and mess of it all.

This excerpt shows a man unwilling to stay the course and deepen existing connections, whether they be with his girlfriend or therapist. Neil is unable to tolerate the ambiguities and ambivalences of intimacy and expects quick, immediately gratifying fixes. One even hears contempt and devaluation in his utterances. His abrupt decision to leave for a distant place speaks for itself. He will go to great lengths to preserve his own defensive mythology as an adventurer. But underneath it all is a man who really cannot allow himself to be found out. He cannot permit himself closeness with anyone. With his abrupt departure he impulsively takes matters in his own hands, reflecting a characteristic narcissistic conviction that ultimately one can expect care only from oneself.

HYSTERICAL

Some people can be described by the old familiar word, *hysterical.* Affects and emotions dominate their behavior more prominently than thought or foresight. Their behavior may be dramatic, with fluid, easily shifting, sometimes uncontrolled emotional states. They may be suggestible and liable to change their minds. Unpleasant or objectionable desires, ideas, and memories are dealt with by *repression*, disregard, or indifference, shallow and vague thinking, or Pollyannaish *denial*. Occasionally this makes hysterical persons charming in a somewhat childlike way. Such people's ability to look at themselves tends to be limited. Exploring their inner world is stoutly resisted, and encouraging them to do so or entertain new views of themselves may produce great anxiety. People with hysterical features tend to avoid seeing themselves as agents of their fate; instead they prefer to see themselves as passive victims. Sometimes they appear childlike and to a certain extent naive, even "clueless." They tend to be much concerned with their bodies and seem to have special capacities to develop certain physical symptoms, which on medical evaluation may be without organic basis. Hysterical symptoms at times appear as additional painful elaborations of actual physical or medical conditions (e.g., incurable coughs long after an infection is gone or continued pain after an injury has healed). In both men and women sexuality and all its subtle or obvious manifestations appear as a source of anxiety, revulsion, moral indignation, and disgust and may be dealt with by apathy, apparent coldness, or conspicuous ignorance. On the other hand it may be expressed in dealing with other people by coy flirtation or manifest attempts at seduction. Such efforts sometimes show themselves in the therapeutic relation too and may serve the purpose of deflecting the therapist's exploration of difficult or unpleasant issues.

Harriette is a woman of thirty-five who entered therapy complaining of "anxiety attacks" and depressed feelings. She is in a relationship with Alex who is "exciting" and who promises to be with her but takes no substantive action in that direction. She works late afternoon and evening hours as an aerobics instructor at a local gym, which is fortunate because she experiences great difficulty waking up in the morning and getting out of the house. Although she is currently of normal weight, this has not always been the case. For roughly five years, from her late teens to early twenties, she struggled with bulimia and her weight would fluctuate. In the last year and a half she has begun to speak of frequent headaches, fatigue, and insomnia. Although tests have come up negative Harriette is sure that her symptoms are connected to something physical. She has been prescribed antidepressant medication but refuses to take it. She constantly asks for "tranquilizers."

Harriette is stuck. She is prone to emotional outbursts. She will deny any anger at Alex and any suggestion that her symptoms may be connected to her feelings. About her past and her family she speaks precious little. Her father and mother live in an apartment in the next town. She has one sister who is "a pain." One day she came to therapy feeling especially anxious.

Pt: I had another anxiety attack, or panic attack, or whatever you call it. On the freeway I thought that I was going to have an accident. My heart was pounding. I was sweating. And I couldn't focus. It was horrible. When is this going to end? What's wrong with me?

Th: What do you suppose triggered the attack?

Pt: I don't know. The day was going fine. Well, as fine as it ever is with these symptoms.

Th: Well, why don't you tell me more specifically about the day, fine as it was. Perhaps there is something we can learn.

Pt: There was nothing special about it. (*Silence*) What do you want to know? (*Silence*)

Th: It seems difficult for you to bring in the details of your day.

Pt: But there was nothing special about it. I got up. I felt miserable, *as usual*. I drank some coffee left over from last night. I was too miserable to make a fresh pot, *as usual*. I got dressed to go to the mall 'cause I needed new leggings. And then I had the panic attack. On the way to the mall. I swear I thought I wasn't going to make it. I don't know what other details to tell you. (*As usual*, the therapist thought, feeling frustrated with her.)

Th: The last time you had a panic attack was when Alex didn't call you for several days.

Pt: Yeah, we were supposed to go out . . . When were we supposed to . . .? Not last night. The night before last. I can't remember anything these days with these headaches. Let's see. I can't . . . I don't know. But his mother got sick, and he had to take her to the hospital.

Th: You had plans to get together.

Pt: Yeah. I was disappointed. (*Silence*)

Th: I see. Tell me more about that—being disappointed.

Pt: That's it. I was disappointed. What could I do? His mother was sick. He had to take care of her. She's okay now.

Th: I've noticed that plans have changed a lot between the two of you in the last few weeks.

Pt: Well, things come up. It happens. I understand. But we're getting together tonight. I called Alex from the mall. He was so sweet. He said that he loved me and that things would work out. We'll see each other tonight. He's so sweet when it comes to my well-being. He says I'll be fine. He's so understanding. My last boyfriend was a mess. He didn't have a good job. He didn't have any direction. I wonder if I ever loved him. Well, I did at the beginning. Or at least I thought I did. But things changed.

Th: You sounded charged up just now.

Pt: He was good for nothing. Just sat on his ass. He never wanted to do anything. (*Silence*)

Th: Can you say what you are feeling now?

Pt: Frustrated just thinking about him. Wouldn't you be? He was like a mule. You'd want to kick him. (*Harriette laughs. Silence. The therapist smiles at the metaphor.*)

Th: Like a mule?

Pt: I know that's awful to say. (*Laughs. Silence*) You're looking at me. You think I'm crazy. I probably am. (*Silence*) I need an aspirin. Do you have an aspirin? You're not allowed to give patients aspirins. Right? I'm getting an EEG next week. I want to get to the bottom of this. (*Silence*) Anyhow I can't wait to see Alex. I love him so much. He's unlike any person I've known. I always feel better around him.

Th: As you were talking I wondered if you sometimes felt like kicking Alex for breaking dates with you.

Pt: No. Not really. There's no point in that. Besides we are seeing each other tonight.

Harriette is unable to access any conflictual feelings. Her descriptions of relationships with people are thin and superficial. She cannot stay with any complex feelings and defaults to teeny bopper–like idealizations and devaluations. She seems very angry at Alex but veers away from such feelings to avoid dealing with her own dependency needs and fears of being alone. Her therapist feels frustrated with Harriette and wishes she could give the patient a push that might dislodge some of her defensiveness.

OBSESSIVE

Obsessive individuals can be pedantic, tedious, ruminative, and often they tend to live by strict, sometimes elaborate, and anxiously held-to routines. They are also known to be conscientious, righteous, and perfectionistic, sometimes espousing an abstract kind of idealism. Adherence to principles, rules, and procedures sometimes overrides live human concerns. Cool and contained aggressiveness may feed into their hard-headedness, rigidity, coldness, and lack of spontaneity. Obsessive people deal with anxiety and conflict by *in-*

tellectualization, emphasizing "rationality," occasionally to the point of absurdity. *Isolation of affect,* the disconnection of feeling from thinking, and *reaction formation* are typical forms of defense. The obsessional's effort to disregard or eliminate feeling can deprive them of guidance for action; this in turn can lead to indecisiveness and paralyzing doubt. Ambivalence appears in many forms and about many things. These individuals will alternately approach and avoid, do and undo, resulting in their inability to make up their minds. Often they fight against experiencing feelings altogether.

Orson is a twenty-three-year-old man who came to therapy feeling depressed and hopeless. He had just graduated from college and was applying to graduate school in English literature. For the last three months he had been dating Adele, a woman his age, also depressed. Orson spoke in a droll way. Unable to express genuine affect he complained of boredom and disillusionment with life and people, including his girlfriend. He was preoccupied with fears of not getting into graduate school, with poor job prospects, and being used by people. He could be brutally cynical and pessimistic. Over time it became clear that Orson was desperately trying to protect himself from overwhelming feelings. He described his mother as critical, demanding, and withholding, and his father as ineffectual. He was scared of abandonment and was both ashamed of and enraged at the intensity of his dependent longings. He avoided emotional closeness because he viewed it as an intrusion to be feared. When there were signs of beginning intimacy with someone he would quickly undo them. He kept other people at a distance by way of his intellectual cynicism and subtly aggressive means of controlling them. But these efforts alternated with expressions of loneliness and wishes to be dependent. Unlike Neil, Orson stayed in treatment. Fears of abandonment and rejection kept him from leaving a therapist who could handle his intensity. See for example Orson's reaction to the therapist's being ten minutes late on one occasion. She inquired how it was for Orson to have to wait.

Pt: Oh, it's fine. (*Orson said this abruptly, followed by quite a lengthy silence.*)

Th: Where did your mind turn?

Pt: Oh. Just to Adele. We went out with friends on Saturday. They didn't like me. I didn't particularly like them either. No one paid much attention to me. It's not like I didn't try, you know. It's not as if I just sat there. I gave it a shot. How many times can a person be expected to make contact? . . . There was this one guy. He started talking about something intelligent, about writing and movies, but ended up talking about something useless. Football. For a moment there I thought something interesting might happen.

Th: You felt left out?

Pt: There was really nothing I wanted to be part of. (*Pauses, then continues without much feeling.*) Oh, by the way here's today's fee and last week's. (*Orson pulled out his wallet and several crisp bills.*) Before I forget—like last week. (*He hands the money over to the therapist who places it on the table beside her, refolds his wallet, and puts it back in his pocket.*) I don't like these things hanging over my head.

Th: You pay on time. It was only last week that you forgot. (*She says this quite casually.*)

Pt: I can't stand it when people don't pay on time. It's inconsiderate. People have no sense of etiquette, of doing the right thing. (*Silence*) I tried to be gracious on Saturday. I tried to listen to these people talk about football, but they all started to behave like morons.

Th: How so?

Pt: How so? Haven't you seen a group of drunk guys talk sports?

Th: What did you observe?

Pt: Well, stupid jokes, stupid comments about women. I'm really not into that. And some of these guys had some college education. I'm surprised that Adele put up with it. Really surprised. She should have just walked out.

Th: Sounds like she was having a good time with the rest of them.

Pt: Well, that's what's so disturbing, to be quite frank. If that's what turns her on then maybe this relationship needs to be rethought. I really don't think I can tolerate this crudeness. I actually took a shower when I got home and did my laundry first thing Sunday so as to get the smell of beer and chicken wings and smoke out of my clothes. I know I'm not going to do that again.

Th: You sound very particular about the way you like things.

Pt: I am. No one has standards that I can see. No one these days has any sense of doing the right thing. Am I the only one?

Th: You express strong feelings but with such a straight face.

Pt: Excuse me?

Th: I said you express strong feelings with such a straight face.

Pt: Well what am I supposed to do? Behave like those morons. I don't think so. (*Silence*)

Th: You strike me as very concerned with doing the right thing. In fact you've used the phrase twice today. You speak of moronic behavior; you make sure to pay me. In that light I wonder if there is more to your reaction to my being late than, "It's fine."

Pt: No. It happens. You're on time generally. I have standards but I can understand that sometimes people are late. No, it's fine. That's not so much what I wonder about as whether I've done as much as I can here. I'm a little less depressed than I was and that's good, but graduate school still bothers me. I don't know why I even applied. I just shouldn't pin my hopes on getting in anywhere. If I get in . . . and that's a big "if" . . . it'll probably be more useless crap. I'll be overworked and used up by professors. I don't think I've gotten anywhere on that front.

Th: You're concerned that you'll feel let down again.

Pt: I don't trust people.

Th: Tell me about that.

Pt: It's the same old same old. People usually turn out to be disappointments. They don't understand me, or want something from me, or don't want to talk about anything beyond the latest film or fashion for that matter. So I don't see any reason to get close to morons . . .

Orson is extremely anxious and conflicted about being liked and fitting in. His yearning for acceptance is huge, but he feels too vulnerable to rejection to take a chance and join in the fun. These things are contained and expressed in his obsessive and cynical preoccupation with "morons" who have few if any standards. The therapist tried to bring Orson's concerns into the here and now when she returned to the subject of her lateness, which she felt must have confirmed his feeling undeserving of anyone's interest. She thought that he was likely deeply disappointed, angry, perhaps even ashamed, and in characteristic fashion retreated into his negative, hostile, and tiresome self-righteousness. Orson cannot address this issue. When he responds, "It's fine," he denies any discontent about the therapist's lateness but follows this with associations to people as disappointments. Orson had difficulty leaving the session. It was hard for him to be with his therapist (his needs were so big and scary) and hard for him to be without her (she offered hope and acceptance). Orson came back the following week.

PARANOID

Paranoid people are motivated by a deep sense of living surrounded by danger, danger deriving from other people's ill will, threats, even persecution. Their primary attitude is distrust; they expect to be misled and deceived and believe in hidden implications behind apparent realities. They are vigilant and alert, try to anticipate betrayal, abuse, attack, or insult by searching out the hidden motives of others or the "real" reasons and meanings of things. In their relations to others they are suspicious, cautious, and guarded. Their way of looking at the world is rigid, often dominated by strange but fixed convictions. Information disconfirming their suspicions is ignored. At the extreme one may see a psychotic loss of realism. Sometimes they see themselves as victims of serious injustice and ruminate about possibilities of obtaining revenge. These people are hypersensitive to feeling diminished and cut down, and issues of dominance and submission are always in play. The paranoid style likely has deep roots in a person's development. Early and conflicted experiences in relation with others may have left the young person insecure, distrustful, and with unclear and conflicted feelings. By means of defensive *projection* such persons attribute some of their own disturbing, especially aggressive, feelings to others whom they tend to fear. In the therapeutic situation such patients can take a long time before they begin to trust the therapist's good intentions. Much depends on her consistency, straightforwardness, patience, and quiet strength.

Perry is a twenty-year-old man seen at a community clinic for "problems with relationships." He lives alone and works at a local bookstore. Perry has been unable to sustain a relationship with a woman for more than a few months. His work history has been discontinuous, characterized by contentious run-ins with fellow employees, even supervisors and employers. Similarly a succession of therapies has ended on a bitter note. Perry has developed something of a reputation among the people who know him. His parents, who live in another state, were divorced when he was eleven years old. Both were strict and withholding. Father could be physically and emotionally abusive. Perry describes having been scared of him. Further he does not recall his two younger sisters being treated as badly as he. Perry is extremely suspicious of people, automatically assumes that their motives are sinister, and he is prone to feeling rejected. He finds it difficult to contain his rage. Recently he has reported feeling quite sad and hopeless. Perry's therapist is female. A male staff psychiatrist, Dr. X, prescribes antidepressant medication and is considering a mood stabilizer or neuroleptic because of the intensity of his rage and paranoia. In this session Perry comes in wearing his characteristic beret but does not take it off, as is his custom. He looks despondent. He sits down and says nothing. The therapist opens the session. In a light way and with a smile she says:

Th: I notice you are keeping your hat on today.

Pt: Yes. I had a haircut.

Th: Oh. And you won't take your hat off.

Pt: It was cut too short.

Th: Oh. What about that?

Pt: I hate it when it's too short. I feel naked. (*Pause*) I really don't want to talk about my hair if you don't mind.

Th: Okay (*She is feeling a little defensive herself here.*) What would you like to talk about? (*Silence*) Where did your thoughts turn?

Pt: Did you and Dr. X speak about me?

Th: What? (*She is puzzled.*)

Pt: Did you and Dr. X speak about me?

Th: I don't know what you mean. Why do you ask?

Pt: When I saw Dr. X yesterday he seemed irritated. I told him that he seemed angry at me. He didn't want to respond. He just wanted to talk about medication. Last week you and I talked about how I can make people angry. It was a big deal for me to talk about that then.

Th: Indeed.

Pt: Then yesterday he gets angry at me. I don't think I did anything to deserve that. It was then that I thought maybe you two talked, and that somehow that affected his attitude. I know he doesn't like me. I got that feeling from him from the first time we met. He didn't want to look at me then. He was busy writing notes. And when he did look at me it was only very briefly. Like he didn't want to make eye contact. But until yesterday he kept things in check pretty well. Until he tells me that he's considering Respirdol. I know what that is. It's for people who aren't in touch with reality. And aren't psychiatrists supposed to meet for twenty minutes? Well, he only saw me for fifteen. If he hates me, he hates me. I'll live with that, but I won't put up with being shortchanged when it comes to medical care. And I think it's unprofessional to talk about patients behind their backs.

(*The therapist is rather taken aback by Perry at this point.*)

Th: Well, what do you imagine we said? (*At this point she is quite annoyed but remains calm.*)

Pt: You were probably talking about what a difficult patient I am. (*Silence*)

Th: Hm.

Pt: I bet you were telling him all about my seeing previous therapists. If you did that, then how can I ever trust you? (*Silence. Perry looks down at his shoes. Then at the therapist. Then out the window. The therapist detects a slight pout.*)

Th: You think I'm sneaky. (*During the silence her attitude toward Perry shifts, as if she is now saying to him, "Okay, let's play." She counters Perry with a direct comment concerning the implications of his words.*)

Pt: (*Perry himself is taken aback at this point.*) That's not what I said.

Th: Sure it is. (*She is feeling more self-assured here, even some-what amused.*) You think I'm a sneak. After all we've been through together. (*She seems to have found her footing.*)

Pt: I just don't understand Dr. X's attitude.

Th: Well, I can't speak for Dr. X, but I'm really struck by your focus-ing on my alleged betrayal of you as if nothing good ever hap-pened between us in our work together. It is as if you erased all of our work together up to this point. How did you imagine I would feel hearing this?

Pt: I don't know . . . I didn't mean to hurt your feelings. Don't be so sensitive. I'm supposed to be able to say whatever is on my mind here. Right? (*Perry is looking quite uncomfortable at this point.*)

Th: That's right. But we're also supposed to think about what you say. I think something made you feel very threatened. Perhaps the idea of going on Respirdol. Maybe something else. And I think you reacted by getting very angry and thinking that Dr. X and I were de-vious and talked about you in unprofessional ways, ways that went beyond the necessary sharing of any clinical information.

Pt: I didn't know what he was thinking. There he was with his pre-scription pad and his pen deciding things about me.

Th: (*Gently urging.*) Tell me.

Immediately upon starting the session Perry initiates a power struggle: he is not revealing anything, thank you—at least not consciously. He feels naked and vulnerable; perhaps his too short hair makes it easier for his therapist to read his mind? As he continues we see clearly his defenses of *projection* and *splitting*. His therapist calls him on these. With regulated af-fect she remarks that he thinks she's a sneak after all they've been through together. If the therapist had been unable to stand back and examine what was happening and had reacted to him by either apologizing or getting an-gry back at him, we would have seen an example of the defense of projec-tion becoming *projective identification*. In this situation the therapist was able to take enough distance to interpret what was happening during the hour. As a result Perry was able to experience his vulnerability in a new and more constructive way.

Psychotherapy is a difficult enterprise. It requires a substantial absorption of requisite knowledge as well as the capacity to remain open-minded and flexible in the face of the new. The strength of our craft is really only as good as a clinician's ability to apprehend both theoretical precedents as well as the great variety of individual human beings who may ever again confront her with the unforeseen. Individual experience often wanders away from general law, as does a child from the arms of its mother. Psychotherapy's valuation of the case study underscores the premium it places on individuality and difference. As much as we need the organizing effects of established knowledge we need the unexpected to pull us into new places of human understanding.

II

CREATING A ROOM OF ONE'S OWN

. . . to have a room of her own, let alone a quiet room or a sound-proof room. . .

—Virginia Woolf, *A Room of One's Own*

Here we wish to address the process of learning to be a psychodynamic therapist, one that involves both personal and professional growth. Inspired by the work of Virginia Woolf, we envision this process as akin to creating "a room of one's own," literally a room in which the therapist works, but also her internal or psychological room. The latter continues to widen and change its shape over the years, reflecting the emergence of a professional identity. The concept of a room of one's own has helped us organize this section of the book.

There really never is a final destination in this process. The potential for learning about ourselves and our work is always present. A patient challenges our well-seasoned impressions and convictions; we experience doubt, confusion; we question what we know, or think we know. We loosen up old ways of thinking and put our thoughts together differently. We learn new things from our supervisors, personal therapy, colleagues, patients themselves, and life at large. We recognize the wisdom and the folly of our mentors and of ourselves. The challenges are on-going; psychological work is perpetual; both patient and therapist are continually evolving; and no two therapies are alike. For those who like their parcels neatly wrapped, psychotherapy may be more a frustrating enterprise than an exciting or enlightening one. In psychotherapy, a parcel unwrapped is likely to disclose further ones, like the children's game.

Part II is an all too brief exploration of how we have begun to think about learning to be a psychodynamic psychotherapist; it could be a volume in itself. We begin by looking at personal experiences and qualities we feel are necessary and useful to potential therapists. We then discuss therapists' training needs, distinguishing between what we call Early Learning, which is formal training, and Later Learning, which succeeds it. While it is likely that some of the underpinnings of a future psychotherapeutic identity are silently laid down in early life, it is most consciously and rapidly shaped during the process of Later Learning. It is during this time in a therapist's career that the task of creating her own room, finding her place in the professional world, gains momentum.

6

The Therapist: Her Personal Experiences and Qualities

It has been asked "Is a therapist taught or born?" If not definitively answerable the question is interesting. While the craft of psychotherapy certainly needs to be a learned enterprise some people clearly have a greater propensity to pick it up than others. Therapists do seem to possess certain talents probably from early on in life, and they appreciate and refine those talents as time goes by and work them into their psychotherapeutic identities. Here we offer our thoughts on some of those experiences and qualities. You may find that some parts of our discussion are personally relevant to you while others are not. And surely you may have observations and thoughts of your own. At any rate here are some of our ideas.

Psychotherapists, like other people, have experienced difficulties in their early lives. They may know emotional suffering, confusion, discouragement, and uncertainty. For reasons that cannot always be traced some future therapists develop particular ways of being able to stand back a little from their own experiences. They question them and look for rhyme and reason. That is to say they begin to do their own individual psychological work. They may have been aided in this by an example provided by a significant other person. They come to use their understandings constructively in their own inner lives as well as in their work with patients. All this adds significantly to the development of their characters, therapeutic skills, and depth. It is up to each one of us to decide how far we go in this journey of self-exploration and discovery.

Having had earlier convincing experiences of being helped and cared for in some manner by another can contribute a good deal to the making of a therapist. When teaching we sometimes ask trainees whether they would share personal experiences of being helped. In one instance a trainee recounted the time he spoke to a college advisor about conflicts related to changing his major. He remembers the advisor's attentiveness, saying "I hear you," and suggesting useful administrative steps. The trainee was deeply grateful. "There was an almost magical quality to it," he said, "an unqualified understanding. An easy, unobstructed validation. She didn't doubt my sincerity. And I was so scared. I really needed extra units and wasn't at all sure that I would get them. I now know that the advisor must have dealt with similar situations innumerable times. But, nonetheless, I felt singularly important. There was now a viable academic future possible for me, and I felt hopeful. She helped me move on." He told the seminar that the words "I hear you" have stayed with him to this day.

This trainee's story puts the spotlight on knowing what it is like to be helped. It shows that some of what we give to others may be predicated upon our having been given it at some point ourselves. Such experience may persist unconsciously for a long time; at relevant moments, however, it may arise into conscious memory, sometimes in a dramatic manner.

The capacity to form an *emotional connection* with another human being is central among the characteristics and skills on which a therapist relies. Forming an emotional connection depends on one's being able, in good faith, earnestness, and skill to *listen to* and *hear* what another is saying. It requires us to be empathic, an ability to be in touch with the inner experience of another, even to feel some of his feelings. The therapist needs to be open and receptive to what is occurring in the patient, to put her own needs aside temporarily, and to withhold judgment. This is not always easy. At times it can be hard to follow a patient's line of thought or to feel at home with some of the patient's convictions, emotions, and affective reactions. We have to *learn* each person with whom we are working, understand him for himself, as different from anyone else, like *no other person*. Being deeply heard is a precious thing: *It* is like no other. Empathic ability is one aspect of emotional maturity. It is spontaneous and intuitive, not consciously calculated or manipulated. The therapist's own individual psychological work may have assisted her in developing that ability. Our trainee was fortunate to connect with a person so empathically responsive. That encounter may have resonated with others earlier in his life, which contributed to his ability to profit from his advisor's help.

Empathy implies recognition of other people's inner lives, of invisible domains of experience that may exert powerful effects. It must be accompanied by a basic attitude of respect; internal life is not much held in high esteem. Interest and curiosity about the internal workings of the mind, and valuing of introspection and self-reflection, are indispensable to the future therapist. She must be able to understand that people have reasons for the things they do even if those reasons are presently unknown, and that these reasons grew from experience, internal as well as external. This curiosity must have also been present early on in the therapist's life, in her questioning attitude toward her own inner pains and confusions, and perhaps toward those or others close to her.

An interest in the human condition and curiosity about exploring it are things that therapists share with artists and writers. They also try to understand and describe how people function, make meaning, and shape their fates. As does the work of artists the work of therapists depends on imagination. While the therapist begins getting to know her patient as he starts to unpack his issues and concerns, she may find herself imagining additional implications and alternative meanings, perhaps even some that would be unimaginable to the patient in his present state. She will develop a picture of the patient in her own mind, but not a fixed one. She will keep it flexible and avoid jumping to premature conclusions. She stays as Suzuki writes, ". . . always ready for anything; . . . open to everything."

Tolerance for the limitations of understanding must accompany the therapist's curiosity and imagination. We try to befriend the unknown: there are many things about the ways of our patients and ourselves that will, despite our best efforts, remain elusive. Often we will be puzzled or confused. Nevertheless, as messy as it can get with paper and string strewn all about, a therapist still wants to open the human package.

Good psychotherapists know, however, that packages cannot be forced open. As much as we wish to look inside we must respect the pace of each individual. We must be able to bear or hold uncertainty and at times great distress both in ourselves and the other. To these ends the therapist must nourish her capacity for patience, for tolerating delay of gratification, and she must recognize the value of contemplation. Each patient proceeds at his own pace, a pace that may vary greatly over the course of the work. A therapy may drift through what can appear to be doldrums for a time, the therapist all the while remaining alert to any hint of movement in its sails. A therapist needs these qualities because quick and clear solutions are not the norm in our profession. As writers and artists who go to their studies, studios, and rehearsal halls, each day we go to our consulting rooms, practice our craft with honesty, and essentially wait for things to come ashore both in our patients and in ourselves.

While this may seem like a thing too obvious to say a therapist should be a person who basically likes people. Only then is it possible for patients to know that they are in the presence of a decent and benevolent human being whose demeanor is one of openness, competence, and kindness; someone who will not rush to judgment.

Having experienced help herself, developing a sensitivity to inner life and an interest in others, identifying with caregivers and so on, all seem to contribute to a therapist's way of being. Yet they are not in themselves explanations of how one comes to choose this profession. Many other experiences and unconscious workings and elaborations, not easily traceable, must act together to form the psychotherapist's identity.

7

Wobbly and Brittle

Finding one's way as a psychotherapist has its rewards, but it is not easy and there can be many stressors. Therapists can react to these pressures in a number of ways. We can try to think about these ways by placing them along a continuum characterized on one side by a tendency to be open to experience and on the other side by a tendency to be closed to experience. We like to call the two ends of this continuum *wobbly* and *brittle*, respectively. At the extreme end of open a therapist can become very dependent on and overly influenced by her supervisors or patients or others. Pulled in different directions she can become very wobbly, moving first this way and then that way, getting disoriented and removed from her own thoughts and experiences. Take the example of setting fees. It is certainly good practice to hear out the patient's circumstances, but it is not such a good practice to yield to a fee much lower than one can live with. Beginning therapists (and not-so-beginning ones for that matter), still measuring their worth and gathering experience, may out of anxiety, agree to a fee quickly and sell themselves short. Yet it must also be underscored that openness to input, if tempered and not extreme, gives a therapist a kind of flexibility that can protect her as a tree that is able to sway back and forth is protected against high winds.

A therapist on the other side of the continuum has the advantage of remaining steadfast and sticking to her guns when challenged. But the extreme, close-mindedness, is like a kind of stubbornness, and under high winds the inability to sway or bend can put her in danger of breaking a limb, as it were. In such a scenario rigidity can render the therapist quite brittle. Taking up the fee example again let's think of a therapist who will not budge from a set rate. After all is she not well trained and gifted? Does she not deserve her worth? This may be so, but for most in the field some negotiation is made for the sake of imparting to the patient that the therapist has some flexibility, that there is meaning to this work, which includes setting a fee. Further, for many, negotiating a fee also ensures a practice and an income.

Both propensities with their attendant ways of reacting have their strengths and weaknesses. In trying to be sensitive to, even tolerant of, a very wide range of experience, therapists as a group are perhaps more vulnerable to wobbling. But one also encounters rigidity and brittleness. Staying somewhere in the center of the continuum would seem optimal: judging when to hold one's own, when to give ground.

8

Early Learning

The process of therapists' acquiring the tools of their craft can be divided into two phases: Early Learning and Later Learning. The course of one's formal training comprises what we call Early Learning. By Later Learning we mean all that occurs afterward—*everything else, forever.*

Early Learning in psychotherapy as elsewhere primarily involves taking in. Beginning students are being newly exposed to all kinds of information, both theoretical and practical. Early Learning depends on developing relationships with mentors: identifying with them, imitating them, joining with them to work on clinical cases, admiring, even idealizing them. Their external as well as internal presence supports the beginner during periods of stress, it being important to have someone there "with her in the consulting room" as it were. Early Learning takes place in four contexts: didactics, direct clinical experience, supervision, and personal psychotherapy.

DIDACTICS

The didactic aspect of training requires study of theories of human development and of the varieties of psychotherapeutic approaches, modalities, and techniques. Much of this may be new for students who have not acquired an academic background in psychology. Didactic learning involves a confrontation with approaches to treatment that are often not clearly distinguishable, that are even quite conflicting. Students must grapple with different views of the nature of personality, psychopathology, and intervention. In time they will begin to extract what seem to them the essential features of different theories and orientations and begin to integrate them into a growing position of their own. In the course of doing so students will come to recognize how their intellectual leanings and choices express their own psychological makeup.

DIRECT CLINICAL EXPERIENCE

Direct clinical experience begins with the trainee's first encounter with a patient. Here she faces a mixture of different challenges. Some of them have to do with quite practical matters: the first telephone call; how to meet and greet the patient in a good way; how to make the necessary arrangements. Other challenges arise in the trainee's own inner world: anxieties, uncertainty of how to behave, coping with unfamiliar emotional reactions of her own. Trying on this new role can be exciting, perhaps even exhilarating, but overwhelming and stressful as well. All these experiences are quite different from those that she encounters in pursuing her academic agenda: reading, teaching, and doing research. Shifting into clinical work can be scary and tiring; beginners, therefore, should see few patients, perhaps three or four, by the end of the first year. With increasing experience they will be able to work with a greater number of patients. Not everything will be new; patterns will come to be recognized, practical knowledge and sound clinical judgment will grow as, with luck, wisdom will too. There is no substitute for the experience of sitting directly with a patient.

DIDACTICS AND PRACTICE

Theory helps therapists organize their perceptions and is a way for them to communicate with each other. It serves as a kind of common language, a reference to shared experience. Problems with using theoretical constructs, however, arise when concepts are ill defined or people mean different things when speaking the same words. Problems also come about when therapists dismiss their own perceptions in favor of what they have read or been told. They begin to wobble. In this case we see a sort of tyranny of theory. Theory should serve as informant, collaborator, not as dictator. Slavish adherence to theory is the killer of creativity. Because theory is intellectual it can be read and learned quickly whereas experience with patients grows more slowly. It is not unusual to find a therapist shifting her theoretical emphasis as she gains experience and changes. In the end therapists are guided by what they have formed as their own theoretical basis, a combination of what they have learned academically and of ideas and conclusions they draw from their encounters with individual patients.

Theory provides us with a set of concepts that name the phenomena we encounter and help guide our thinking about what we are doing. As such it orients us and gives a measure of coherence to our experience. It is interesting to speculate why a particular theoretical position attracts us. Intellectual proclivities are at best only a partial reason. More likely we gravitate to a certain theory because it somehow meshes with our character, has immediacy and personal significance for us, and therefore a special vitality.

In certain ways then theory can inform, that is, give definition to, our intuition. But theory can also guide us in ways that go counter to our intuition or personal experience or impulses. Take, for example, the situation in which a patient comes feeling very distraught, hopeless about therapy and everything else, and pulls for support. The therapist picks up on the distress and responds in a gentle and nurturing manner. The patient leaves the session apparently more consolidated and calm. The next session he comes in sullen, angry, and oppositional. Not what the therapist expected. She thought she was being understanding, but upon reflection she wondered if in her zeal she took a less than neutral stance, that is, addressed only one side of the patient's set of feelings toward her. Yes, the patient wanted to be close to her, but he was also frightened of just that. Upon further exploration the patient was able to say that he was angry at the therapist because the closeness he felt stimulated a need for more contact, even physical contact, with her, which he knew he could ultimately never have. The therapist realized that to have been more fully empathic would have required being less sympathetic. Such is hindsight. Hindsight can, however, develop into useful foresight. Theory then can suggest alternatives which intuition itself might not provide.

New therapists often remain quite conscious of what they have learned theoretically; they hold on to such knowledge to feel more secure. In time, and with increasing therapeutic self-confidence, theoretical ideas are less in the forefront of consciousness, although still they guide the therapist's activities and interventions. Clinical teachers and mentors must recognize this fact, namely, that they themselves are not so conscious anymore of how theory affects their work. They will have to explain to trainees what they do in their own therapeutic work, even though they do not always explicitly account for it themselves. Seasoned clinicians should respect and support the beginner's intense early efforts at integrating the theoretical material she learns in class with her initial patient contacts. What is she to focus on? How is she to sort through the barrage of information coming her way? Or understand and bear awkward silences?

Whatever theoretical position you embrace at any given time it is important to remember that theoretical terms have no place in therapeutic conversation. The essence and power of psychotherapy lie in the patient's experiencing feelings and new ways of being, not in intellectual exchange.

SUPERVISION

Supervision is the one-to-one guidance given to a student in her dealings with patients, and along with one's personal psychotherapy is key to learning this craft. It is part of the experiential component of training and is not purely intellectual. Supervision can, and perhaps should, extend throughout one's career. Later in one's learning it may take on a different flavor—it is perhaps more collegial—but its essential functions remain the same.

Supervision, in most instances, consists of the therapist-in-training reporting the story of her work with the patient to a more experienced clinician. Both she and the supervisor can then review this material and think and talk about it together. For beginners the supervisor often takes on a more active and directive role, given that early clinical encounters bring so much that is new, and attempting to integrate all of this can be very difficult. It is the function of supervision to help the trainee organize what she is experiencing, both in terms of the content and the psychological processes involved. Supervision should provide different perspectives and ways to think about therapeutic work as well as help a trainee read her own reactions and use them clinically.

Each supervisor will impart a somewhat different way of working with patients, from varied theoretical orientations to turns of phrase. It is important to experience this variation because it will give you a feel for the range in clinical styles, and it is from this range that you will pick and choose as you develop your own personal style. Unfortunately in many training sites the opportunity to see practiced therapists in immediate clinical action or presenting a case is rare, often nonexistent, even though it might offer invaluable information to trainees, a kind of learning by example. After all, for better or worse, singers listen to other singers perform publicly or on record, pianists listen to maestros, baseball players watch their heroes on TV or in the ballpark, surgery residents accompany their teachers to the operating room.

Over time supervision can underscore strengths and help develop clinical capacities and comfort in working with problems that may seem strange, incomprehensible, or even repugnant. It can also define areas where one has, for the time being at least, empathic limitations. A productive supervision is one in which both strengths and current limitations can be explored and developed with the least amount of intimidation.

Supervision, especially early supervision, is important insofar as an effective supervisor can help set a tone for learning as something that is ongoing and never complete. Keeping ideas and formulations organized not as certainties but as possibilities is a way of keeping us honest, honorable, and humble. If our supervisors don't teach us this our patients will.

Supervision is not personal psychotherapy to be sure. And different supervisors will have different thresholds for the amount of personal information they wish to deal with from their trainees. There is no hard and fast rule here, and a supervisor ultimately does what she is comfortable doing. But there are some ways to think about the situation. There is much that goes on in the process of supervision that directly relates to the clinical process. Foremost in our view supervision is ideally a protected space, in some ways like the therapeutic space, where the trainee can speak openly and safely about her own experience and feelings. Indeed much of her imaginative thinking flows from these places and can enrich the therapeutic process. Generally speaking a trainee can hardly be expected to speak freely and retain an empathic and nonjudgmental stance toward the patient when she finds no similar attitude in the supervisor's stance toward her.

PERSONAL PSYCHOTHERAPY

We have always been taken aback when a trainee asks if personal psychotherapy would be valuable or necessary. The answer should be yes, if you seriously want to work at this craft. Experience with one's own personal psychotherapy is the single most direct and potentially powerful part of one's training. There are several reasons for this. First, the therapy will provide a demonstration of what the therapeutic situation is like, how it is conducted, and what it feels like to be a patient. After all you are learning a craft that involves the sentient presence of another human being. Personal therapy lets you see another therapist in operation, providing a model for identification. The vivid experience in your own therapy of creating, carrying on, and finally terminating a therapeutic relation prepares you for successfully carrying through relations with those who have and will come to work with you. Second, the therapy is very important in clarifying for you the issues involved in work with other people, the prejudices and biases you might have and their origins. Coming to know more about things that we have tried to disregard or fend off in ourselves prepares us for greater sensitivity and tolerance for things in other people that otherwise would have been very strange to us. Self-knowledge is essential to this work. Knowing yourself is critical if you are to maintain your focus and your standards. Clinical work will bring up personal issues. This is inevitable. This is the nature of the beast. Personal therapy will help you sort out your reactions to patients, determine what the patient is stimulating in or pulling from you. When we speak of self-knowledge we speak of some understanding of who we are and where we stand: our identity; our patterns of relating; our needs: relational, intellectual, financial, recreational, spiritual; and our values. Every therapist must work this out for herself. Each has a different personal history and different present circumstances. Third, therapy also provides a situation in which a future therapist comes to form impressions of what are the possibilities and limitations of psychotherapeutic progress. She will determine for herself who is most suitable for what method, what are realistic aims, and when the course of a particular piece of work may reasonably come to an end.

9

Later Learning

After formal training many of us are faced with the loss, sometimes stark, of a relatively protected environment. As we begin to find our place in the world, as we begin to build our own rooms, we actively search for other structures within which to work. We may experience a shift in status within our training site, make a move to another clinical setting near or far, perhaps open a private practice. Initially, especially, this is a time of transition, of tremendous novelty and change. It is a time of rapid learning and has its own share of exhilaration and very real stressors. This is Later Learning.

Although the foundations for the room we are building are being laid throughout our training it is really during this stage in professional development that the concept of *ownership* truly begins to come into prominence. In our view ownership primarily means the development and refinement of a professional identity and with it a clarity of vision and voice.

As we have said Early Learning is characterized primarily by taking in information, idealizing mentors, identifying with them, and internalizing certain of their ways. In the puzzling new world of the clinical encounter these processes are essential because the trainee needs something to hold onto, to orient herself by. Although taking in continues, the process of internally differentiating herself from images of her mentors and supervisors becomes a major part of Later Learning. During this time the therapist will learn more about her craft, herself, and her needs and how she handles them, as well as the particular circumstances, internal and external, emotional and material, that affect her life and practice. Later Learning involves finding ways to cope with the new and multiple challenges of making a living at her profession. In so doing she will make choices that will reflect a set of values about what is important and how she wants to run her life and work. As she integrates her general knowledge and her developing identity with gradually accumulating clinical experience and self-knowledge she develops a style of work and a model of practice that fits best with her individual needs and circumstances. In doing so she may find that every so often particular pieces of her training become freshly relevant.

Importantly Later Learning asks that a therapist conduct herself honorably, in ways that she can live with. Although there are the inevitable compromises she is ultimately accountable to herself. All of this can be a daunting task. It may take her a few, perhaps many, years to find a situation that seems to work. The therapist's overall benevolence and sense of control are the two qualities that give most convincing evidence that she has things in hand.

Let us consider some of the major stresses and strains that have to be coped with during this period of gaining professional maturity. First, she is now quite on her own and must rely on herself to make formulations and interventions with patients. Although supervision may be available it may not be as easily obtained as dropping by a faculty member's office. It must be deliberately sought and often paid for. Related to this independence is the constant awareness of a clinician's responsibility to others, her patients. Second, she must adjust to physical restraint, that is, sitting for long periods of time and being encapsulated in the same setting. She has essentially removed herself from the stimulation that comes from being out in the world, choosing to live with the stimulations and satisfactions that come with experiencing her patients' and her own inner worlds. Third, she must observe emotional and verbal restraint. She must watch her words and not position herself with any one aspect of a patient's dilemma. That is, she must maintain her clinical neutrality, the careful consideration of all sides of a patient's conflicts. For some this can at times feel like a significant deprivation. Fourth, if she owns an independent practice she must deal with the responsibilities of running a small business on which her livelihood depends. This includes maintaining a referral base, managing overhead costs, and ensuring that her "customers" pay.

There may be hard moments when the therapist feels driven to the wall, feels helpless, is at the limit of what she knows, and is losing confidence in the power of her craft or her capacity to perform it. Any therapist can find herself in such a position at certain times. It is impossible to offer general ready remedies; they will always depend on the kind of problem at hand, and on the staying power and ego resourcefulness of the therapist. But we can bring up the importance of self-care. Self-care is an umbrella term covering many significant aspects related to the therapist's overall effectiveness at her work. It is important that each therapist work out for herself ways to maintain physical and psychological health. Times of replenishment and refreshment must somehow be woven into the design of each therapist's individual circumstances. This is both an obligation to herself and to her patients. If not, the result will likely be burnout. Her steadfastness as a worker and the solidity of her identity can, amongst other things, be supported by her developing congenial, even some close relations with professional colleagues. It is helpful as well to make use of opportunities in continuing education such as seminars and workshops, and perhaps especially important, keeping herself active in the network of professional conversation and general wisdom. In some instances turning to consultation with a trusted colleague may be helpful and indicated. Sometimes this involves the decision to resume personal psychotherapy. And, of course, time spent with family and friends and on personal interests separate from psychotherapeutic work is essential. You are not in formal training anymore.

In chapter 11 we will continue to discuss issues involved in Later Learning. But first we will turn our attention to the psychotherapeutic frame.

10

The Frame

Well, there's no quick fix, no sure way to order up the flash of inspiration. What you can do, however, is create a set of circumstances that will increase the likelihood of its happening . . . [that] can . . . load your creative dice.

—Anna Held Audette, *The Blank Canvas: Inviting the Muse*

What conditions are necessary for the creation of works of art?

—Virginia Woolf, *A Room of One's Own*

Developing a psychotherapeutic relationship rests on the patient's ability to bring very personal material into conversation with the therapist. Although people come to therapy with varying capacities to do this, generally speaking, it is not an easy task. For many people psychotherapy is initially an unfamiliar situation and the therapist an unfamiliar person. The newness of the situation can be anxiety provoking and understandably get in the way of speaking freely and openly about oneself. The prospective patient is likely to have all sorts of questions about what is expected of him as well as about the kind of participation and flexibility he can expect from the therapist. A patient may wonder, for example, whether sessions will be of variable length. Can he call the therapist when he wants? Can they meet for coffee? Will appointments be scheduled regularly? What will he have to pay? Will the therapist ask him questions? Tell him what to do? Say nothing at all? Can he speak in confidence?

Setting up the *psychotherapeutic frame*, hereafter referred to simply as "the frame," is a responsibility that rests with the therapist. The frame is comprised of the aforementioned work rules. They are among the most essential and far reaching of those in our craft because once the frame is negotiated it conveys to the patient some idea of the structure and boundaries of this unusual situation or "workshop." Most fundamentally the frame defines psychotherapy as something other than a social encounter. Although psychotherapy may share some borders with other forms of psychological engagement such as religious and artistic pursuits, as a method it comes with a certain set of arrangements or conventions that differentiates it from them. The details of these arrangements have been worked out over the years and are based on clinical experience and theoretical soundness. It is this set of arrangements agreed upon by both the therapist and the patient that constitutes the frame. When we speak of work rules in the context of the frame we are referring to the ways in which the therapist sets up and protects these arrangements.

The conventions of the frame articulate what is to be expected of its participants in terms of confidentiality, time, place, fee, and cancellation policy, among other psychotherapeutic matters. It is not, however, expected that the therapist present all these conditions to the patient in one initial legislative act. Neither is she obligated to a single blueprint of how psychotherapy should proceed nor to the conditions remaining rigidly steadfast for the duration of the treatment. The therapist ideally hopes to work out arrangements with the patient that take into account the circumstances of the individuals involved. After all we live in a world that exacts of us many and complex demands. Negotiating around these demands requires the therapist to be skilled enough to convey her openness and flexibility without undermining the basic structure necessary to do psychotherapeutic work. It is likely that, over time, if the two parties work well together, the frame is quietly taken for granted and nearly forgotten. It will reappear in their consciousness only at times when changing external circumstances or inner developments touch upon its conditions and boundaries.

The frame can be a source of tremendous stability for the therapist as well, especially in the face of what can at times be considerable emotional onslaught. Feeling anchored and in command of her situation she has a better chance to listen open-mindedly, think freely, and remain able to be flexible in her reception of the patient, and to understand that he arrived at his present adaptational dilemmas for reasons of his subjective history and experience.

The frame, therefore, serves to facilitate the work of both the patient and the therapist.

PREDICTABILITY

The psychotherapeutic frame sets up conditions in which a person may come to explore thoughts and feelings which at first he is not always accustomed to recognize. He may gain access to preconscious aspects of his inner world that he has avoided or denied so far or pretended not to exist; now, however, he experiences flickers of new feelings, imaginings, and thoughts that enter his awareness or come close to being expressed. Anxiety and unease may arise within the patient and his sense of inner security may become diminished. The steadiness and predictability of the therapeutic situation can then be a significant provider of feelings of safety. The frame ensures that the patient will not encounter anything so destabilizing that he must mobilize urgent defensive measures, that would interfere with the emergence of preconscious material. Predictability in areas such as the therapist's continued interest, time and place of the sessions, and practical routines, supports the patient's as well as the therapist's expectation that whatever may happen in the sometimes rough and tumble world will be contained and safely held in the therapeutic setting and in their relation. Patient and therapist carry this understanding during their work and as they go about living between sessions; it is there in the back of their minds, perhaps even viscerally. In his story, *The Little Prince*, Antoine de Saint-Exupery refers to the impact of predictability when he speaks of observing "proper rites."

> The next day the little prince returned.
> "It would have been better to return at the same time," the fox said. "For instance, if you come at four in the afternoon, I'll begin to be happy by three. The closer it gets to four, the happier I'll feel. By four I'll be all excited and worried; I'll discover what it costs to be happy! But if you come at any old time, I'll never know when I should prepare my heart . . . There must be rites."
> "What's a *rite?*" asked the little prince.
> "That's another thing that's been too often neglected," said the fox. "It's the fact that one day is different from the other days, one hour from the other hours. My hunters, for example, have a rite. They dance with the village girls on Thursdays. So Thursday's a wonderful day: I can take a stroll all the way to the vineyards. If the hunters danced whenever they chose, the days would all be just alike, and I'd have no holiday at all."

CONTINUITY

One of the central provisions of the frame is that of continuity. Walter Mosley, a writer, addresses its importance when he discusses the process of writing. He speaks of how ideas are "shifting renditions of possibilities that have not been resolved, though they have occurred and reoccurred a thousand times in your mind." The ideas, he says, have no physical form; they are "smokey concepts," like "vapors." Writing, Mosley says,

> is gathering smoke . . . It's an excursion into the ether of ideas . . . you have to return to tend to your flimsy vapors. You have to brush them, reshape them, breathe into them and gather more . . . One day you . . . pick up the pencil or turn on the computer, but no new words come. That's fine. Sometimes you can't go further . . . You have reentered the dream of the work, and that's enough to keep the story alive . . .
>
> The next day you might write for hours; there's no way to tell . . . All you need is to keep your heart and mind open to the work . . . Returning every day thickens the atmosphere. Images appear. Connections are made . . . Reality fights against your dreams, it tries to deny creation and change. The world wants you to be someone known, someone with solid ideas, not blowing smoke. Given a day, reality will begin to scatter your notions; given two days, it will drive them off.

Mosley's words about the process of writing describe so well an atmosphere that also seems to dominate at times the therapeutic work. His "smokey concepts," "flimsy vapors," and "ether of ideas" refer to forms of preconscious thought that often emerge in therapy. To sustain access to this preconscious domain we ask of ourselves and our patients that the rite of continuity be observed so that emergent vapors are not blown entirely away by the realities of life between sessions. We ask the patient to show up with the frequency agreed upon. The more frequent the sessions, the more available this preconscious realm, the thicker the atmosphere. In psychoanalysis patients are seen up to five times a week. The therapist has a responsibility of her own in maintaining continuity by keeping in her mind the patient's ever growing story together with her sense of things as yet only hinted at. In this way she develops an organizing, inner picture, which will guide her interventions.

CONSTRAINTS AND FREEDOMS

The frame imposes certain constraints on behavior while permitting certain freedoms. Both of these qualities, constraint and freedom, work together to provide a "holding environment." This means a space, both physical and psychological, that is safe and secure enough to facilitate and tolerate the presence of intense affects and wide-ranging imaginings; it will also contain the patient's and therapist's gradually developing joint understanding of the patient's inner life. Let us look closer at both of these aspects of the psychotherapy situation.

FREEDOMS: LETTING THE "LINE DOWN INTO THE STREAM"

A basic freedom facilitated by the frame is that of self-expression. As our reference to Mosley suggests we think of psychotherapy as a creative process allowing a person to open doors to his inner life and express what he sees and experiences through them. Freedom of expression requires that the patient have confidence in the frame—the therapeutic arrangements and the therapist's ability to receive without judgment or criticism what may emerge. A secure frame enables the patient to relax and reduce his defensiveness. In most customary social interactions, with some exceptions of course, speaking one's mind fully, even thinking and feeling in similarly unrestrained ways, may feel like a transgression of what is socially acceptable and workable. Psychotherapy offers the patient the potential to express himself uninhibited by ordinary social convention and judgment, but it may take time before the patient can believe this. While the therapist has a concept of what she is up to, the patient usually lacks an equivalent understanding when he first enters the therapeutic relationship. His trusting the offer of security and freedom eases the emergence of material from within, makes it possible that later in the treatment previously unspeakable things will be spoken, unthinkable things be thought, and new feelings be discovered and felt. The safety of the frame invites the patient to speak to the therapist more freely than as if he were speaking to himself. Should, on the other hand, a patient feel endangered, particularly at the outset of the psychotherapeutic process, he is likely to absent himself mentally or physically. He may censor and inhibit his communications, shape them artificially in the form of disguises and compromises, dissociate, or physically leave.

Within this psychotherapeutic space the patient can temporarily abandon connection to reality in the service of increasing his self-awareness; he can loosen up and allow the more primal aspects of his mind to emerge, those that fantasize, imagine, want and wish, think magically, feel intensely. Without having to worry about being rational or realistic, he can make his inner world vivid. The process of allowing our minds to wander without conscious control is known as *free association*, a concept introduced by Sigmund Freud. It is a process similar to daydreaming and serves a good purpose. As one thought leads to another we can find ourselves arriving at places quite far from where we began, places we might never have reached otherwise. Think of a piece of driftwood, which having ridden many currents, finally washes up on a distant shore.

Relinquishing conscious control of one's thoughts, but within the safety of the frame, is a form of regression in the service of the ego and linked to the creative process. Virginia Woolf spoke to this very beautifully when she wrote of "Thought [having] let its line down into the stream." Free association, of course, is never "free" in the sense of being random. Emerging sequences of associations may at times and to some degree be free of conventional or logical order. But to the extent that they are they can be expected to be determined by unconscious, private meanings that define their connections and aims. Nonetheless, we hope that when a patient settles into psychotherapy he enters a space that will allow him to let his "line down into the stream" of conscious and unconscious feeling and imagination. Maybe only a little at first, then deeper perhaps, then deeper.

CONSTRAINT: PULLING THE LINE BACK UP

Even within the safety of the psychotherapeutic frame not everything goes. Indeed a number of the arrangements that make up the frame come in the form of constraints. They assert and remind the participants that, although the bounds of civil communication are made more flexible in psychotherapy, they are not done away with entirely. In this light an important difference between what is expected of the patient and of the therapist should be noted. Although the therapist must be empathically communicative and even allow her own thoughts to wander she is not expected to regress in the same way as the patient. Although the frame facilitates access to her own inner world as well she must, nonetheless, retain and safeguard the connection to reality, which she does in large part by enforcing therapeutic constraints or boundaries. The patient needs to have a secure sense of the stability and reliability of the therapeutic arrangements and feel safe from manipulation and unwarranted intrusions by the therapist. At the same time the patient may resist these constraints, especially if they are experienced as interfering with his wishful fantasies of sexual or other kind of union with the therapist. It is precisely because therapy allows access to intense and sometimes irrational aspects of one's inner world that these constraints are necessary. Without structure and boundaries psychotherapy can easily devolve into an amorphous enterprise: distracted, disorganized, and dangerous.

Many of the constraints imposed by the therapist can be managed with some flexibility. A patient must pay a fee, for instance, but the amount can be negotiated as can meeting time and place, even cancellation policy. Other constraints, however, are absolute. Examples of absolute constraints include prohibitions on physical aggression and sexual contact and apply to both parties. The premium placed on confidentiality, of what has been said and what has transpired, is an example of a constraint that applies to the therapist. Only with the competent patient's specific permission can therapeutic information be released. Confidentiality can be breached only in extreme circumstances, such as when either or both parties are threatened or the safety of other persons is at risk. For other kinds of behavior, such as verbal aggression, somewhat more latitude than is usually tolerated is granted the patient in the service of freedom of expression.

BACK AND FORTH

The psychotherapeutic process profits from the patient's moving back and forth between two places, keeping one foot in fantasy and one foot in reality, avoiding extremes. Too much fantasy and we can become lost and disoriented or worse, especially if we lose sight of reality. Too much reality and we become mired in the concrete, unable to think and feel in broader and less restrained ways. The psychotherapeutic frame, with both its offering of expressive freedom and its constraints, establishes conditions that facilitate this dual endeavor in a dynamic kind of balance.

Psychotherapy not only provides a place to regress, it also provides a means to return from the regressive depths to the surface. In therapies that are working well the patient can fluctuate between regressed and rational states, between reality and fantasy. We want to let the line dip deep, but never so deep that the light from the surface vanishes. We also want to pull it back up again. Being in therapy requires that a person be able to suspend or control regressive forays, that they may be observed, wondered about, explored. This is what we mean by being able to "stand back" and engage in psychological work. "Pulling the line back up" enables us to see and think about what has been hooked. The preservation of reality is critical because our lives are to be lived outside the consulting room. There is the world in which we work and love, make our way, and to which we must ultimately adapt.

It is hoped that over time the patient will internalize the frame and be able to wander back and forth with less and less prompting by the therapist. Patients can vary greatly in this regard.

THE LION, THE WITCH, AND THE WARDROBE

Let us revisit C. S. Lewis' children's story, *The Lion, the Witch, and the Wardrobe*. It gives us a wonderful example of what it is to wander into the imaginative. As you will recall, this is a story of four children sent to the country house of an old Professor, away from the air raids in London. The children enter the fantastic world of Narnia through a magic wardrobe, which they find in a spare room. They make their way through rows of soft fur coats that give way to branches and the crunch of snow underfoot. Lewis is decidedly aware of the importance of keeping one foot in reality, reminding the reader each time a child steps into the wardrobe toward Narnia of the importance of leaving the door open and that it is a "very silly thing to shut oneself into a wardrobe."

Adding to the image of the open door and the fur coats Lewis also describes a lamppost. Seen from the wardrobe the lamppost acts as a beacon signaling the world of Narnia ahead. Seen from the world of Narnia the lamppost signals the nearness of the wardrobe, the light from the spare room shining through the open door. It serves as a beacon indicating the way back to the real world. To us the lamppost represents a lighted reminder of two realms of experience, flexibility of access to both of which is necessary if we are to avoid getting psychologically/creatively stuck in some kind of darkness that makes living "always winter . . . and never Christmas . . ."

It is fun to think of some of the characters in Lewis's book as representing players in psychotherapy. There is, for example, the old Professor in whose vast house the children are staying. In a way he assumes a therapeutic stance by "being quite at their disposal." He is logical yet able to embrace the possibility that someone could experience "other worlds" *without assuming them mad*. We have Lucy, the youngest, able to enter Narnia knowing when it is time to return and that she must keep the wardrobe door open in order to find her way back. In contrast we have Edmund, who seems completely unaware of what he is doing, carelessly shuts the wardrobe door, overindulges in the sweetly seductive but dangerous offerings of the witch, and barely finds his way back. And then there are the two eldest children, Susan and Peter, who approach the Professor with serious questions concerning reality and Lucy's hold on it.

Psychotherapy provides a setting where its participants, like the four schoolchildren, are permitted to wander into fantasy and feel and imagine in expansive ways. Shaped as they are by their experiences and expectations people come into psychotherapy with different capacities to be creative in this way. For some, often those who are out of control, more reality-based therapies are in order, at least initially—until they tighten up a bit. The frame then is like a portal that makes possible a ritual of entry and leave-taking. The constituents of the frame are, if you will, akin to wardrobe doors, lampposts, and fur coats. They are constants that guide the transition from the realities of day-to-day life into a psychotherapeutic space and back again. If the door to reality remains ajar one is in a fantasy; if it closes for a short while one is in a dream; if it closes for a long time one is in a psychosis. Conversely, if the door to fantasy is closed one can become ponderously grounded in the juiceless pulp of the day to day. Returning to Lewis's story it is as if Lucy has been able to internalize the frame whereas Edmund, given to indulging his impulses, is at least at the outset in need of someone to maintain it for him. His hold on reality is at first rather shaky. As for Susan and Peter? Well, initially they are bound by the conventions of reality but eventually loosen up.

Different patients will, of course, bring to therapy their different subjective experiences of transitions. Let's contrast C. S. Lewis's description of his characters' entry into Narnia with Lewis Carroll's description of Alice's entry into Wonderland. Alice enters Wonderland by literally falling down a hole. In both stories there is the element of the unexpected, but to our reading, whereas Alice literally loses her footing and falls, this is not the case with Lewis's characters whose experiences are less jarring. They walk upright through a softness, the fur coats which soon transform into something else—branches. Patients will experience beginnings and endings with different amounts of ease or discomfort. Some patients will start talking right off the bat, sinking into the chair as if it were made out of fur. Others will find the transition more challenging as though they, like someone falling, have nothing to hold on to. Still others find ending sessions variously difficult. One patient, a woman in her mid-twenties with a history of childhood molestation, would spend the last few minutes of the session sitting on the edge of her seat then bolt out of the office when the therapist would remark that they needed to stop. Nonetheless, this patient was able to continue coming to therapy until she could tolerate the therapist's observations and speak of her fears. It became clearer, then, that her fears were informed by her inability of years ago to leave her molester, who could be sweet and caring as well as vengeful. She bolted not only to escape him but also her own shameful and guilt-ridden need for care.

Here we have put forth reasons why a frame is needed in order for good therapeutic work to be possible. In the following chapter we take a closer look at the constituents of the frame. These are the very practical arrangements having to do with time and place, fee, confidentiality, and the like. Concrete in a way that thoughts and feelings are not, these arrangements and the manner in which they are established have, nonetheless, very broad significance.

11

Setting Up a Practice

This hour, this quiet room, and my small thought
HOlding invisible vastness in its hands.

—Siegfried Sassoon, "The Power and the Glory," *Collected Poems 1908–1956*

For many of you Later Learning will entail starting your own private practice. While the following discussion focuses on the building of an independent practice we think that portions of it can be usefully applied to work in other settings such as a hospital or community clinic.

In my (Angelica Kaner's) second year out of training I was asked to speak to a group of pre- and postdoctoral fellows on the topic "Starting a Private Practice." The thought of this was both daunting and compelling. I was certainly in the thick of it, and it was only getting thicker, so who better to speak than someone for whom the task was literally at hand? After much wondering about how to go about this I decided I would turn it over to the group and encouraged them to imagine what they would need to set up shop. I asked them to just speak off the top, whatever came to mind. Sound familiar? And this is roughly what emerged, one person saying this, another saying that, some of it serious, some of it tongue-in-cheek, all of it relevant.

"A room. Two chairs—or more if you are seeing couples and families. Toys if you are seeing children. A desk. How big of a room? How big of a desk? A couch if you're a psychoanalyst. A chair for the desk. Pencils. Pens. Stationary. Personalized business cards. Where should this room be? In an office building? How about a rug? Pictures. What kind? Landscapes. Flowers. Something profound. Oh please! What about diplomas? A fax machine. A copier. A clock. Fax machines make noise. A computer. An answering machine. How about voice mail? What about an answering service? Some people like to hear a real human voice. How about two rooms—one for officey stuff? Two clocks. A plant—maybe. I've heard there should always be something living in the room—aside from you of course. (*Laughter*) A book shelf. Books. A file cabinet? Too officey? Goes in the other room, if you have one. A sound machine. A space heater or an air conditioner if there is no central air. A coat rack. An umbrella stand. Lamps."

(*Silence*)

"What else?" I asked.

"Insurance. What kind? Malpractice. Where do you get that? Health insurance too, if you are self-employed—and single. Parking. A car! A rest room. Maybe a separate one for patients. A license. A psychiatrist to prescribe medication if you're a psychologist or social worker—a male and a female preferably. An accountant. A supervisor. A supervision group. Your own therapist. A kitchen facility. What if you get hungry? Want a drink? Somewhere to keep a vacuum cleaner if necessary. A waiting room. Windows. Two doors would be nice—one to enter, another to exit. Security. A cupboard. Did some one mention pictures?"

(*Silence*)

"What else?"

(*Silence*)

"You're leaving something out."

(*Silence*)

"Patients?" someone offered tentatively.

"And where do we get patients?"

This last question ushered in the second half of the colloquium.

When setting up a practice you are immediately and in a concrete way confronted with establishing the therapeutic frame. We will first offer some general guidelines about setting up the physical space using the trainees' comments and associations as we go. We will then address the question "And where do we get patients?" because it is important to have some idea of the business of psychotherapy and the ramifications of the many decisions you must make. Here we also offer some thoughts, especially in view of the almost total absence of comments related to money and finances. Indeed the word *patients* barely got air. Hardly surprising, of course, given the common refrain amongst students, namely, "They don't teach you this in training."

THE PHYSICAL SPACE

Therapists have different ideas about how they wish to set up their offices. Although the guidelines we present are somewhat conservative a therapist must ultimately do what is most comfortable to her. Before getting into specifics we encourage you to be mindful of four general and important considerations. These are that therapy requires (1) a regular and stable environment, (2) safety, (3) recognition of the transference, and (4) understanding that it is not a social situation. Since we have already discussed the last of these we will only reiterate its importance, recommending that one avoid those accoutrements that might suggest a living room, bedroom, kitchen, even a coffee shop. The qualities with which a patient, of his own accord, imbues your office are another matter.

A regular and stable environment means a fairly benign space that provides basic physical ease and comfort. This means an office that is literally not too warm or too cold or drafty, that is clean and calm and quiet within reason; a room to which there is easy access for able-bodied people and, if possible, people with physical disabilities. And of course provision of an accessible and well-maintained restroom is essential. Needless to say the requirements of safety overlap with those of a regular and stable environment, but since this is such an essential aspect of therapy it must be allowed its own prominence. Here we will focus only on what is physically necessary, keeping in mind that physical and emotional safety are connected.

Most important, the consulting room should be protected from physical intrusion. We speak here of the obvious cautions such as making sure the building and the room are secure with the necessary locks and lighting, especially if one sees patients at night. It is generally not a good idea to schedule first appointments at night. But there are also other kinds of intrusions. The ring of a telephone, for instance, can be jarring; the sound of a fax machine is annoying at the very least; and, of course, incoming phone messages should never be audible. Unfortunately additional space for such "officey" things is often not possible. Further, connected to the principle of safety is privacy. Some office suites are built in such a way as to have private waiting rooms, separate doors for entering and exiting patients, and even double doors. Although not every office has these features, whatever can be done within reason to protect a patient's privacy should be done.

The third consideration is the transference, about which we will speak at much greater length later. For now a definition will suffice. The word *transference* literally means "carryover" and refers to the patient's unconsciously carrying experiences and feelings deriving from earlier relationships to newer ones. In the favorable environment of therapy the patient essentially recreates features of past relationships also in his relationship with the therapist, which can then be explored. Given the centrality of the transference in psychodynamic psychotherapy you may wish to avoid clueing the patient in to aspects of your life in order to allow his fantasies to emerge with the least interference. This facet of our craft may take the most getting used to. Other lines of work generally permit, even expect you to display your diplomas, awards, family photos, and interests and hobbies in the office. The space is often treasured as an expression of its occupant, of ownership, of someone with a personality and a life beyond work.

Taken to the extreme, of course, anything you do to your office, diplomas and photos notwithstanding, is some statement of who you are and how you practice. Even placing fresh flowers in the room conveys at the very least something about your aesthetic. The important thing is to remember the implications for the transference of what you do. We suggest that you keep these considerations in mind as you read the following and make decisions about your own office space.

FURNITURE AND ACCESSORIES

The psychotherapy office should look professional, with furniture and accessories chosen for comfort and a calming influence. It ought to be easily accessible; its door conveniently located and the corridor wide enough so that patient and therapist do not find themselves involved in a traffic jam as they enter or leave. Inside, offices typically contain a desk, bookshelf, and seating. Seating is most important. Focusing on individual psychotherapy, two chairs comfortable enough to sit in for fifty minutes are basic. Having another comfortable

chair or two available is also a good idea. In one training site a therapist remembers sitting in a chair with her feet unable to touch the ground. Legs dangling in the air do nothing for one's sense of groundedness or comfort, let alone
one's credibility and until she hit upon the idea of a footrest the discomfort interfered with her ability to concentrate. Chairs should also be arranged so that
they are neither too close nor too far from each other. Sitting too close may feel
intrusive, too far apart may leave one feeling disconnected, even exposed. Given
that rents can be very high and office spaces small the former is likely more of a
concern. But if one is innovative enough such spaces can usually be worked with
in creative and clinically uncompromising ways. Chairs can be positioned either
facing one another or at an angle. Some therapists prefer the former, there being something open and direct about face to face contact. Placement at an angle, on the other hand, allows the patient the opportunity to face away from the
therapist with greater ease should he wish to do so. Also, for some patients a
face-to-face encounter may feel like something of an interrogation, which can
be unnerving. Opinions are divided about whether it should be left to the patient to select his seat. Some feel that there is useful clinical information in what
the patient does, others that it is important for the therapist, considering all that
she must cope with, to be able to count on her own seat. Patients who are new
may prefer not to have to make an immediate decision. Wherever the patient sits
a box of tissues should be within close reach, as should a wastebasket.

Accessories, that is, pictures and other decorative items, should be chosen
with care. Much good art can be provocative. You may want to bypass pieces
with overtly sexual and aggressive images since these are often overstimulating. Think twice about furnishings such as lamps with tassels, ornate window
treatments, or frivolous upholstery. Some therapists decorate their offices
with great reserve; others are variously less restrained.

Therapists also have different ideas about the placement of clocks. Some prefer that a clock or two be in sight of both parties. Others prefer not to show their
patients the time, placing one clock behind the patient so they can observe it un-
obtrusively. As we have touched on in our discussion of the frame dynamic psychotherapy respects both the preservation of time as a coordinate of reality as
well as the suspension of time in the service of promoting a feeling of timeless-
ness and expressive freedom. What you decide to do with your clock or clocks
should be informed by how you think about the frame and how you wish to
weigh reality versus fantasy. We suggest selecting a clock that is neither too large

nor overt in appearance nor that chimes or makes some such noise. Should there be more than one clock in the office make sure they are set to the same time. Many patients are anxious about the clock. For some the ability to see the clock is paramount and related to feelings of control. For others not seeing the clock is significant. One patient would put his drink directly in front of it. When asked about this he said that he didn't need to see the clock because he had a watch. When the therapist pointed out that he never seemed to look at his watch the patient responded by saying that he did not want to exercise any control. He preferred to remain passive and have the therapist call time.

Telephones come in all shapes and sizes, and you may want to consider the aforementioned discussion when you choose your model. But beyond issues of style it is important to note that a patient's first contact with you is usually on the telephone, via voice mail, answering machine, or service. Your recording should be clear and not too lengthy, inviting the prospective patient to leave a message (some like to say explicitly a "confidential message"; some like to add "with a few good times to reach you") and giving pertinent information about how else you may be reached. Some therapists include what to do in case of emergency. If you are out of town let the caller know the dates you will be away, who is covering for you and how to reach her. When hiring an answering service make sure that personnel have experience with psychotherapy practices. Care should be taken to turn the ringer off before a session and certainly the volume if you have an answering machine. Should the phone ring inadvertently during an hour calmly excuse yourself and turn off the ringer. Your patient might react openly to such an event. He might also keep his reactions to himself. So listen for references to intrusions in what he says. Sometimes it may be useful to inquire about the patient's reaction if he does not express it spontaneously.

In our seminar a student thought she might place a candy dish in her office. It was a lovely notion that brought out many important points having to do with the provision of food in therapy. Providing candy or some such food is certainly a common social nicety, and platters and bowls can be quite decorative. Offering food is a gesture of welcome and may, as does a cigarette or a cocktail, allay social anxiety. But anxiety in psychotherapy is another matter. Food in this context can be used to avoid talking about issues and uncomfortable feelings. It can also be a temptation and too stimulating for some. Further presenting food or other offerings might, in the patient's mind, define the therapist as a provider or caretaker, perhaps as a maternal person and thus reduce the spontaneity of imagination that would help the development of the transference. Patients, though, do sometimes ask for water and it would be fine to oblige. Even so try to keep in mind when and how the request is made especially if it is a habitual one for it likely has its motivations.

As for the therapist herself it is theoretically not advisable to eat or drink during a session, except perhaps for water as needed. Admittedly this can be felt as rather depriving, especially early in the morning or later in the day. Different clinicians are variously ascetic in this regard. Many will sip some tea or coffee. The idea is that food and drink introduce sensory stimulation, which may interfere with the therapist's attention and may be a defensive way of dealing with difficult feelings aroused by the patient, such as anger or boredom, even sleepiness. It is better to understand what is transpiring than to eat or drink the feelings away.

Sharing Office Space

It is common when beginning to see private patients to rent space from an established clinician. Understandably the income derived from an initially small number of patients would argue against investing in your own office space. When deciding from whom to rent keep in mind how this clinician sets up her office; it might not be your style. You and your colleague should be very clear about scheduling patient hours and ending on time. Arriving at the office to find some conflict is upsetting, leaving you at best without needed time to settle into the space. The last thing you need to deal with is uncertain boundaries, with the frustration, even fear and anger, this often generates. Also poor boundary management may raise valid concerns for your patient. These are important frame issues. If you find yourself in a situation where you are dealing with an unpredictable colleague and cannot resolve it quickly with her, go and find another space with a clinician who has it more together.

"AND WHERE DO YOU GET PATIENTS?"

. . . a good dinner is of great importance to good talk.

—Virginia Woolf, *A Room of One's Own*

Referrals

Perhaps fifteen or more years ago one could finish training, hang out a shingle, and more or less hit the ground running. Because of a number of factors, sweeping changes in the management of health care and the large numbers of people entering the field, this is not necessarily the case for most practitioners today. Going about establishing and developing your referral base thus becomes an important aspect of Later Learning. Referrals, at first, may come from friends and family members, then from colleagues, physicians, the telephone book. Insurance companies or the managed care companies with whom they contract can come to provide a sizable gateway for referrals. As a new practitioner you may find that with some of your patients you will need to work under contracts with insurance companies that to some extent become your employer. The establishment of the frame must take into account some terms to which you are legally bound. If one elects to participate, learning how managed care companies operate is necessary and can take some time.

Fees

Starting up a practice requires that the therapist adapt to a set of economic realities different from those in the past and different in many respects from those found in training. In training one does not have to develop one's own referral network, for example, and fees are not usually transacted directly between patient and therapist.

Discussing the financial part of psychotherapy involves a willingness to engage in the topic of money, which is usually not much done in training. A psychodynamic psychotherapy practice is a small business generally built over time. It can take several years for a practice to reach a critical mass in terms of number of patients and referrals. But even when running on a roughly forty-hour-a-week maximum (which for many practitioners is a very heavy load) psychotherapy is essentially a limited, low volume enterprise that puts a premium on quality and requires time and a high level of skill and concentration. Psychotherapy, like the production of anything unique—a painting, a fine piece of handcrafted furniture—is costly partly for this reason. When anticipating potential income overhead costs such as health and liability insurance, rent, annual licensure fee, and so forth need be considered. There are also those uncertainties endemic to an enterprise in which no one signs a contract binding him to payment or number of sessions and that must deal with such variables as weather and illness. Other factors affecting fees are credentials, practice location, use of insurance, and the laws of supply and demand.

When negotiating a fee both therapist and prospective patient bring a wide array of experiences and attitudes toward money. They will bring issues connected to how they value themselves, the meaning of getting and giving help, their sense of entitlement and deservingness, greed, control, and more. In the practical and emotional environs of this encounter they are both asked to assess their resources. What are their assets and earnings potentials? Their obligations? Are they single? Do they have children? Do they have loans? How much are they willing or able to invest of their time, money, and psychological energy in a psychotherapeutic enterprise with this individual? How necessary and valuable is the therapy felt to be? A complicated equation needs to be worked out between them involving their needs and wants and realities. Sometimes these things can be settled quickly, sometimes they will take time.

Settling upon a fee, therefore, is a complicated matter with notable significance. The issues connected to fees can present ongoing challenges and at times can be quite stressful for therapist and patient alike.

Who Pays?

Either the patient himself or a third party will pay for therapy. If the patient is paying you directly, that is, "out of pocket," then you can discuss the amount and the issues involved one to one. Some therapists choose not to negotiate their fee. Setting a nonnegotiable fee is a definitive statement about an aspect of the frame and may indeed provide a necessary and stable expectation. The patient knows what is required; he can take it or leave it; and the lack of any ambiguity can be very useful. In our experience most clinicians do negotiate. The negotiation, although involving some uncertainty, may impart to the patient that the therapist is flexible, within limits.

A fee ought to be felt by the patient. Some sacrifice needs to be made. Otherwise the process is meaningless, without value, too easily come by. Therapists starting out are perhaps more inclined to undercharge. This is often done in the service of getting their practices going, but it may also understandably reflect an initially wobbly self-confidence. When patients pay too little they may not use therapy as well as they could. They may not be investing enough psychologically because they may not be investing enough financially. As a therapist it can be very disconcerting to see a patient pay you a relatively small amount while coming in with the latest fashions.

But a fee should not necessarily impose undue hardship on the patient. A patient agreeing to something he cannot afford may signal all sorts of self-damaging, compliant, or irresponsible tendencies. Sometimes it takes a patient a while to find a therapist whom he likes and with whom he can work something out financially. This may entail his paying for several consultations along the way. Therapists can sometimes agree to see a patient for a reduced fee stipulating that it will increase along with the patient's income. Whatever the scenario it is often a good idea to ask the patient what it is like to talk about money. He may or may not be able to engage around this, but asking does impart to him that no subject is beyond discussion.

Third parties do not always come wrapped in insurance packages. There are variations on this theme, which have their own implications. Here are two examples. Jerry is a college senior who was seen at his college-counseling center for depression. Once stabilized he was advised to continue therapy with a private clinician. He discussed this with his parents, and they agreed to pay. It turned out that this arrangement had great meaning for Jerry. Although he and his therapist made a good connection Jerry soon began to miss sessions. When the therapist inquired into this Jerry revealed that he felt guilty for being a financial burden to his parents. It became clear that his lateness was a way for him to undo this burden and "take care of himself," which was even more imperative now that he faced graduation.

In another instance Sharon, also a college student, sought treatment because of a serious problem with binge eating. Sharon made a strong initial connection with her therapist and came promptly to her sessions. But it soon became apparent that her parents, though financially secure, were, nonetheless, irresponsible about payment. This put the therapist in a difficult position. On the one hand she had a patient who clearly needed help and on the other parents who were not cooperative.

Who Gets Paid?

In the above examples the therapist gets paid directly. An interesting variation on the third-party issue arises in the context of agencies in which a therapist is assigned patients. Fees are essentially paid to the organization and not the therapist. Money is given to a receptionist in much the same manner as it is in a physician's office. The patient is often not even aware of how much the therapist is paid (this can also be the case in private practice situations involving third parties). The clinician may be paid a set rate by the agency. The patient remains relatively remote from the concrete experience of paying a debt and handing money over. Important emotional issues may come to be bypassed.

Presenting the Bill

When does the therapist give the patient the bill and how? Again therapists have different ways of handling this. Some present the bill at the beginning of the session; others at the end. Some mail out their bills. Our preference is not to mail (except in circumstances where there will be some interruption in the work) but to hand the bill to the patient. In this way money and its emotional contents are kept within the frame and are not sidestepped. The closeness of the experience allows the therapist to listen for any reference to money, gratification, deprivation, greed, anger, and so on and if appropriate to comment and give the patient an opportunity to discuss the issues involved.

CHARGING FOR FIRST APPOINTMENTS AND CANCELLATION POLICIES

First Appointments

Some therapists feel that they should charge for all their professional time, including first appointments or consultations as they can be called. Others do not charge for first appointments. Of these some feel that the first appointment is "pre-contractual," that is, prior to any agreement concerning fees.

Cancellation

Cancellation policies are put in place to protect the therapist's income and convey to the patient that missed sessions be acknowledged and not taken lightly. Therapists vary on how much notice they require, some forty-eight hours, some twenty-four. Ideally cancellation policy should be clarified at the outset of treatment. But there are times when so much is going on that the therapist forgets. In such cases one can say to the patient who calls at the last minute, "Well, let's not worry about it this time. After all we never discussed this. But for the future let's have an understanding that you will give me twenty-four hours so as not to be charged." This amounts to a gesture of good faith. In life there are, of course, those "acts of God" such as weather, illness, accident, or death that may require a therapist's understanding and flexibility.

Some patients, however, will exploit the "acts of God" criteria and put the therapist in a difficult position. In such cases it can be useful to think of the behavior conveying something about the transference and communicate this to the patient in an appropriate manner. At such times clarifying the conditions of the frame may also be in order.

Worrying excessively about bills and retirement is an excellent way to stifle creative thought. Too much reality. The therapist's freedom to think and contemplate broadly is essential to the enterprise and can suffer under financial pressure. Her clinical judgment and flexibility of associations are cramped if she is overly anxious. Sometimes this anxiety is neurotic. But no one can deny the real importance of financial security. An orderly financial house and the peace of mind this engenders is, therefore, an important aspect of what the therapist brings to the clinical encounter.

PRIVACY AND CONFIDENTIALITY

In our discussion of the physical space we referred to the importance of privacy and confidentiality. These issues come up again here in the business section because third parties want to know what they are paying for and if the therapy is doing any one any good.

All of this is particularly important in the context of managed care. With most companies sessions must be justified clinically, and here concerns arise over access to confidential information. Some patients want to be very involved in the process of reporting. Some are aware of the ease of access to such data, and the possible risk of being denied future coverage based on a "preexisting condition." These patients may elect to forego use of their benefits on these grounds. Other patients are less concerned; some don't care, or appear not to. Yet others have no choice.

III

OPENING THE DOOR

In part III through part V, we describe in detail what therapists refer to as "the work." What, in short, does the therapist do? Who is sitting with her in the room? What guides her thinking and her actions? What are the contributions that she will make? How does she really go about assisting in bringing the therapy to useful results?

12

The Patient

. . . go forth to greet
What world within you lies.

—Siegfried Sassoon, "Silly Sooth," *Collected Poems 1908–1956*

Into the prepared space enters the *patient*. Encountering him the therapist faces several questions. Who is this patient? How does he arrive at the door? What does entering into therapy mean to him? What are his expectations? And, given what she has to offer and what the patient is seeking, are they suited to each other? Will there be a successful *therapeutic match*? In what follows we will try to address these questions.

First, "who is the patient?" He is someone in a more or less uneasy or painful state. He has been unable to resolve his dilemmas himself by means of his own psychological work. He may feel depressed, anxious, confused, lonely, and isolated. Life seems not as full, enjoyable, or as promising as it once did, and he asks himself perhaps "Is that all there is?" To some degree or in one form or another this person is suffering. What is more, difficult situations in which he finds himself keep repeating themselves.

When a person feels paralyzed in this manner he may start searching for help from the outside, for assistance in resolving his difficulties, perhaps a "cure." Experience tells us that people try a number of different solutions depending on

115

how they understand their subjectively experienced states of impairment. Is it fate, illness, possession, being defective, being a sinful person? If they view anxiety, depression, sleeping difficulties, or similar discomforts to be medical problems they will seek medical assistance, try to change their diets, perhaps try various herbal remedies, or begin exercise programs. If they see their situation in terms of emotional conflict they will seek some form of psychological assistance by pursuing various self-improvement programs, perhaps self-help books. They may also turn to religion, especially if their suffering involves existential questions or their sense of self-worth. Finally, if they are aware of its existence they may turn to psychotherapy.

The potential patient enters therapy by one of a number of means. He could have looked in the phone book. A family member, friend, a physician, or an insurance company might have referred him. The referral agent is of no small consequence and can have great meaning for the patient. You should ask how the patient got your name and be attuned to his emotional connection to the source. The recommendation by a close relative or trusted friend who may have had personal experiences of therapy is likely to have a much different significance from someone in "customer relations."

Surely the patient comes with questions. Some of them may be clearly in his mind, others only vaguely. Some will be asked, others concealed. The idea of therapy is often experienced as quite foreign, if not intimidating, and considering therapy can resemble entering an unfamiliar culture where things are done in different ways. He may worry, "What can I expect?" "What does entering psychotherapy say about me?" "Does it mean that I am crazy?" "What do I do here?" "How long will this take?" "How does this work?" "And what of this person—my therapist?" Efforts to answer these questions will influence how a patient settles into the therapeutic work.

These sorts of questions are on the therapist's mind as well. To explore and clarify them and to assist the patient in broadening self-understanding she brings her skills to bear. Only at the end of therapy is it sometimes possible to appreciate what really worked in the particular patient-therapist combination. The answer can truly only be related to the specific case, and it has to be worked and suffered for. Nonetheless when a patient asks questions about what he can expect he deserves a response, even though it cannot be one that is definite and detailed. To "What can I expect?" or "How does this work?" one might say something like, "Well, you come here with troubles and have not found satisfying resolutions. So we will talk about your situation, what seems to be getting in your way, and see whether we can come up with something. Two heads are often better than one."

A patient's views of treatment are manifestations of his character, dynamic patterns, and unconscious wishes. Sometimes they are also shaped by his having been in therapy before. The therapist should, therefore, inquire and attempt to form an idea of what that had been like for the patient. What was or wasn't helpful about that experience? How does he currently understand his problem? Has he a theory or intuition or even a hunch about its beginnings, and what does he imagine it will take to deal with it? One might, if it feels right, probe the patient's expectations of what a therapist does, of the effort required, and of what the necessary investments in time and money are.

The therapist, however, cannot expect that the patient will always respond in a manner to her liking. Some patients may be able to engage the topic, saying something perfectly logical but in an intellectualized way such as, "Well, I'm here to talk about my problems and you will listen and give me feedback." Others may spontaneously begin to talk about their concerns: "Will you just sit there?" "Will I have to be politically correct?" "Will you be capable of understanding me?" "Do you accept the principles of Alcoholics Anonymous?" Some expectations, certainly those that are vocalized, are conscious. Others are not. These would include disavowed and fended-off wishes and fantasies, such as to be absolved from feelings of guilt, to be loved, to be told the purpose of living. By means of such questions the patient uses a first opportunity to hint at his experiences and anticipations; the same issues may be seized with greater productivity later in the therapy, usually in connection with the transference. A patient angered by the therapist's silence, for example, may be reacting on grounds of unarticulated passive-dependent wishes and the expectation that the therapist take the active role. If only by briefly acknowledging some of these issues at the start a point of reference is set, a piece of the groundwork laid down.

Expectations about psychotherapy, both conscious and unconscious, are formed from a variety of sources, from popular cultural stereotypes such as books, television, and movies, as well as the individual's own more immediate circumstances. These include models of help derived from family relationships, social encounters with friends, experiences with medical doctors, tutors, guidance counselors, and other therapists. They are as relevant to the therapeutic process as they have been for the patient's development, whether for better or for worse.

Perhaps the most fundamental and far-reaching expectation is the patient's readiness to believe in the ability and willingness of another person to help. It implies a kind of hope that something favorable can happen and exerts a strong influence on the viability of the treatment. If not immediately apparent, over time the nature and strength of such a belief or trust can be explored and elaborated via the patient's fantasies. Such trust likely depends heavily on the person's earliest preverbal experiences of being mothered, cared for, and of favorable parental concern. Bringing such trust into a new relationship is a basic example of transference.

This benevolent belief, however, may never have sufficiently developed. It may have been shaken and thrown into doubt. Disappointments and conflicts experienced during some period of development may then reemerge as part of the person's present crisis and come to be encountered within the therapeutic relationship. Hope, for instance, may struggle with distrust; a patient who has had to adapt to a world of exploitation and chaos may not be able to fully apprehend or emotionally tolerate a relationship defined by clear guidelines and expectations of close cooperation. Such disparities can create difficulties in establishing and maintaining a therapeutic relationship, which are not always overcome. Many people never even make it to a psychotherapist's door for such reasons.

Some patients assume that the therapist will be very active, do something to or for the patient, reassure him, think for him, even take over in order to manage or solve his problems. Such expectations may stem from experiences with other helpers of various kinds who offered primarily suggestive sorts of treatment. The very term *patient* still carries the idea that an authority, the doctor, with special knowledge, skills, and materials, will diagnose the complaint and formulate a treatment, which will be dutifully followed toward a "cure." By her way of responding the psychodynamic therapist will try to assist the patient in gradually becoming an active partner in the examination of his story and experience instead of remaining a passive recipient of ready-made "help."

Some patients ask what they can expect from therapy in a forthright way and do so with feeling. Some, directly or indirectly, want more than just an explanation of how therapy works.

Olivia, a young woman of twenty-eight, comes to therapy because of a series of failed relationships characterized by her feeling betrayed. Near the end of the first hour she asks the therapist how therapy works. At first the therapist tries to answer her question by saying that people find talking helpful, that there are often aspects of our lives that we are unaware of, and so on. Olivia nods and an uncomfortable silence ensues. Knowing that this response is not going anywhere, the therapist is able to shift gears quickly and offer the following: "You know, I wonder if you are asking me this because you want to know if you can trust me to help you." Olivia smiles spontaneously. "I've been betrayed," she says, "I have difficulty trusting. I wonder if I'm capable of it anymore." In Olivia's case it is clear that, answering as she did, the therapist empathically and tactfully touches one of her central concerns. The face value of the question masks Olivia's true worry, which she had been unable to articulate. In this instance therapy will likely "work" as a consequence of the two participants' addressing issues of trust and betrayal.

Others come to therapy feeling that it is their last chance. Veiled attempts may be made at asking the therapist if she thinks there is any hope for them.

Marcus, a man in his late forties, who had been unsuccessful in love and social relations, is quite persistent in pressing the therapist about what he can expect. After he describes his relationship failures and abiding loneliness for the third time, the therapist wonders aloud if he isn't really asking whether therapy is, to put it bluntly, worth it. Marcus smiles, then cries at this comment, and then says, "If I can't connect with you then I'm doomed. And I won't be able to connect if I feel that you feel hopeless about me. Do you?" To this the therapist replies, "Well, life holds no guarantees, but between the two of us we will try to come to some understanding of what has been getting in your way all these years." Thus the therapist does not say outright that she has hope, but by conveying that she will try to engage with him and help him, that they will work together, she nevertheless honors his needs.

Some people may ask in an aggressive manner what they can expect, as did Neil from chapter 5. Remember how he walked to the door at the end of the first session, stopped, turned to the therapist, and asked in a way that caught the therapist off guard, "What can I expect from you?" We saw how the therapist had quickly come to see that Neil habitually dealt with his anxiety by throwing people off balance. But at the time it was unclear what the question and its method of delivery meant, what he was asking for or checking out. Perhaps "Can you handle me?" or "Do I intimidate you?" What could the therapist have said at that point? Perhaps, after collecting herself, she might have come out with, "You ask me this good question just as you are leaving. Let's take it up next time" or "Hmm, I wonder why you ask me now on your way out?" Of course it is easier to think about such things in retrospect when not in a state of acute surprise.

13

First Encounters

After having made various efforts to obtain assistance, a person may arrive at the office of a potential psychotherapist. Even if the referral is based on an evaluation, the therapist still wants to get to know the potential patient herself and evaluate him in her own way. She is interested in hearing the patient's version of his difficulties and circumstances in his own words. She wants to form an impression of his impairment, the degree of his difficulties, and how well he manages his life and himself. She needs answers to questions she has in her own mind: What is the patient's immediate "presenting problem" and how does he view it? To what extent is his current state of adaptation significantly compromised? Is he sufficiently able to contain feelings or control powerful affects and impulses, or is he likely to act them out? Has he been in need of psychiatric consultation? Should referral for psychopharmacological evaluation or treatment be considered? Have earlier attempts at treatment brought good results or at least shown promise? Does the patient seem motivated for undertaking psychotherapy on his own or has he come under pressure from family, public agencies, or the law? Is psychodynamic therapy the therapy for him? Would another therapist be better able to help him? The therapist is also watching how the patient presents himself—that is, his *manner*. How does he comport himself? Is he well groomed? Does he speak clearly or in a confused way? The patient's manner will be revisited by and by.

The therapist, in other words, is still making a kind of assessment. She needs certain kinds of information to form an opinion of what she, by her training and experience, can offer the prospective patient in his particular situation, of the chances for the therapy to be successful. In some respects she may agree with the views of prior clinicians but take issue with others. Occasionally, both patient and therapist may continue for some time in an evaluative mode to clarify relevant issues and also to find out what kind of work relation can develop between them.

At this stage the therapist primarily tries to form an idea of whether the patient has sufficient capacity to do psychological work and whether she feels that she could work with him. Ideally the patient should be willing and able to talk, to have at least minimal ability to look at himself, to take occasional distance from his experience, and be somewhat open to the therapist's comments. He must show some capacity to tolerate the frustration of hopes for quick relief or change. He needs to cope with the difference between a conventional social situation and what goes on in the more intentionally ambiguous, less specifically defined relation offered by the therapist. And he will be required to bear up under possible pressures from disturbing affects, painful memories, and seemingly unsolvable conflict. All this, of course, amounts to a very tall order and is rarely filled in practice. But minimal amounts of the described assets might usefully be looked for. All the while the therapist, having presumably greater self-knowledge and self-control than the patient, keeps in mind her own system of supports (consultation, supervision, medical backup), which can sustain her equanimity during difficult phases of the work.

Besides making inquiries necessary for evaluation therapists are likely to begin employing more specific therapeutic techniques, even in the first session. Attempting to prepare the patient for the kind of work that will have to be done the therapist sometimes gives the patient a sample of her wares, a demonstration of her expertise, a foretaste of what therapy, *her* therapy, offers. She may, for example, inquire into some hesitation shown by the patient, ask him to clarify something he said, connect seemingly disparate ideas, or empathize with the patient's feelings, thus demonstrating her interest and participation in their meeting. And she assesses how he responds to these offerings.

The first encounter then is essentially a hybrid: partly assessment, partly a beginning of therapy via establishing a mode of conversation and developing mutual involvement. In a skillfully handled first meeting the two parts can dovetail nicely. The distinction put forth here is, of course, best understood as conceptual. In the practical situation it doesn't fall quite as neatly.

As a result of the first encounter two things can happen: the patient leaves or he stays. On the one hand it may come about by one party's decision or by joint agreement that the two will not enter into a therapy with each other. This could be for practical or emotional reasons. After discussion of alternatives and possible referral elsewhere contact is terminated. On the other hand the two parties may conclude that they might be able to work with one another and want to do so. Here they enter a *therapeutic understanding*. Although this understanding will develop further in the course of the work it may still be fragile and be yet broken or abandoned. From now on therapist and patient find themselves in a new kind of relationship. The therapeutic process, with its own qualities and circumstances, begins. Before discussing the therapeutic understanding, however, we will address the concept of the therapeutic match.

14

The Therapeutic Match

It is always something of a mystery why some patients and therapists work well together and others do not. The *therapeutic match* refers to some compatibility or "goodness of fit" between a patient and a therapist, an indication of how well the two might work together. Thoughts of promoting a good match affect how referrals are made. Therapists, even nontherapists, think seriously about whom they would refer a potential patient to. A practitioner's known and demonstrated expertise and reputation are certainly one factor. Additionally, though, a referral will sometimes be based on "a good feeling" or a more specific sense such as "this person needs a very kind male therapist" or "that person could benefit from someone who doesn't take any nonsense."

A good therapeutic match also depends on the right modality of the work. For person's wishing to resolve a troubled marriage seeing a couples' therapist might make the best sense. An adolescent would do well to see someone familiar with that age group. Persons with substance abuse problems or eating disorders would do well to consult someone with experience in those respective areas. A match may also be provided by the particular personalities of patient and therapist. One could imagine a shy person working well with someone who has a sympathetic nature and is not too brusque, or a person not very psychologically minded doing well with a therapist who could initially focus on available practical, here-and-now matters. An adolescent boy struggling with feelings about an absent father might profit from work with an older male therapist.

Compatibility on the surface is part of, but not identical with, what in the end really makes a good therapeutic match. This is so because as therapeutic exploration continues new topics come to the fore, issues arise, and dormant conflicts are stirred up and come into prominence. The therapeutic relation can become invaded by unsuspected desires, misunderstandings, conflicts, and may become fraught with disturbing emotions. Patient and therapist will show themselves well matched if they can maintain their curiosity, skepticism, patience, and commitment to the task.

Besides the therapist's overall intelligence and skill, her ability and willingness to learn from the patient are important ingredients of the match. It is fair to say that with each case we always have to "learn" the patient, just as even an experienced performer has to learn a given piece of music. Some patients keenly sense this process of mutual adaptation. In the middle of a complicated and disturbing phase of his treatment, during which both partners had trouble understanding each other, a certain patient said, "I'll have to train you to be *my* therapist!" In his own mind the therapist knew as well that this was the truth. Sometimes, somehow, both patient and therapist know there is more going on than they understand and they tacitly agree to bear with each other in order to reach and come to know it. Here we come to appreciate the invisible but powerful unconscious mesh between two people. The quality of such a connection, then, may or may not coincide with what appears obvious at first glance. However elusive, the concept of match seems to have certain vitality, validity, and intuitive appeal and remains compelling.

A good match can be the luck of the draw. It may not always seem present early in a given therapy. It is not unusual for people to come into therapy with ambivalent feelings, even suspicions about it and the therapist. But some may stay because on some level they begin to feel safe and listened to, and because some curiosity about themselves or the therapist has arisen. Enough of this must happen at the outset for the patient to want to give the process a chance. Whether a good match has come about can really be determined only after the therapy has progressed a little or a lot, with the benefits of hindsight. The match alone does not guarantee that the therapy will be successful, but it is a significant extra card that stacks the deck in its favor.

A therapy that does not take off or go well can be painful and discouraging for beginners and experienced therapists alike, although the latter may have the advantage of being able to remember past successes and the resulting larger perspective. The beginning therapist must realize that the skills of her craft are still new but will probably develop. Especially with continuing supervision she will come to understand the nature of the difficulties that had prevented better results, and this will help in future work. Finally it is important to realize and keep in mind that psychotherapy is no panacea that can take care of everything, and that no psychotherapist should believe that she be able to work successfully with any patient or problem.

15

The Therapeutic Understanding

Whether a person seeking therapy and an available therapist decide to work together depends on their having reached a *therapeutic understanding*, that is, some meeting of minds about what is involved in the psychodynamic process. Such an understanding includes something of the nature and implications of the method and of the definition, negotiation, and settlement of the frame. It establishes the therapist as the experienced assistant able to create conditions favorable to collaborative exploration of the patient's distress and the possibilities of beneficent change. "Experienced" does not mean omniscient or having fore-knowledge of the developments and changes that will be encountered or brought about. Although it is very likely that the therapist, on grounds of what she has heard and seen from the prospective patient, will have formed some preliminary ideas about his particular needs and what has to be done, and while the patient may have come for a solution to particular dilemmas, specific results cannot be guaranteed. Both parties are setting out on a journey, and there is no way of knowing where the work may lead. At times during the therapy it can be helpful to remind the patient of the exploratory nature of the work: "It is interesting where your thoughts have taken you today"; "I don't think we can know how the hour will unfold"; "Let's just see where your thoughts and feelings take you"; or "What's it like not to know where the hour will take us?"

This understanding of which we speak also involves certain expectations for the patient's behavior, there to impose a measure of predictability and stability on the process for both participants. They are spelled out by the psychotherapeutic frame. The understanding further extends to the patient's commitment to potentially far reaching self-disclosure, certain frustration (no immediate magical help), active participation, and persistence in the work throughout difficult and discouraging periods.

This understanding can begin to develop during a successful first contact and become more or less specifically verbalized. As with the frame one ought not to expect to get all its features out at once. For any particular patient certain aspects of the understanding, such as that there are no magical cures, are implicitly retained while others need to be openly stated.

Some patients find it very helpful if the therapist provides some amount of "consumer information" during first contacts, especially if the patient has certain expectations or seems puzzled or mystified by what is happening or going to. There is no need, however, to do this in any standard form or in every patient's case. Generally, though not always so, such information is best brought forth in response to a patient's inquiries. Educating or informing a patient of certain aspects of psychotherapy has its own implications, so it needs to be weighed. Technical explanations might put a didactic tone into the therapeutic situation. Any explanations are best given in minimal amounts; lessons in the theory of psychotherapy are generally not suggested because they tend to shift the therapeutic relationship away from its *emotional* immediacy toward abstract intellectualizing. And finally these questions often veil some deeper issue. Recall Olivia and Marcus in chapter 12.

In some cases the therapist may elect to give some information based on how the patient impresses her. For example, Ann spends much of the first session both showing and telling the therapist how she has trouble controlling her feelings, saying that she wants to do something about this now. The therapist notes to herself that Ann has obvious difficulties with affect regulation. At one point the therapist says, "You are telling me that your feelings go from zero to sixty pretty quickly and that more often than not you can't bear their intensity. I agree, and I think it is very important that you work on these issues. But, really, life holds no quick and easy answers, you know. Really, these kinds of things take time." In this way the therapist addresses a concern and adds a piece of reality to Ann's expectations. Interestingly she also takes the heat off psychotherapy itself by situating her comments in the broader context of "life," and by assuming what resembles the stance of a grandmother who carries a benevolent resignation about her and a "listen to me; I've pretty much seen it all" attitude. Incidentally the therapist's approach worked like a charm and probably did so by somehow tapping into a piece of the transference, namely, Ann's need for "grandmothering," with a tough calm and an aura of charitable control. Like any good therapeutic move made at the appropriate time a circumscribed piece of education can get things moving, thereby implicitly imparting to the patient a feeling of mobility, that he is not irrevocably stuck.

The majority of patients, if not all, will most assuredly encounter disappointment somewhere along the way, more than once actually, maybe even a lot, and about different things. In terms of the understanding psychotherapy may not be as they imagined: resolution not as quick perhaps, interaction not as interactive, therapist not as directive. For any given individual these expectations may have been fostered by a culture that is reductionistic, blasé about inner life, and that cannot stand a process that spreads out and deepens. Or perhaps these expectations are the result of a "marketing pitch" by the referral source who in a push to "sell" psychotherapy exaggerates the "surgical strike," a problem-focused bias. And in many instances patients react with some anger at any challenge to their expectations. One patient remarked, "I feel I've been a victim of some false advertising about what psychotherapy is. As it turns out I feel I'm getting something out of it, but not at the speed or the way I expected. It's taken some getting used to. And I'm still getting used to it." Another patient said, "This is not what I wanted. I don't feel I'm getting anywhere," and left. For those who carry on in therapy disappointment must have been mitigated by the experience of a process, certainly slow going and frustrating at times, but also profoundly careful, connecting, affirming, challenging, insightful, and powerful. Even at times exhilarating. For many patients, and for many reasons, something of this just does not click into place. Here it is very important to note that the therapist invite the patient to look at himself.

Before a basic understanding can be established, however, several things need to happen. There must be some evidence of a workable match. A decision must be reached that the particular therapist's professional training and experience provide the expertise relevant to the nature of the patient's psychological makeup and problems. And the patient must feel that she is personally someone with whom he can work. It would do little good to proceed, for example, if it turned out that a patient needed substance abuse counseling for which the therapist had minimal training; or if he could not abide the therapist's expression, the shape of her nose, or the tone of her voice. This work is hard enough. In some instances the therapeutic contact may need to be conceptualized in terms of an extended evaluation, with an understanding that for the moment the two will work toward yet defining an appropriate course of action, perhaps in a different setting. In general this is not such a bad idea. An evaluative frame acts as a kind of emotional vestibule within which the patient can acquaint himself with the therapeutic process. He can peer in a noncommittal way into the rest of the house as it were, perhaps even test out a bit of his adaptability to the process (*can* he, *does* he want to enter the wardrobe?). The patient must also feel some confidence in the therapist, both in terms of her professional ability and personal manner. They come across in the therapist's exercise of her skill and humanity.

At some point a "good-enough understanding" is either reached and the process continues, or it is not and the process ceases. Whether it is reached by the end of the first session or not until after the first few contacts it will remain throughout the process of the therapy and occasionally go through periods of crisis. It could be that a patient's particular conflict may come to play itself out against a piece of the frame (for example, the patient cancels appointments) or it turns out that a piece of the frame was not discussed (for example, payment for missed appointments). His conflict may also show up as a feeling of stuckness that he attributes to the therapist's reserved demeanor, a topic we take up in much greater detail with the concept of *clinical neutrality*. Inasmuch as a "good-enough understanding" has been reached it forms the beginning of the *therapeutic alliance*, also to be discussed later.

Upon reaching this understanding and resolving to accept psychotherapeutic assistance a person copes with a complex situation requiring a new stance. While he enters the therapeutic relationship as a fully competent contractual partner; abides and complies with the practical arrangements that were made, and commits to open his own psychological work to intimate participation by the therapist; he also assumes a state of partial surrender, acknowledging a degree of helplessness and expecting a somewhat superior competence in the person offering herself as the therapist.

To illustrate the therapeutic understanding, consider this example of the opening encounter between a patient and therapist.

Mrs. Jones is a woman in her mid-fifties. She calls Therapist J to ask if she is taking new patients. Therapist J inquires how she might be of help. Mrs. Jones remarks that she is greatly upset and goes on to describe the molestation of her daughter by a family member. She divulges some details of the trauma in a clear but rapid and pressured way, adding how guilty and saddened she and her husband feel, and how she looks forward to her "blessed sleep." She feels it is very important that she, herself, get help.

Mrs. Jones then asks Therapist J if she takes a certain insurance. Therapist J says no, but that she would be happy to negotiate some out of pocket payment, if that interests her. Mrs. Jones seems to feel a connection with Therapist J, repeats how important her getting help coping with these circumstances is, and they agree on a time for consultation.

Mrs. Jones comes to this first session well groomed. She is a tall woman, polite, but rather forceful. She recounts the details of her story, remarking that she is a very moral person and that she likes to be in control. At one point she begins to cry, telling Therapist J how much she loves her child. Therapist J says that Mrs. Jones seems to be in shock over the incident, but that she also seems able to function at work and that her "blessed sleep" comes across as restorative rather than excessive. Mrs. Jones smiles. She continues to speak openly with appropriate affect. Therapist J says that this is indeed a very hard time for Mrs. Jones, that perhaps she will need more time to discuss her concerns and the practicalities of therapy. Mrs. Jones agrees wholeheartedly, and an appointment is set for the following week.

The second session finds Mrs. Jones in much the same condition as the first. She smiles upon entering. Therapist J asks about her reactions to the first session. She responds that she thought Therapist J to be intelligent and that she had offered some very helpful comments. As with the first session Mrs. Jones speaks without much assistance. About two-thirds of the way into the session Therapist J tactfully brings up the fee. She likes Mrs. Jones and is prepared to work out a mutually fair arrangement. She tells Mrs. Jones that her usual rate is $100 a session but is open to hearing what Mrs. Jones can afford. Mrs. Jones discusses her finances briefly, saying that she can afford the full fee. Therapist J is a little taken aback by this. She says that if it is something Mrs. Jones feels she can do then they would proceed with that understanding. Mrs. Jones assures her that this is so because therapy is important and she continues to talk about the issues that brought her in. Therapist J has to tactfully stop her from going beyond the hour.

The next morning, a little before 8:00 A.M., Mrs. Jones leaves Therapist J a message saying that she discussed things with her husband, who felt that it was silly to pay so much for therapy when they had insurance. She thanked Therapist J for her time, leaving her number in case Therapist J needed to contact her.

Mrs. Jones had appeared to be quite engaged in the process. She expressed understanding of the importance of therapy for her at the time and that difficult feelings would be encountered. She also showed a degree of confidence in the therapist, and seemed to feel some connection to her. Therapist J was empathic and flexible. She took the time to develop some connection before addressing the fee. Mrs. Jones even reassured Therapist J that she could afford her rate. Thus the patient accepted the terms initially but then rejected them ostensibly after a discussion with her husband. What is puzzling is the abrupt about face that occurred after the fee was set. How does Therapist J set about making sense of this? And what should she do? There is no one way to approach these questions.

What Therapist J decides to do will depend on how she understands the situation and how she feels about it. Mrs. Jones did not appear to be a compliant woman. She stated that she needed to be in control. Yet she left therapy because, as her husband reportedly said, it was silly to spend the money when they had insurance. Was money the issue? Or was it a convenient screen behind which Mrs. Jones could hide her mixed feelings about being in therapy? Did she feel some loss of control? What about her leaving her phone number? Was she hoping to receive a call back? If so what might she have been expecting or wanting? And what would Therapist J wish to say to her?

Not quite convinced that she was doing the right thing, Therapist J decided to leave things as they were. This had been a particularly tiresome month for Therapist J and her energy reserves were low. At any other time she might have called Mrs. Jones. So she would send Mrs. Jones a bill for the sessions along with a note acknowledging her decision to stop their work and inviting her to return if she felt the need.

Here we touch on the fact that the therapist's life and reality are also a part of the wider therapeutic situation. It is good to be reminded of that every so often, that we cannot think about therapy only within a theoretical bubble.

16

The First Therapy Session: Setting a Tone

In opening a first session a therapist can, in theory at least, do any number of things that either *set a tone* conducive to prosperous conversation or interfere with bringing it about. She can, for example, say nothing and sit expectantly. Although doing so may at times serve a purpose once the therapy has developed some momentum, most people would experience this as rather weird for a first encounter. And they would be right. For one thing it's just not very good manners. We do indeed step into a different space when we enter therapy, but it ought to bear some resemblance to the decencies of human interaction. Also silence at a first meeting would do nothing to promote feelings of safety and trust in the therapist's interest. Beginning by presenting the frame and all the conditions of therapy might not be such a good idea either; therapy might come across as a stiflingly rule-bound enterprise. It is generally best to wait to discuss the practical and administrative matters until at least some mode of conversation has been established. Sometimes it is useful to start with what is known about the patient from a prior intake or the referral source. One might begin with something like "I understand that you met with Therapist X. Could you tell me about that meeting?" Occasionally a patient will come in and ask,

"Did you speak with so-and-so?" or "I take it so-and-so told you about my problems?" or "Did you read so-and-so's notes?" To this one can simply say, "Yes (or no as the case may be), but I would very much like you to tell me in just your own words." If a patient asks, "How do I begin?" you might say, "Perhaps we can start by your telling me something of what brings you to therapy."

Essentially the therapist wants to encourage the patient to speak, to attempt gradually to extend his communications, pursue lines of thought, feeling, or remembering, and to think and explore a bit further than he has been accustomed to do by himself. It is as if the therapist's comments are accompanied by a subtext entitled "tell me more." Such a mode will continue to dominate the therapy because we always want to assist the patient in approaching matters of which he is generally not fully conscious. Setting the proper tone for accomplishing this is an important task from the very first hours onward. We do some of this in ordinary life as well, such as in meeting new people, when a friend comes to us with a concern or exciting news. Some of us are certainly more skilled than others at this; they have a little more natural "savoir faire" than the rest. As therapists we continue to develop our capacities for widening conversations. We exercise them in assisting our patients to express themselves more and more fully.

Patients present in many ways. Some take the bull by the horns and ramble on right away. Others theorize about their issues in abstract terms. Taciturn types might not know what to say. There are patients who are overwhelmed by anxiety, depression, or confusion. They leave it up to the therapist to find ways of helping them, even imploring her to do what is necessary to make them feel better. There are also the therapy savvy, who seem to know what it is all about and what is generally expected of them. Overall one can say that the first therapeutic hour is one in which the two parties are checking out each other in a preliminary way. They are trying to find a way of working together and, possibly, reaching a *therapeutic understanding.*

Most of all, however, first hours must set a tone, an abiding tone that will echo through the entire therapeutic process. This tone is primarily one of *freedom of self-expression.* It is a protected freedom, safeguarded by the frame as previously discussed, and encouraged by the initial communications and reactions of the therapist. Here we are not only referring to words but to attitude and conduct put forth nonverbally. It may be in an expression, a gesture, or just in sitting quietly and listening. The kind of listening spoken of here is characterized by an open, unprejudiced, and receptive quality that conveys to the patient several very important things: (1), that it is safe for him to speak; (2), that he is being heard; and (3), that he is being heard in a manner very different from what he has known. Furthermore the therapist tries to provide minimal definition to the conversation. Her nongratuitous and considered use of words allows the patient to follow any train of thought with the least influence from the therapist's preconceived ideas. Again it is the content of the patient's own internal world we want to hear about. Of course what is deemed minimal will vary according to the specific needs of each patient. The therapist must weigh the appropriateness of her reserve against her assessment of the patient's level of anxiety. How much structure and guidance does he need to feel safe? It would be hard to imagine any first encounter devoid of anxiety. Those who have previously done some psychotherapeutic work and thus already have some idea of the process might feel somewhat less anxious. Finding themselves with a new and still unknown therapist, however, may create anxieties of its own.

This tone of which we speak must also ring of the essential notions that therapy is both a *mindful* and *active* endeavor. Psychotherapy is active in the sense that it asks the patient to look inward and examine the ways in which he lives, the ways that have brought him to the consulting room. With its emphasis on improving and assisting the patient with his own psychological work, psychotherapy tries to engage his curiosity about himself. Viewed in this light, the first hour should deliver the expectation that the patient will participate rather than be a passive recipient of the therapist's knowledge. So, from the first moments of the opening session, it is the task of the therapist to guide the potential patient into treatment by creating a safe therapeutic atmosphere that facilitates and introduces the work as an active and mindful process.

In the following we present three opening sessions that demonstrate how the therapist sets a proper tone and facilitates the therapeutic work.

MADELYN

Madelyn (Ms. M) is a twenty-two-year-old senior in college. She is about twenty-five pounds overweight by conventional standards and seems self-conscious. The therapist's immediate sense of her is of a young, pleasant woman, hiding. She wears a pair of blue denim overalls, flat sandals, and a soft narrow-brimmed felt hat over what appears to be a head of thick blond hair. Rather large tortoiseshell glasses frame very blue eyes, and large dangling earrings the sides of her face. She greets the therapist with a smile, which although genuine cannot hide her obvious anxiety. She looks about the room and at the therapist. Then she sits on the edge of her seat clutching her haversack to her chest for some time.

Th: What brings you to the clinic, Ms. M?

Pt: A lot of things I guess. (*She pauses and looks at the therapist expectantly. The therapist nods.*) I have less than one year in college. And there are a lot of things I have to think about. I have to think about what to do next. What's going to happen? I have a lot of questions. Time's gone by very fast. It's all gone by in a flash it seems. And I'm not sure where I'm going to go from here. I have a lot of questions about what's going to happen.

Th: (*She observes how extremely anxious the patient is; she feels anxious herself. She responds empathically.*) What next?

(*"What next?" has a double referent here, speaking not only to Madelyn's articulated fears about the future a few months away but also to her anxiety about what may happen next in the session. This latter meaning likely exists beneath awareness in both the therapist and Madelyn.*)

Pt: Yes. (*Smiles.*) So that's one thing. I also have difficulty making connections. I really feel uncomfortable (*Pause*) around men. I haven't been able to have a relationship with a man, even friendships are difficult. (*Patient is going very fast here and her anxiety level seems to be increasing. She does not seem to be in control.*) I haven't had a boyfriend really. I'm not a teenager anymore, and my friends have all had or have boyfriends and . . . (*Uncomfortable pause*) Should I go on or what?

Here the therapist has to make some very rapid assessments and decisions. She will not comment on Madelyn's anxiety because that would be coming in too close and they have just met. After all, Madelyn has just finished saying she has difficulty making connections. Such a comment would likely only increase her anxious self-consciousness. The therapist would like Madelyn to slow down. At some point she also wants to inquire about any past therapy experience. She decides on the following:

Th: Well, you've begun to talk about your last year and the difficulty you have making connections with men. I would be interested in hearing more about either of those things but certainly feel free to tell me something else if you wish.

Pt: Well. (*Pauses and thinks.*) I've never been able to make a connection with a guy. It's very uncomfortable for me. It's difficult. What I'd like is a relationship that's sort of like what I have with my girlfriends.

The therapist's comment appears to have helped Madelyn. She is able to engage in prioritizing even when anxious. And this is important and encouraging. Madelyn demonstrates a capacity to stand back and, if only temporarily, to control her feelings; she pauses to consider what she has said and then makes a decision. Facilitating this the therapist may have affirmed to Madelyn that she was indeed listening and that all of what she was saying was important. Also the therapist's comment asked Madelyn to take an active role in the conversation. Because of Madelyn's anxiety the therapist senses that she will have to continue to make the appropriate effort to help her feel more at ease.

Th: Aha! And how would you describe that?

Pt: Well, it's different with different girlfriends. With my friend Mary it can get contentious but not in a bad way. I kind of like that. We'll fight. But it's not really serious. We can kid around. Kind of . . . I like to argue and go back and forth like that, but playfully. And with Alice and Jenny and others I may not argue but it is comfortable. I don't know how else to describe it. So it would be nice to have something that is a mixture of those things.

The therapist herself is feeling a little more relaxed. Madelyn is speaking more fluidly and describing the quality of certain relationships. She does not seem to lead an isolated life.

Th: (*Nods.*) But it hasn't been that for you.

Pt: No. I can't seem to get past the superficial. Sometimes, not often, I'll ask someone out to coffee. But it gets uncomfortable so quickly. I don't know what to do, where to go. How is something like this done? I get very . . . I don't know. And then things just end or go nowhere. And I'm not sure what to do.

(*Short silence*)

Th: (*Smiles.*) Something seems to be stopping you here.

There are many salient aspects to Madelyn's story. She comments on how interactions get uncomfortable quickly, on not being able to get past the superficial, and things just ending and going nowhere. The therapist's last comment addresses this. Similar to her earlier comment ("What next?"), "Something seems to be stopping you here" is both empathic and ambiguous. "Here" could refer to Madelyn's experience with men or what is happening in the session as she recounts her story. Where will Madelyn go with this?

Pt: Yes. And that's what I don't understand. I don't know what the discomfort means. Is it becoming sexual? Should it be becoming sexual? And if it is then what do I do? Or am I reading things wrong? I don't know whether it is a friendship or something more or what, and I can't figure out what to do.

In Madelyn's case there seem to be two areas of concern at present: the future and connections with men, the latter being predominant for now. With empathy and encouragement Madelyn is able to begin to convey to the therapist more of her story regarding men. Thus far the therapist seems to be succeeding in facilitating self-expression, Madelyn's active participation, and the mindful nature of the encounter. Let us continue by turning to some other vignettes.

JEFFREY
Jeffrey (Mr. J) is a twenty-five-year-old lawyer. He has dark brown hair and eyes and an overall boyish look. He is well built and in good physical condition. For some reason the therapist notices at once that he has beautiful hands, dark slender fingers, and nailbeds that are deep and with pronounced half moons. He comes to the session in a fashionable suit and tie. He looks about the office immediately upon entering.

Pt: (*He begins to speak on his way to his seat.*) This is like in the films.

Th: Oh. How so? (*The therapist smiles. She is responsive. Her comment suggests that nothing is too trivial to talk about.*)

Pt: (*He sits.*) The big chairs and all. (*He pauses and looks to the therapist.*) So how do we start?

Even in this short exchange a lot is going on. The patient opens the session. The therapist wonders about the kind of films he is imagining and his comment about the big chairs. She will "file" these thoughts. She is not, however, fully aware that she has noticed his hands, of the level of detail she has registered. At some later point she may ponder her reaction.

Th: Sounds like we already have. (*Joint laughter.*) Why don't you tell me what brings you here?

Pt: Didn't Dr. X write something down?

Th: Yes, he did. But it would be useful for me to hear this in your own words.

Pt: Well, I have this problem. (*Pause*) I haven't had much success with women. I think I am a reasonably attractive man. I work out. I'm intelligent. I'm a lawyer. I have a very good job. I'm used to doing research. So if I have a problem I will look, get a book, read it, and understand the mechanics of the problem, and solve it. So . . . (*Pause*)

It is interesting how Jeffrey comes right out with it, telling us a lot even here. The therapist wonders why he isn't more hesitant. Is this a way of compensating for feeling anxious?

Th: I take it that this strategy is not working with this particular problem.

Pt: That's right. I am very puzzled why. It has worked before. (*Pause*) I think I'm the only one with this problem. And you know I don't want to set up a pattern that I will always come to counseling for my problems. Like I say I am used to figuring out my own problems.

Th: I see. Can you say more about your thoughts about counseling? (*Therapist capitalizes on patient's bringing up counseling.*)

Pt: I'm really not sure what I think. I have this friend who swears by it. She's been in counseling for a very long time, maybe a year or two. And I've heard of people who stay for much longer than that. Years. Another friend is an English professor who's really into psychoanalysis. I don't think he'll ever get out. I really can't get behind all of that. (*Pause*)

Two of Jeffrey's comments are worth noting here: "I don't think he'll ever get out" and "I really can't get behind all of that." Both express some anxiety about counseling and what he is getting into. Perhaps not even conscious that she has made a choice of which comment to go with or why the therapist continues with . . .

Th: . . . all of what?

Pt: All of . . . well, the Oedipus thing. Penis envy. Wanting to sleep with your mother. It seems far-fetched to me. (*Pause*) Is that how you think? What do you think of all that?

Th: I think you are asking me what you can expect from this process—far-fetched ideas or ones that you can relate to?

Pt: Yeah. That's right. (*Pause*) So what are your ideas about counseling? (*Asks this tentatively.*) What can I expect?

Th: (*Although she thinks this is a very interesting question, she also feels that Jeffrey is not making the work easy for her. Trying to preserve as much anonymity as possible without alienating Jeffrey she focuses her comment on his manner.*) You ask me this in a very tentative way.

Pt: Yeah. Yeah. I'm not sure if I should ask you this.

Th: You can ask me anything you like. To answer your question I think theories are all well and good, but I generally base what I do on what the person in front of me is saying and experiencing. What you are, would be, saying and experiencing.

The therapist might still have been on solid ground continuing in relative anonymity with something like "Tell me more about that," or "What's the hesitation?" rather than answering directly. Such comments might have extended the nascent exploration of Jeffrey's expectations and concerns about therapy. But she instead proceeded by imparting to Jeffrey some consumer information, a decision likely motivated by her assessment of his and perhaps even her own level of anxiety. As an aside, although we may take some issue with how a therapist goes about her work it is she, after all, who is there in the session with the patient. We are merely looking in. The actual therapist, along with the patient, is an "insider," as opposed to a supervisor or other commentator, and is sensing firsthand all sorts of anxieties and agendas to which an "outsider" is not directly privy. For better or worse she is making her own way. As it turns out in this case interesting information emerges.

> Pt: (*Nods.*) Okay. Yes. Okay. (*Pause*) What do I say now? (*The patient opens up quickly and now is unsure of himself. Is this how he engages with women in general?*)
>
> Th: Perhaps you can tell me why you chose to come to therapy at this point in time. Clearly you have been worrying about this issue for a while now. (*Therapist decides to continue to structure the conversation for now.*)
>
> Pt: I'm afraid that people will figure this out. What if they start putting two and two together. You know, "Come to think of it I've never seen Jeffrey date." Or "Why doesn't Jeffrey have a girlfriend?" If they decide to ask me these questions I'll soon run out of excuses.
>
> Th: That's an interesting choice of words—excuses—as if you've done something wrong.

VINCENT

Vincent (Mr. V) is a thirty-six-year-old man recently hired by the city to trim trees. He is a strong, handsome man who, from the start, comes across as extremely agitated. He taps his left foot and hand and speaks in fits and starts, smiling as he does, sometimes stopping to ask for help. It took a while for Vincent to make his way to the therapist's office. When he called to set up an appointment he asked the therapist many questions: what her specialty was, how long she had been practicing, and so forth. Two appointments were made and cancelled before Vincent showed up. When the therapist walked into the waiting room he was looking out of the window, a magazine opened on his lap. Hearing her enter Vincent looked up with a start. The therapist said hello, asked if he was Mr. V, and then introduced herself. Vincent commented on the "nice building" and asked if she had been here long. He was anxious. She responded politely in the manner of small talk. When they sat down she opened the session formally:

Th: Perhaps we can begin by your telling me what it is that brings you to therapy.

Pt: Well, I've been real anxious. I think my girlfriend is cheating on me. We've been going out for six months now, and well I just have this feeling that she's cheating on me.

(*Vincent is silent. He looks at the therapist, shrugs his shoulders, and smiles with a sigh.*)

Th: What makes you think she's cheating on you?

Pt: Well, I just got this feeling. She goes on the internet for hours. We don't live together, but I spend a lot of my time at her place. She has these three dogs, and I take care of them a lot. I don't mind. I love animals, especially dogs. The dogs and I, we get along. Animals and I just have this thing. Well, she sometimes doesn't feed 'em because she's kind of scatterbrained. She forgets about them. Also I think that maybe when she's out she's seeing someone. I don't have any hard proof, if you know what I mean. But she's not caring at times. I think maybe I've had it with her.

Th: She is not caring.

Pt: She doesn't seem to care about what I am feeling. I wanted to talk to her about us the other day, and she said that she was tired. She wasn't tired. She went out with friends an hour later. She won't pay attention to me. She's not sensitive. (*He pauses.*)

Th: (*Smiles.*) Why did you stop? What happened then? (*Here she demonstrates her continued interest as well as calling attention to his behavior. Her smile shows her benevolence.*)

Pt: I played with the dogs, then went out for a walk, then I went back to her house and watched some TV and waited for her to come home. I know what you're thinking.

Th: What am I thinking?

Pt: Why am I still with her?

Th: (*Smiles.*) I think that you're thinking that. But since you mention it . . .

Pt: Yeah. (*Smiles.*) We have a lot in common. We have a spiritual thing. We like to go to church together. We did that early on. I want to go to church. I feel a need for it. And it's not every woman who feels the same. Only we haven't been going lately. That's another reason I think she's seeing someone. We're not close anymore. (*Stops, shrugs again, looks at the therapist.*) What can I say, we're not close anymore and I don't know why. (*Pauses, shrugs, and taps his foot.*) Help me out, doc. I don't know what to say. I'm stuck.

Th: (*The therapist notes Vincent's distress and responds immediately.*) All this must be very stressful for you. It is really causing you a great deal of anxiety.

Pt: You can tell, doc, huh. (*Smiles openly.*)

Th: Why don't you tell me more about your feeling anxious.

Pt: I don't want to be alone. I'm nearly forty, and I want a family. It makes me sad. I get very sad. I know she's cheating. She won't admit it.

Th: You've asked her.

Pt: Yeah. She says no she isn't. I know she's lying. I just know it. She turns hot and cold. She can be really warm, and we can be getting along great. And then she's cold. I don't understand.

Vincent is getting agitated again. The therapist is getting the picture of a man who needs a lot of support both in his life and, it seems, in the session. Whatever is going on in his relationship the idea that he could be alone is terrifying to him. She is also sensing how angry he is but decides to let that go for now unless he brings it up. At some point she would like to ask him about his need to go to church and what he means by "a spiritual thing."

Th: Go on. Tell me what you don't understand.

The therapist offers encouragement. Its beginning to look like Vincent will need a lot of it. She feels pressured and wonders if she wants to take him on. She wonders if this is not how his girlfriend is feeling. But for now she will just make note of her feelings and continue.

Pt: I think that she turns hot when she needs me. If she's feeling lonely herself. Or if one of the dogs needs to go to the vet. It hurts me. Things will go good for a few days, maybe a week if we're lucky (*smiles*), and then we get to fighting. Can be about anything. And then she's cold. Hot and cold. I feel jerked around. Why did things change? That's what I don't understand. Things were very good when we met.

Th: How did the two of you meet?

Pt: We met at a bar (*smiles*). It's not what you think.

Th: What do I think? (*Smiles and notes that this is the second time that the patient "knows" what she is thinking.*)

Pt: That I just pick girls up. Well, I have, actually. But it was different with Connie.

A little later in the session the therapist says:

Th: You know, I thought I would ask you about your curiosity about me over the phone. It seemed to me that you had some concerns about me, that something was on your mind.

Pt: (*Smiles.*) Yeah. You remembered that, huh? Well, I was in therapy once before, about five years ago after my dad died. I was pretty upset. In a state of grief you might say. I didn't think he understood me. He didn't say much.

Th: The therapist?

Pt: Yeah, the therapist. (*Pause*) I gave it a shot, but I just felt that he didn't care. He was a good guy and all. He had a kind face. But I guess he expected me to do all the talking. We'd just sit there in silence sometimes, and I felt uncomfortable.

Th: This is the second time you've referred to someone not caring about you. The first was your girlfriend. (*She thinks this person really needs to know that others care about him, that he is not forgettable perhaps. And that he probably experiences silence as being disregarded.*)

Pt: Yeah, that's why I cancelled. I got scared. I don't want to be ignored. I didn't know if that therapist was paying attention to me. I don't know what to expect anymore. I get ignored a lot, by my girl-friend, my parents—especially my dad when he was alive, and my girlfriend in the last two months. What happened?

Th: I think you're telling me that there are times in the relationship when you feel treated like her dogs—forgotten, uncared for. (*There is something appealing and engaging about him, she muses, as well as infuriating at times. She notes how often her reactions to Vincent have shifted during the hour.*)

Pt: I tell you the dogs are treated better than me . . .

The previous excerpts illustrate some of the points raised at the outset of the chapter. Both Madelyn and Jeffrey come to the session without any prior experience of psychotherapy, whereas Vincent has had one previous "shot." Jeffrey, however, does allude to an initial intake with a Dr. X. It is unclear what Jeffrey is expecting with his question "So how do we start?" but the therapist's subsequent comment conveys several things. She is letting him know that it is he who must be active and speak, and that his words are important. This issue comes up again a little later when she responds to his questions about theory. Essentially the same message is imparted to Madelyn when she asks, "Should I go on or what?" The therapist's response communicates to her that she has been listening, that the two themes Madelyn has brought up, namely, concern about the future and men, are both worthy of elaboration, and that it would be good if she chose. Or she could bring up something else altogether. Having Madelyn choose is, of course, informative in its own right because it lets the therapist know that the topic of relating to men is likely the most pressing for her right now. The therapist subsequently encourages her to follow this train of thought. Responding in such a way also carries with it the idea that Madelyn need not confine herself to any one topic, that she can speak of anything she likes. Jeffrey as well is given *carte blanche* when told that he may ask the therapist anything he likes. These comments all serve to encourage self-expression and to open up its possibilities. With Vincent the therapist is doing essentially the same. Sensing his level of anxiety she has chosen to be quite overtly empathic and structuring in response to his request "Help me out, doc. I don't know what to say. I'm stuck" in order to encourage him to continue telling her about himself and his circumstances.

By drawing attention to details of their patients' behavior, these therapists are asking them to be mindful of what they are doing and saying. In Jeffrey's case the therapist calls his attention to the tentative nature in which he asks her a question. She also highlights his choice of the word *excuses.* In Madelyn's case the therapist points out that something seemed to have stopped her. That Madelyn goes on to speak of her confusion around men confirms the correctness and empathic quality of the therapist's observation and the connection that is quickly forming between them. In Vincent's case the therapist, in a tactful and gentle way, encourages him to think about his own questions and comments, including those expressing his preoccupation with what she is thinking.

It seems evident that all three patients are quite anxious as they come to the first therapeutic hour. Madelyn shows this by speaking rapidly, speaking before she has taken off her coat, by sitting on the edge of her seat, and pausing uncomfortably. She also has many questions about what to do next, both in her life in general and within the hour itself. Jeffrey comes across unsure about his ability to relate to women and the process of psychotherapy. Unlike Madelyn, who waits for the therapist to begin, he opens the session with a comment on the room. He also has questions, these being directed squarely at the mechanics of therapy: How does it work? How long will the process take? Years? And what of the therapist? Will he be able to relate to her? Is she Freudian? What about penis envy and sleeping with your mother? Jeffrey is concerned about becoming dependent on therapy. How far can he go in this enterprise? Will he be sucked in and never be able to get out? Will this be yet another failed effort at relating to a woman? Vincent is arguably much more anxious than either Jeffrey or Madelyn. His rapid speech, his questions both on the telephone and in the office, his body language all attest to his feeling frightened, hypersensitive, and feeling uncared for. The therapist makes it a point to bring up Vincent's phone call and cancellations and inquires about their significance; this yields quite a bit of information. She also demonstrates an ability to understand him with her comment that at times he feels treated like his girlfriend's dogs. Also sensing a passivity about Vincent she deliberately uses the words "I think *you're* telling me . . . " in order to underscore to Vincent that he is actively conveying something to her. This will no doubt need to be repeated.

In all three cases it appears that the therapist has succeeded in engaging the patient's curiosity and creating a safe atmosphere. The processes are moving, and we get more and interesting information.

Therapists can indeed feel anxious, too. Really, no therapist, not even the most practiced, ever becomes immune to a patient's anxiety. Nor should she, since personal reactions can serve as important barometers of a patient's internal states. Over time, though, therapists can become accustomed to anxiously generated questions and behaviors when encountering a new patient. They will become better able to catch their own reactions on the wing so they don't fly away. This allows them to sit *receptively* with the patient and think *expansively*. In due course a therapist will come to know what she needs in order to anchor herself, and will develop her own array of orienting responses. They will vary in their particulars with each patient, because each one brings something uniquely challenging to the hour. As for the patient he may or may not feel that the stated arrangements (arrangements that pertain to the frame, that is) are workable and accordingly will make a decision whether to continue. For novice practitioners, however, unaccustomed to these often complex and at times intensely provocative situations things can become unsettling very fast. They may discover that some patients may be set at ease by almost any response, the fact of the response itself and not its content being the crucial factor. Other patients may always be ill at ease and, regardless of the response, unable to settle. We said before that there are reasons for a particular therapy not getting off the ground. The patient may react to something about the therapist; the therapist, for her own psychological or educational reasons, may not be cueing into an important aspect of the patient's presentation. Or the patient may not be ready to do further psychological work. One can never know for certain.

In the seminar we ask trainees to think about their experiences of the first hour. They are usually quick to say that they feel excited, curious, and hopeful on one hand, uncertain and anxious on the other. Their concerns are many: Will they live up to their patient's expectations? Can they help the patient? Might they have difficult problems with him? Indeed some have stated that they are glad not to have "fouled it up yet." Let us turn to situations in which what might have become a therapeutic relationship came to an early and unexpected end.

17

The First and Only Hour

The first psychotherapeutic session is an interaction of great complexity that may or may not lead to another meeting. Both therapist and patient feel certain apprehensions, and they may express or fend off these feelings in a variety of ways. It happens in every therapist's experience that a first hour with a patient is to be the only one. Sometimes this becomes quite clear during the session. In other instances a patient will cancel or simply not show up for the next session, and this will come as a surprise to the therapist. There are many different agendas that people bring to a first session, and it can be difficult to know what is transpiring, especially if the patient has trouble putting thoughts and feelings into words or chooses not to do so.

Actually we are speaking of the "first and only hour" in part for dramatic effect. The events to which we refer may in fact draw themselves out over two or more sessions before the relationship comes to an end. The point is that therapies that end before they really begin are quite different from therapies that experience a rupture later on. In those, there already is more of a connection, more of a basis for understanding what happened, and for a better chance for repair and working through.

The following vignettes are intended to illustrate some of the ways a therapy just does not get going. We decided to present a few scenarios familiar to most therapists, along with a brief discussion of each.

MR. A

Mr. A, a man in his mid-twenties, comes to see Therapist A. He begins to talk almost immediately about the recent breakup of a relationship. He speaks obsessively, leaving Therapist A little room to join the conversation. Each time she tries to say something Mr. A pauses for an instant and then continues over her, leaving Therapist A feeling as though she is trying to force open a door that is kept closed by a strong wind of words. Her attempts are futile, and so she stops and simply listens. There are about ten minutes remaining in the session. The therapist is aware of the time and manages to indicate that Mr. A seems overwhelmed by all that is on his mind. She reflects back to him what she has heard. Mr. A remains quiet, nods, says, "Yes, that's right," pauses, and then begins to speak as before. Therapist A wants to say something about the process but does not quite know how to do so. She feels that if she does she will somehow hurt the patient. She anticipates that they will run beyond the time, and she wants to contain things as much as possible. Therapist A makes another go for it, saying that they will need to shift gears as their time is almost up. She asks Mr. A if he would like to set up another appointment. He says yes. Therapist A then brings up some of the practicalities of meeting. Mr. A is able to agree on them but is also a bit flustered. When their time is up, Therapist A says that they ought to discuss the fee at the next session. Mr. A puts on his coat, says thank you, and leaves. Therapist A stands in the empty office feeling somewhat dazed. She feels uneasy about having brought up the fee and wonders if Mr. A will show up next week.

The following day Mr. A leaves a message on Therapist A's answering machine saying that he would be cancelling the next session and that he would not be making any further appointments.

Mr. A's anxiety showed itself in his pressured speech. Given how Therapist A felt that she was trying to force open a door it is possible that Mr. A unconsciously tried to communicate to her that he was defending against feelings of being intruded upon. It is understandable, then, that she chose to let him go on speaking, because that was one of his ways of maintaining control. Her uneasiness at bringing up the fee is also understandable. For Mr. A, negotiating a fee could have been freighted with all sorts of struggles relating to control: he may have been afraid of what he was getting into, the costs of involvement, issues of commitment, and more. Therapist A might better have said something like, "It sounds as though we need more time because you have so much on your mind" and not gone into any practicalities short of setting a time until more of a tie had been established between them.

This kind of situation is difficult in many respects. Mr. A is anxious. Therapist A is taking in all sorts of information, reacting to the person of the patient and needing to make some quick decisions. Furthermore she may have had her own anxieties about money. Among other things a therapist may have to ask herself how much she is willing to risk financially, an issue that may be approached differently by different practitioners. Although one can't let the fee issue go unresolved for too long, sometimes more latitude is necessary in the service of creating more of an interpersonal tie and getting further clinical information. In this case the money issue was perhaps forced through the door, and this interfered with establishing sufficient connection.

This situation also brings up a clinical paradox. We have emphasized that in order to do therapy one needs a "frame." Yet in order to discuss the frame an atmosphere of cooperation is required; its establishment takes place in a *preliminary phase* of the relationship. That is to say, developing a portion of the relationship encourages conditions favorable to negotiating the frame. Discussion of money introduces a harsh bit of reality and a pinch of structural antagonism to the hour. In some cases one can discuss such matters in the first session. In others it requires more time and more of a balancing act. It ought to be kept in mind, however, that any patient may leave the therapy for a host of known or unknown reasons no matter how carefully a therapist proceeds.

MRS. B

Mrs. B is referred by the Employee Assistance Program at her husband's workplace. She is a woman in her early forties, tall, quite heavy, and looking tired and pale. She comes to the session about twenty minutes late saying that she did not expect traffic at 9:00 A.M. She sits down and takes off her coat. Therapist B asks what brings her to therapy. Mrs. B explains that she is having difficulty with her marriage of six years. She has two children, one of whom has ADHD. She takes on most of the responsibility for raising the children and caring for the house. She explains that her husband is a good man "basically." He provides well, but he can be mean to her. He does not hit her, she is quick to add. But he is rude: he calls her names and tells her she needs to lose weight. She is also rude to him, but only in response to his meanness. She tells him he needs to spend more time with the kids, that she cannot do it alone. But he is good in many ways, she insists. He does provide for his family. He drinks though, on weekends, rarely on weekdays. Mrs. B goes on to say that she was put on Prozac two weeks ago by her internist, who recommended that she seek counseling. She is very depressed, mostly because she has no life of her own. The therapist asks Mrs. B how she feels about coming to therapy, whether she has some mixed feelings. Mrs. B replies that she thinks she did the right thing by coming. She is surprised when the session ends, saying that she just got started. She agrees to meet next week at the same time.

The day before their scheduled meeting Mrs. B calls to say that she cannot find a babysitter. She would like to reschedule, however, and leaves her phone number. Therapist B calls back only to speak to her answering machine. Mrs. B calls again saying that she will be in all day. Therapist B calls twice. Finding Mrs. B absent both times, she leaves two messages and sends a brief note inviting her to return when the time is right. She does not hear from Mrs. B again.

Mrs. B is entrenched in a complex and tightly woven family system. She speaks of a husband who provides, but drinks, probably more than she is letting on or letting herself know; who can be "rude and mean"; and who does not help out with the house or the two children. She is doubtlessly unhappy and so overwhelmed that it is unclear how she can have a life of her own. It is possible that her present state is a form of adaptation that is quite ingrained and that provides her with some kind of equilibrium. Even though she thinks she did the "right thing" by coming Mrs. B seems to have had very mixed feelings, expressed perhaps from the very outset by her arriving late, which may have been a way for Mrs. B to communicate how overburdened her life was. This is not a woman who has time to sit in a waiting room reading *Glamour* for ten minutes. In hindsight Therapist B might have empathized more with how pressured Mrs. B felt and explored her ambivalence more. Remember, though, that the session was cut short twenty minutes.

Although therapy may have given Mrs. B some venue in which to express her resentment, that itself may have intensified feelings of guilt and anxiety that were in sum more than she could handle at the time. And the "right thing" may have been a compliance with her physician. It is hard to see what could have been done in therapy at this point. Something very likely may have to shift in her inner world or her external circumstances for Mrs. B to be able to make use of the process. Things may need to get worse or better. For now it seems that she was repressing her conflicts in order to stay afloat.

MS. C

Ms. C is a single woman in her late twenties. She arrives at Therapist C's office early and takes a seat in his waiting room, noticing the fine furnishings. She wonders if Therapist C is anything like his waiting room. When Therapist C greets her on the hour, Ms. C is immediately taken aback by his presence: young, handsome, well dressed. Indeed, he is as fine as his furnishings. She is visibly anxious from the start and unable to think clearly. Her rate of speech increases rapidly, and material seems to just tumble out. About ten minutes into the hour she asks if she can have a glass of water because her mouth is dry. She is told where to obtain it. Therapist C tries to structure the hour, but he still has difficulty. He points out that something seems to be making her very anxious. That only increases her discomfort. Therapist C feels at a loss. Both silence and attempts to engage seem only to increase her anxiety. From what Ms. C is able to say, he gathers that she has had a traumatic past with multiple moves and hints of untoward sexual advances from a family friend about which her parents know nothing. Ms. C is overwhelmed. As the session draws to a close Therapist C asks if she would like to continue. She says yes, she would, and they schedule an appointment for the following week.

Ms. C calls several days later to cancel the appointment. She leaves a message on Therapist C's answering machine thanking him for his time. She adds that she is not ready for therapy and to please send her the bill. Therapist C puzzles over whether he should call her. Although she interests him and needs help he decides to do as she asked, that is, send her the bill and leave things as they are.

It seems that in an unconscious way and over a background of sexual abuse, Ms. C may have immediately sexualized the encounter with Therapist C. For Ms. C the hour was intensely overstimulating; she was unable to control her speech and her mouth became parched. She was extremely anxious and overcome. Aspects of the *real* situation, especially the person of the therapist himself, likely acted as a stimulant to a neurotic problem. She is shocked to find Therapist C as fine as his furnishings. As Therapist C opens the door fantasy and reality merge or in this case collide. The intensity of her reaction, therefore, may be unique to Therapist C and will not inevitably be repeated with another male therapist. These kinds of situations, although unusual in their immediacy and intensity, do happen. Therapist C definitely felt Ms. C's anxiety. It is doubtful that he could have done much to help steady her, because he himself was the stimulus.

Ms. C is able to leave a message several days later to cancel the next appointment. Notably she does not act impulsively but likely gave the situation thought. By canceling she protects herself from further overstimulation. She also asks Therapist C to send her the bill, which is not a passive or submissive move. It is a statement that she understands the boundaries of the relationship and is also one of closure. By taking these actions Ms. C gives evidence of initiative. Although Therapist C thinks about whether he should call her, it seems that he intuitively understands the importance of letting her call the last shot.

MR. D

Mr. D is a twenty-four-year-old medical student who came to see Therapist D for depression. When Mr. D entered the office he looked about the room carefully. He told Therapist D that he had been in therapy once before very briefly, but that it had not been very helpful because the therapist seemed more interested in his medical education than in him. He went on to describe his symptoms, which included low self-esteem, decreased appetite, and bouts of lethargy that kept him in bed an entire weekend. He was worried about the impact on his studies. About halfway into the hour Mr. D began to ask Therapist D questions about his nonmedical degree and whether he has had much experience treating medical students. He wanted to be very sure that his therapist could empathize with the medical student experience—the pressure, the competition, the long hours studying. Therapist D felt immediately derailed, that anything he said could somehow come across as inadequate, even defensive. He chose to inquire further into Mr. D's concerns, but Mr. D essentially repeated himself. Therapist D tried to remain empathic, adding that the pressures of medical school were intense and real. Mr. D seemed pleased and wished to continue. Therapist D then tactfully asked him why he had not chosen to see a psychiatrist. Mr. D answered by saying that Therapist D had been highly recommended, and that he wanted help immediately. They settled on a time and a fee.

Several days later Mr. D left a message saying that he found another therapist who understood him better. Therapist D felt puzzled and taken aback. But there was something else that resonated with feeling which had arisen during the session, albeit very briefly. Now that he thought about it he had felt diminished and hurt.

It appeared that Mr. D had an insecure, narcissistic involvement in being a doctor. Being in therapy with a nonmedical therapist may have stimulated his own anxieties about making it in medical school. His initial onslaught might well also have stirred certain insecurities on Therapist D's part. Here we may have an example of *projective identification.* Mr. D projected his low self-esteem onto Therapist D, who then felt diminished. He also expressed his hostility in the way he chose to let Therapist D know that he would not be continuing. He was hurtful by emphasizing that he had found a better therapist. It is likely that Mr. D was expressing a pattern of interpersonal involvement and behavior that leaves people unsteady and feeling belittled. It is also likely that he will attempt to belittle even the "better" therapist, if indeed there is going to be one. At any rate, for competitive reasons he may not have wanted to see a psychiatrist at all.

It would have been interesting to see what would have happened had Therapist D said something like, "What do you have in mind when you ask me about my experience and wonder whether I can understand you?" If Mr. D persisted in wanting to know then Therapist D could have said something like, "I guess there will be some things I can understand well and other things you will have to explain to me." It is possible that Mr. D would still have experienced this kind of response as too threatening.

MS. E

Ms. E, a young woman of twenty-eight, arrived at her first two sessions twenty-five minutes late. When Therapist E observed this to her, Ms. E was able to say that she was ambivalent about therapy. Encouraged to go on she spoke of her inability to trust. Ms. E was the daughter of very troubled parents who could neither let her get close to them nor bear to see her separate from them. Furthermore they would deny her sense of what was real and refused to recognize any difficulties on their part. She was an engaging, attractive woman who longed to get close but who was terrified of doing so, resulting in her anxiously cramming the abbreviated sessions with a lot of material. During the second session Therapist E recalled to Ms. E how difficult it was for her to end the last hour. Therapist E noted that Ms. E was again speaking in a pressured way and, given that they didn't have much time left in the hour, suggested that they discuss what Ms. E thought about continuing in therapy. Immediately upon saying this she felt that she had misjudged something, maybe phrased something incorrectly. Suddenly Ms. E became very angry, saying that she did not want to make any decision right now. Wasn't that premature? Couldn't she just talk? Therapist E felt her heart pounding as though something terrible had just happened. She deferred to Ms. E quickly, saying that nothing needed to be decided right away and that by all means, she could just talk. Ms. E proceeded to do so without any apparent shutting down. Mindful of the frame Therapist E could not see ending at fifty minutes without further harming any developing connection between them. When she, a little sheepishly, asked Ms. E if she wished to set up another appointment Ms. E hesitated, then restated her concern with trust. Therapist E responded saying that she felt it would be helpful for Ms. E to talk about her worries and that she would be happy to continue with her, but that she could also respect whatever decision Ms. E came to. Ms. E then asked whether Therapist E had times available later in the day. An evening appointment was made for the latter part of the following week. Therapist E then brought up the issue of the fee, which involved insurance and a copayment, which Ms. E paid. Ms. E asked if she needed to provide a copay for the first session. Therapist E said yes, and Ms. E asked if she could bring it next time. Therapist E said this would be fine. Ms. E then looked serious and asked quite suddenly what Therapist E considered important for her to work on. Therapist E mentioned that they would have to stop in a moment but would answer her question. Giving it some thought she responded by repeating and underscoring Ms. E's stated concerns, including some specifics from the previous session, adding that there was always the element of discovery in this work. By that time they had gone about ten minutes over the hour and bade their farewells. When Ms. E left the office Therapist E, feeling quite wobbly, sat back down in her chair, glad that no other patient had been scheduled that morning. The day before the next scheduled meeting Ms. E called to cancel, saying that she did not wish to do therapy.

Therapist E was initially quite disturbed by the encounter. She was not at all without experience, and it came as a bit of a blow to her that she could be so easily caught in the web of this dynamic. But she knew that such things happen: they keep one humble and on one's toes. She wondered whether Ms. E would seek out another therapist and if the same dynamic would recur. She wondered how she would be portrayed. What would "the other therapist" think of her? As the initial upset dulled, Therapist E was better able to sort out what likely occurred.

She remembered that during the session she had been aware that Ms. E's ambivalence and distrust showed themselves immediately around the frame, that is, in her coming late. She was also aware of Ms. E's alternately drawing her in and pushing her away, leaving her somewhat off balance. Therapist E felt that she was walking a tightrope, neither wanting to come off as intrusive nor as uninterested. What she recognized less was her own ambivalence about working with such a patient, how anxious she had made her. She feared she might say the wrong thing. She realized she had to think quickly and carefully because the push-pull dynamic was repeated often throughout the hour, like a fast-paced swing with many intricate steps and turns and in which Ms. E was clearly, so it felt, the leader. She decided to let Ms. E speak beyond her time in the service of establishing a connection but also addressed one frame issue, the fee, as well as their need to "stop in a moment," in order to establish boundaries and the professional nature of their connection. With Ms. E's need for "space" in mind, she scheduled the next appointment ten days hence. Ms. E was aware of being able to call in and arrange an earlier time if the need arose. And then she cancelled.

It appears that Therapist E was trying too hard with this confused and hostile patient. She was attempting to be all things to her, to appease all sides of Ms. E's conflicts. In other words, she got caught up in doing something rather than reflecting on it. There are many reasons why a therapist will find herself in such a position with a particular patient. It is possible that Therapist E's vulnerability derives from some inadequately worked through need of her own to hold onto a relationship. Another therapist, still early in her practice, may experience vulnerability on grounds of needing an income and a sense of herself as a working professional. Still another may worry about disappointing a supervisor by "losing" a patient. Whatever the situation, the therapist must learn to catch herself in these dynamics, loosen her grip, leave it up to the patient do more of the work, or quit altogether.

MR. F

Mr. F is a forty-five-year-old lawyer who comes to therapy because of difficulty with his new girlfriend. He wears an engaging smile and speaks in an eloquent, if not rather pressured, way about his concerns. The woman he is seeing is coping with an emotionally troubled daughter. This requires that she spend time with her, sometimes with Mr. F, but also alone. Mr. F feels very resentful, even angry at times, despite his girlfriend's reminders of her love for him. Mr. F asserts that he had been in therapy before and that "understanding himself had gotten him nowhere." He wants some advice this time round. He is having a terrible time dealing with his "frustrated need" to be with his girlfriend, and when they cannot get together he is beside himself, does not know what to do with himself. Nothing helps, not even going to the gym or speaking to his sister, which he often does. To his request for advice Therapist F says that whatever he could offer would likely be something that Mr. F had already thought of, and that he could probably be more helpful facilitating a process by which Mr. F could understand himself better. Notably on several occasions Mr. F asks his therapist how he should address him. Each time Therapist F responds by saying, "whatever makes you feel comfortable."

Therapist F inquires about the specific nature of the frustration and what it is like not to know what to do with the feelings, which Mr. F describes as "like falling down a dark hole." He gently explores Mr. F's references to his family and gains some clinically important information. After the third hour, Mr. F calls to cancel their next appointment, saying that he would not be continuing because their connection did not feel right to him. He was very polite, grateful, but resolute.

When Therapist F received the message he was a little sad because he had liked Mr. F. If he was really honest with himself, though, it didn't come as a surprise. Although he felt that the liking was mutual it was undeniable that Mr. F was asking for something that for one reason or another Therapist F did not give. Upon reflection it occurred to Therapist F that his patient was basically asking for a human connection. He thought he was providing this—by way of a smile, a colloquialism now and then, the comment, "Whatever makes you comfortable," and genuine interest in his current and past life. But he had obviously missed something. Perhaps it had to do with not responding more directly to Mr. F's requests, such as by telling him what to call him or giving some advice. Therapist F was misled by his patient's eloquence and education into thinking that he could tolerate more exploratory work. Further, a number of his recent referrals had all required quite structured, supportive, and directive approaches. So he might have hoped that Mr. F would be different. But Mr. F really wasn't interested in Therapist F's "facilitating a process" whereby he could "understand himself better." He probably didn't even care what sort of advice he received as long as he got a human response that honored his situation of feeling deprived, frustrated, abandoned, and angry. He needed to be *held* so that he didn't feel so alone, so that he didn't fall down the dark hole. Therapist F kicked himself (not too hard!) because he had prided himself in being open-minded and attuned. The scary part was that he had thought he had been so with Mr. F. He also knew that an initially more supportive approach that tends to a patient's sense of safety and trust can gradually and seemingly almost by itself lead into wider exploration of his inner world. Later Therapist F wondered whether things had gone as they did because he was not paying attention to his own "frustrated need" to do the kind of in-depth work he wanted to do. Perhaps he needed to make changes in his own professional life? Obtain consultations, have more training or further supervision for himself? Mr. F's leaving didn't seem all that surprising in retrospect.

18

The Initial Version

What begins to develop during the first therapeutic hour and continues into subsequent hours is the patient's *initial version* of his situation. We distinguish the initial version as told by the patient himself from what is commonly referred to as the "presenting problem." The presenting problem is formulated by a clinician to be documented in an intake, referral, or progress note. Although some such notes may tell a kind of story about a patient's situation others will stop at a diagnosis or diagnostic history, such as "major depression, severe, with psychotic features," "panic disorder without agoraphobia," "cocaine dependence," and so forth.

An initial version amounts to a narrative account through which a patient presents his situation to himself. In recounting his situation he describes aspects of his internal development up to the point of entering therapy. The initial version arises and broadens in the conversational interplay between patient and therapist. The patient will describe in his own way the nature of his difficulties and the reasons why he is looking for assistance. It may include important parts of his own life's story, his views of himself and others, and it can vary widely in the degree of complexity and consolidation of its different parts. He is telling his story. One person may begin by describing the painful feelings from which he is unable to free himself. Somebody else tells of his inability to make a difficult decision, his hesitations and his doubts about it. Still others may remark how they continually find themselves in frustrating and disappointing situations with people around them. And so on. An initial version consists of what is available to the patient's conscious awareness. It is essentially a product of consciousness, of remembering, imagining, thinking, rationalizing, maybe even of fantasy and theorizing.

The initial version can be seen as representing the end product of the patient's psychological work up to a point, from which onward he is unable to develop further or to accomplish certain necessary changes. Some people will have carried this account around with them for some time and in more or less detailed or thoughtful ways. Now, however, it is being told to the potential therapist, a fact that in itself influences the form and content of what is brought forth. If a good-enough therapeutic understanding is reached and accepted and the therapy continues the initial version will change. It will widen and be transformed and be supplanted by new versions or narratives.

Patients can present their initial versions in all manner of ways and styles. These ways and styles begin to tell us something about the organization of a patient's inner world—what he has put together or synthesized, what he keeps apart or defends against. We begin to discern his symptoms, his emotional state, and the individual psychological work that preceded his coming to treatment. Gradually the patient may include a wider range of his feelings: fragments of his memory; observations about himself that he was unaccustomed to being aware of. In time some details emerge that, because of their unpleasant, embarrassing, or puzzling nature, were at first withheld.

Some patients seem to be formulating their stories for the first time upon the therapist's opening inquiries. Others appear to be reciting well-rehearsed presentations. They offer a detailed, thoughtful, elaborate, well-defined, and edited statement, which indeed they may have presented on prior occasions in their search for therapeutic assistance. In the extreme are those coming in with rigid, unshakable, and righteous outlooks. Some present their versions in the form of an apparently permanent state of confusion, telling their discomforts and problems in shifting, fluid ways, befuddlement and disorientation being the only consistent elements in their communications. Others are overwhelmed and cannot find words. And there are those who bypass any detailed telling of their situation and instead turn quickly to the therapist for advice, relief, explanation, diagnosis, or a "cure."

From the well-defined and detailed to the confused and shifting, initial versions give the therapist a general picture of where the patient is psychologically— of what he has been able to accomplish, of where he is stuck. They convey the limits of the psychological work the patient has been able to do on his own. As products of consciousness they can serve the person in a manner similar to a ready "press release," coherently reporting only what is admissible to himself and to the public. As the therapist listens carefully to the initial version she begins to hear the patient's helplessness and, sooner or later, what amounts to a kind of admission of defeat and a surrender to another person's assistance.

The Therapeutic Formulation and Agenda

Careful listening and paying attention to the patient's developing story are important activities in doing psychotherapy. But they are not aimless. They are embedded in the wider context of the therapist's desire to be helpful to the patient in assisting him to alleviate his difficulties and distress as well as can be done. This is her basic and general *agenda*. How she is going to carry out this agenda depends on her *formulation* of the patient's situation, both in terms of his inner world and of his practical circumstances. The agenda then is analgous to a survey of the overall lay of the land and the formation to a more close-up and detailed mapping of the terrain. The therapist's formulation itself accrues to a kind of narrative or story as she forms it in her mind, drawing on the patient's initial version. She brings to it her impressions of him, her previous experience with other patients, her theoretical knowledge, and her views and understandings of life and its problems and challenges. There is no single way to conceptualize a formulation, in part because it will never be altogether fixed and finished. As the body of information from and about the patient changes, as his story widens and deepens, as new issues emerge and understandings develop, the therapist will find her formulation changing as well.

The agenda with which she approaches the patient is also a process in flux. In its most general terms, especially in her wanting to be helpful to the patient, it will and should remain consistent. With regard to specific developments in the course of the therapeutic work it will undergo adjustments and modifications. Various and different agendas may be pursued, depending among other things on a particular stage in the therapeutic process. In each case they provide a temporary *focus* for the work and are informed by how the therapist assesses the patient. Early on, for example, the therapist's agenda may be mainly one of assisting the patient in finding the confidence necessary to speak about himself, to follow trends of thought further than he has been accustomed to, to pay attention to how he feels about what he says. Later her agenda may be one of directing his attention to how he unknowingly interferes by various means with freely expressing what he thinks or feels, and to what his reasons for doing so might be. She can pursue such an agenda because she has arrived at a formulation of some of the patient's ways of functioning and lets it guide her in doing her work. The therapist is engaged in a constant interplay between new formulations and agendas. How she manages that interplay will define her way of conducting the therapy.

A well-practiced therapist may experience herself as making formulations and setting agendas by means of her observations, intuitions, her preconscious assessments, her habit of looking at conflict situations. Just as she hopes to assist the patient in widening his awareness it is important that she try to be as aware as possible of her own thoughts and intentions for the patient.

Without focus or agenda therapies are in danger of becoming aimless, disoriented, and disorienting, sometimes with bad consequences, for both patient and therapist. If this happens it is important for the therapist to regroup and rethink the agenda. Sometimes this amounts to her reflecting on the material by herself. At other times she may wish to elicit the patient's thoughts and feelings about where they are and how they wish to proceed and add her own observations as well.

The following are examples of formulations followed by agendas regarding Madelyn, Jeffrey, and Vincent sketched out after first sessions.

MS. M

Ms. M is a twenty-two-year-old Caucasian woman born and raised on the West Coast. She describes a "pretty stable" childhood and adolescence, the transition to an out-of-state college being her first major move. This is her first psychotherapy contact. She comes on the advice of two friends, in therapy themselves. Ms. M presents as very anxious, yet able to articulate concerns about what she will do after graduating and her discomfort with men. She also expresses some confusion about how to read sexual cues when dating. Her anxiety shows itself primarily in her pressured speech and how she conceals her body. Her carriage and dress reveal Ms. M's seeming discomfort with her physical self. Further the slightly "bohemian" quality to her dress suggests some struggle with identity.

Ms. M did not appear depressed or socially withdrawn. She established a positive rapport and expressed an eagerness to meet regularly. A brief inquiry into her family history revealed a mother who appears to be dysthymic, with a major depressive episode about ten years ago when Ms. M was entering puberty. Father was characterized as a "nice man who could get lost in his own world." Ms. M is an only child who excelled academically, had many female friends growing up, including a best friend, but no male friends.

The therapist's agenda at this point would likely consist of assisting Ms. M articulate her thoughts and feelings, especially her anxiety about graduating, her physical self, and men. Her openness to being helped, intelligence, psychological-mindedness, and ability to trust are favorable factors.

JEFFREY

Mr. J is a twenty-five-year-old Hispanic male who comes for his first-ever psychotherapy. He comes from a large intact family—three sisters, two older, one younger, and one younger brother. Both parents are well-respected professionals. A lawyer himself, Mr. J has been practicing for two years.

He comes to therapy because he hasn't had "much success with women." He is able to articulate that he is stuck, but unable to figure out what to do. Mr. J does not appear to be depressed, but rather very anxious, particularly so about what he can expect from therapy. Thoughts of becoming dependent on therapy, perhaps getting in over his head, and having to comply with far-fetched psychoanalytic claims were especially concerning to him. These concerns may reflect and parallel as yet unconscious concerns about getting involved with a woman. Mr. J also seems self-conscious with some doubt about his adequacy as a man. All in all he is a very likeable, well-educated person, apprehensive to be sure, but also eager to engage.

Mr. J needs help feeling safe. An opening agenda would likely involve assisting him in further articulating his concerns about therapy and involvement with women. For Mr. J feeling accepted by an interested female therapist will likely be of great benefit and open the way to increased exploration of his concerns and conflicts. Mr. J tends toward abstraction and should be encouraged to speak of his experiences with women in as concrete a way as possible.

VINCENT

Mr. V is a thirty-six-year-old single Caucasian male who was recently hired by the city as a tree trimmer. His father died five years ago; his mother is still alive. He has two older brothers. Mr. V comes to therapy because he doubts his girlfriend's fidelity. He presents as extremely anxious. He also comes across as dependent and angry, but without much awareness of either. In addition, Mr. V seems to have generally very poor self-esteem. By and large he feels inadequate in most domains of his life, uncared for and ignored, and is concerned with how he comes across. He appears to be somewhat depressed. However, the extent of this is unclear. There is a somewhat flirtatious, perhaps even hysterical, quality to Mr. V, as well as a touch, maybe more, of paranoia. Overall he does not seem to be in control of his life.

On the face of it Mr. V does not appear to be very psychologically minded and likely projects a great deal. Odds are that he will benefit from a therapy that is supportive and structuring. A preliminary agenda would need to focus on trust. Mr. V has difficulty trusting and he may not be so trustworthy himself. His own ambivalence about relationships, including the therapeutic one, will need to be addressed at some time or other so that the work has a chance of continuing. Close attention needs to be paid to the experience of his father's death, its recency, and its meanings.

20

Widening the Conversation

The net of images is cast wider and wider; thought
searches more and more deeply.
The writer spreads the fragrance of new flowers, an
abundance of sprouting buds.
Laughing winds lift up the metaphor; clouds rise
from a forest of writing brushes.

—Lu Chi (261 A.D.), *Wen Fu: The Art of Writing*

The development, widening, and enrichment of the patient's initially available order of experience is a basic aim of psychodynamic therapy.

The patient's *initial version* represents the understanding of his internal situation and of his actual circumstances that he has formed on his own. This understanding has its limits, and many patients sooner or later seem to come to an end of their story, have nothing more to say, become uncomfortable and anxious, perhaps feeling frustrated and resentful. Some, then, turn to the therapist, demand that she as the expert take over, provide explanations, advice, help, do something. In turn, therapists also can come to feel stumped, helpless, and cornered at such times. It seems as if their relation with each other has reached a critical point.

Some patients deal with the exhaustion of their own initial version, and with some of their anxiety, by trying to find ways which in their view might please the therapist. Perhaps she might be interested in early memories, in talking about sex, perhaps in trauma or insult? Others do the opposite and seek satisfaction, even safety, in criticizing or diminishing the therapist. Some even take their leave.

In other cases something different happens. Having fully told their initial story they come forth with new and unexpected topics and, perhaps aided by the security coming from the therapist's presence, experiment with new and so far unaccustomed points of view with regard to themselves. They seem less constrained by a need to stay with familiar formulations or even with their story itself. New things come ashore. A patient starts a session by talking about seemingly minor events of the day before or describes a "funny" thought noticed on the way to the office, a dream of last night. He expresses interest in questioning himself and wants to explore feelings and ideas. A sense of curiosity and playfulness crops up; the patient "lets himself go." They seem to derive relief, enjoyment, or aggressive satisfaction from doing so. Sometimes the therapist will sit back and follow with relative ease. At other times she finds herself confused and puzzled, searching to find some aim and focus in all the material, and her tolerance feels strained.

Abandoning strict formulations and seemingly rational and stable positions, giving room to imagination, fantasy, perhaps even to somewhat childlike modes of feeling, thinking, and expressing them, can be seen as manifestations of *regression*, a turn to less "mature" and organized forms of being. The term "regression," as used in certain contexts, has a pathological flavor, but in the context just described we are speaking of a regression in the service of the ego, which holds creative potential. Letting himself "go" the patient allows more into his consciousness in a less controlled way, gives freer range to his associations, is less bound by logic or sequential thinking. Every so often, nevertheless, he can "stand back" from his looser psychological meandering. Such regression in the service of the ego is different from processes of pathological disorganization or rigid holding onto adaptive modes of earlier developmental stages. He is letting his line dip deep into the stream but retains basic control of emotions and manifest behavior.

Enabling a person to open himself to a wider range of his inner experience and to include it in his consciousness can alter his previously maintained state of adaptation. It can thus be one means of bringing about therapeutic change.

The point at which a patient reaches the limit of the initial version of his circumstances and difficulties can, therefore, be *a point of potential regression*.

He experiments with drawing back from accustomed and habitual modes of feeling and thinking. How much and what kind of regression will occur, how useful or "serviceable" it may be, depends on several conditions. These include the patient's character structure; the severity of his problems and of his anxiety; how the therapist responds to the patient; the kind of collaborative interplay they can develop. At the end of telling the initial version, the patient in a way is on his own. He has arrived at the edge of something new, albeit unknown, toward which he may head, from which he may retreat, or both. This is an important, interesting, often scary, time in the work. Like a ship's captain, the therapist is trying to steer the patient through choppy waters in which, unfortunately, some therapies run aground.

The therapist needs to find a good balance between letting the patient present the initial version of his story as freely and originally as he can and wishes to do, and at the same time retaining her position of benevolent skepticism. She can do this by letting him know her interest in his story and by asking him to explain things that are unclear or confusing to her. At times she may gently interfere with the patient's apparently seamless and unquestioned narrative that comes across as fixed and unalterable. She will not criticize the patient's story but wonder about further implications in it. At times she may offer additional perspectives but not insist on them if the patient disagrees. While thus the initial version may indeed come to be exhausted the therapy meantime may have entered into a cooperative flow of musing, guessing, and of trying to understand.

Psychodynamic psychotherapy, with its aim of exploring a person's impairments of adaptation due to such things as misunderstandings, inhibitions, and conflicts in his inner world, depends to a significant degree on his capacity for such constructive regression. The safe therapeutic situation itself may contribute to its further development. But such capacity does not sufficiently exist in everyone. Developmental deficits such as lack of experiences of closeness and of care in early life, overwhelming anxiety and fear of feelings, prevalent tendencies to act out impulses and affects, and certain features of character all may prevent controlled relaxation of defenses and regression. They may present insuperable obstacles to psychotherapeutic work. In making her initial assessment the therapist has to estimate whether the patient has sufficient capacity to do the work. If he has not she may have to think of altering her approach or providing referral to other forms of intervention that might be of help to him.

IV

THE DYNAMIC INTERPLAY

21

Resistance and Anxiety

I resolved, therefore, to adopt the hypothesis that . . . some idea occurred to Elisabeth or some picture came before her eyes, but that she was not always prepared to communicate it to me, and tried to suppress once more what had been conjured up. . . . Either she was applying criticism to the idea, . . . or . . .she found it too disagreeable to tell.

—Sigmund Freud—Fraulein Elisabeth von R., *Studies on Hysteria*

The time comes when emotions strangle . . .
there are times when the spirit freezes. . . .
The dark inside of the mind lies hidden; thoughts
must be brought like a child from the womb, terrified
and screaming. . . .
The truth of the thing lies inside me, but no power
on earth can force it.
Time after time I search my heart in the struggle;
sometimes the door slowly opens, and sometimes
the door is bolted.

—Lu Chi (261 A.D.), *Wen Fu: The Art of Writing*

We speak about *resistance* when we observe that a patient becomes hesitant, reluctant, or unable to confront certain thoughts, feelings, or other aspects of his inner life. Experience and theory suggest that *anxiety is the motive when resistances appear.* Resistances can be engaged on various levels of consciousness. One patient may be quite aware that his resistance is related to anxiety. He may consciously avoid talking about disturbing issues even though they are very much known to him. Another patient may appear completely oblivious to how he avoids or omits important topics or feelings. Resistances can also fluctuate greatly in their quality and intensity depending on the kinds of issues approached and the state of the therapeutic relation. Coping with them demands a great deal of the therapist's perceptiveness, patience, and ingenuity.

Resistances appear in two contexts: in the patient's relation to his own inner experience (an intrapsychic context), and in his relation to the therapist as well as other people (an interpersonal context), especially when they try to direct his attention to those matters he does not want to acknowledge. They are stimulated in the therapeutic situation when thoughts, feelings, and issues that the patient tries hard to keep out of awareness come closer to be recognized. The patient will fight the therapist's attempts to bring them into consciousness and into the therapeutic conversation. The safety of the therapeutic situation, one of its hallmarks, is particularly important here: it makes it easier for the patient to approach grounds upon which he feels endangered.

Resistances can manifest themselves in numerous ways. Some patients might shift their focus onto relatively inconsequential matters. Others may not be able to talk at all. Some may begin to attack the therapist by expressing lack of confidence in her and accuse her of being withholding or incompetent. They express disillusionment, show anger at the therapist, threaten to leave the therapy or actually do so. It is easy for the therapist to experience resistances as bothersome, even infuriating, complications. Resistances can be so interfering at times that it may seem as though the work is seriously teetering. Nonetheless, resistances are important, inevitable, and unavoidable phenomena that no therapist escapes. They are an integral part of the patient's present efforts at adapting to the unaccustomed therapeutic situation. The therapist can rely with confidence on the assumption that when a patient resists, it is for good reasons. It is crucial that she keep this in mind. She must know that, as with smoke and fire, where there is resistance, there is anxiety. The patient is afraid of something within himself or in his surroundings, especially also in the therapeutic situation. The therapist must, therefore, tread carefully and with forethought if the therapy is to remain viable. Comments such as "you are resisting" or "you are being defensive" are insensitive, too abstract and general, and should be avoided. Detail is needed. We discuss ways for the therapist to respond to this kind of situation in the next chapter.

Resistances then, in common parlance, are a patient's way of "not going there." Like other psychological processes they can be thought of as communications and as compromises. While they tip the therapist off to the nearness of painful or conflictual issues that the patient makes efforts not to notice, they also foil attempts at therapeutic progress, indeed the therapy itself at the same time. While they put the therapist on the alert to that unsettling, truly scary something in the patient's inner world, often as yet unnamed, they also hamper, diminish, or obscure the flow of experience and communication. While they may intimate troublesome issues, they also amount to an effort against letting these issues be brought into awareness at the same time. In extreme situations, resistances may block all expression in a certain area: "sometimes the door is bolted." Let us look at a few examples.

BOLTED DOORS: VALERIE AND ANDREW

Valerie is a young woman of twenty-six who has been in therapy several times for short periods. She tries very hard to achieve what she calls the "southern California ideal" of attractiveness. She sports chemically bleached hair, is tanned in winter as well as in summer, has had her hips reduced through liposuction, and is immaculately dressed even in sweat clothes. She exercises regularly but denies any eating problems. Despite this description, Valerie does not seem at all like an airhead. She has a very responsible job that she does well. Valerie has been in therapy for about four months now, coming at the insistence of her psychiatrist, who put her on an antidepressant, one of those that also target anxiety and obsessive thoughts. Initially Valerie spoke of her self-esteem, depressive feelings, and social anxiety. She was and remains preoccupied by her hopelessness about ever getting married or even meeting someone "nice."

Valerie's therapist is having the darnedest time getting her to open up. She wonders why this young woman still comes because it truly feels like pulling teeth. Valerie can be often heard remarking, "I don't know what else to say." At these times she will sit on the edge of her seat with a worried expression on her face. When asked what she is experiencing inside, Valerie will say, as if in an endless refrain, "I'm just afraid I'll never find anybody to marry. I'm afraid of being by myself forever." Her therapist has come to see that Valerie resists going deeper by staying vague. Although she can ruminate, she does not care to look at things in much detail. As long as Valerie stays vague, she doesn't have to take a more comprehensive view of her circumstances; she doesn't have to draw any conclusions. Nor does she have to experience any more anxiety than she is currently. At one point, Valerie noted that she and her previous therapist couldn't find anything "negative" in her past to account for her low self-esteem. In tentatively formulating Valerie's situation, the therapist was drawn to wonder whether, between her concerns with her body and her attractiveness on the one hand and her preoccupations with possible marriage on the other, she might not be hinting at so far unexpressed sexual conflicts. Only in the further course of therapy might it become possible to approach such issues.

Andrew, twenty, is an only child. He is tall, lanky, with an ashen complexion, looking badly undernourished. His eyes are pale blue. Andrew is terribly depressed and on Prozac. He will typically wear jeans and a black leather jacket over a black shirt buttoned all the way up. Black leather boots and belt are adorned with silver studs. He came to therapy at the urging of his mother, because over the last year he had been feeling increasingly depressed, intermittently suicidal, anxious, and unsure of where his life was going. Both parents are alcoholic. They divorced when Andrew was sixteen years old. Whereas his father has remarried, his mother remains single, dating occasionally. Of average intelligence, Andrew performed below average in high school. Over the last few years he has taken various retail jobs, mostly in record shops. He reportedly drinks and uses marijuana on weekends.

Andrew is profoundly withdrawn and his capacity to determine what he is feeling has been seriously undermined. Andrew's resistance shows itself in the following ways. He is typically 5 or 10 minutes late for his sessions. During the hour, he will often sit silently for long periods of time appearing to have "spaced out"; sometimes he will fall asleep. Nonetheless, he continues to come. Almost three months have passed since the beginning of therapy and Andrew continues to be late. Indeed 10 minutes have become 15 and the 15 have become 20. Sometimes he misses sessions altogether. His therapist has tried heroically to engage Andrew and has grown increasingly frustrated and irritated by his lateness.

RESISTANCE AND CHARACTER

The style of a patient's resistances corresponds to the particular features of his character and its associated defenses. Whilst some patients have a wide repertoire of ways in which they ward off anxiety, others, such as Valerie and Andrew, have rather predictable, characteristic styles. Valerie demonstrates features of a hysterical character, although perhaps not stereotypically so. Like Harriette in chapter 5, she relies primarily on repression, experiences in internal void, remains vague, is redundant, or can't think of anything to say. Consequently her stories are sketchy and proceed in fits and starts. Andrew, in contrast, shows features of a depressive character. He is prone to recoil from difficulty by not showing up at all or dissociating—that is, withdrawing into a passive, wordless, likely guilt-ridden and brooding inner state. He can also use substances to dampen feelings. For another example recall Perry from chapter 5. Perry's character shows predominantly paranoid features. He manages to remain unaware of his motives by means of projection. Instead he perceives them in the behavior of other people. Such patients may be suspicious about the therapist's training, qualifications, and intent. Often they insist on asking many questions about her theoretical "school," how therapy works, or how she views the patient himself.

By means of their particular character features, patients such as Valerie, Andrew, and Perry appear to successfully *resist exploration and broader awareness* of sadness, anger, deprivation, or other internal discomforts. By means of a much-reduced assembly of their inner resources they may achieve, at least for certain periods of time, what appear to be reasonably serviceable but narrow, possibly vulnerable, states of adaptation.

We have referred to anxiety as the force that motivates resistances. Anxiety is experienced as unease, a vague tension, physical discomfort, avoidance of certain situations, dislike, apprehension, "angst," fear, and finally panic. Panic is the extreme form of anxiety. It overwhelms the person, temporarily paralyzes his thinking and judgment, and disorganizes efforts at response. Anxiety, furthermore, may at times be displaced or projected away from an internal concern onto external objects or circumstances. A person telling you he knows what he is panicked about will not usually be able to be consciously aware of the actual origin and source of his feelings.

Anxiety can derive from various sources. In the therapeutic situation, anxiety is behind the patient's efforts to avoid recognition or communication of forbidden and troublesome wishes, fantasies, preoccupations, and conflicts both conscious and unconscious. More specifically, it can also arise in the patient's relationship with the therapist, which may closely reflect those that govern the patient's life at large. Therapist and patient will have to try to come to a joint understanding of what the sources of anxiety are in the particular case. And of what might happen if the patient "goes there." Is he worried about being exposed, criticized, embarrassed, ashamed, humiliated? Is he afraid of becoming overwhelmed, even disoriented, by his feelings? Is he afraid of losing love, respect, and the support of others, including the therapist? Will he be punished, betrayed, abandoned? *Will new understandings require that he change his ways?*

Anxiety then motivates resistance to change, the patient seeking safety by remaining in his current state of adaptation. (Temporary regressions to less organized and chaotic modes of functioning are also sometimes encountered in therapy where they play a role in serving the patient's resistances.) And it can happen that resistances become directed against the therapy itself. This may be true especially if the patient was forced into treatment by outside pressures. Like Andrew, patients may refuse our encouragement to continue by coming late to appointments, starting to miss them, or quitting entirely without warning or explanation. They may not pay their bills on time or at all. In such situations the therapist may be forced to end therapy with them. In other instances, patients report feeling suddenly very much better and that the work has been sufficiently successful. They take a "flight into health." And the list goes on.

Gradually recognizing the sources of the patient's anxieties becomes a primary means of identifying some of his major, not necessarily conscious, needs, desires, aims, and motivations. In the process the patient might find himself involved in conflict within himself as well as with the therapist, whom he experiences as being disruptive to his inner order. The therapist is now confronted with the important task of providing the necessary atmosphere of safety and collaboration in the service of awakening the patient's interest in pursuing further aspects of his own story.

22

A Frequent Clinical Situation

The following is a type of clinical situation that arises as a regular and essential phenomenon in the course of psychotherapeutic work. It exemplifies yet again the concepts of anxiety and resistance. It concerns those moments in which a patient expresses a preoccupation with painful things that he is extremely reluctant to talk about, that are disturbing and unmanageable to him. These may be inner experiences that seem bewildering and peculiar to him or things about himself that he feels would be quite unacceptable to others if they came to be known.

In such circumstances a therapist may wish to "go for the content." She may feel that an important issue requires exploration. She is tempted to encourage the patient to bring forth whatever he has in his mind, to reassure or coax him. She feels an urge to bring important material, perhaps still partly unconscious to the patient, to the forefront. This attitude may derive from certain notions of *abreaction* and *catharsis*. These involve the belief that by forcing issues into speech the patient can be made to let out his accumulated feelings, "discharge" them once and for all.

Such forcing is almost always contraindicated. Extracting painful confessions is not the primary goal of psychodynamic therapy. Instead it aims at recognizing and exploring the patient's resistances against thinking about, talking about, and understanding painful aspects of his conflicts. Becoming more familiar with his anxieties and resistances and their reasons for being may gradually enable him to approach painful material at his own speed. The therapist's continuing sensitive, empathic but objective interest is designed to assist the patient in doing so.

Premature revelation of the therapist's assumptions of what might motivate the patient's concerns or of what it is that he avoids may amount to an invasion and disruption of the patient's boundary. The patient's privacy is impaired once previously fended off, intimate, and secretly held concerns are now talked about and become, so to speak, joint property of patient and therapist. Jumping the gun in such a manner pitches the patient against himself at a time when he is not ready to engage in such a confrontation. By this we mean he is too soon asked to face what he doesn't want to know and grapple with inner conflict. Defensively the conflict then very often shifts or is displaced from an intrapsychic arena into an interpersonal one between therapist and patient. They find themselves in an adversarial position vis-à-vis each other, and progress may be foiled. Rather than pursue content there are a number of things you can say. For example:

"Something seems to be getting in the way of your speaking about such and such."

"You are conveying to me some real fear about telling me of such and such. I think we have to pay attention to that."

"Well, why don't we slow down for a moment and address your worries about telling me such and such."

"Let's not put the cart before the horse. Certainly what you have to say is important, but it seems to me that what is most immediate right now is your fear about saying it."

"You are anxious about telling me what's on your mind. Can you tell me about that?"

"What do you imagine would happen if you told me what was on your mind?"

Even, "You are reluctant to give yourself the permission to speak your mind, I think."

"You seem to have very mixed feelings about telling me what is on your mind."

This approach conveys empathy for the patient's anxiety and an understanding of where the work lies. It also facilitates the therapeutic alliance, without which the therapy will not really deepen. It potentially addresses the transference and may be a transference test in which the patient is asking whether he can trust that the therapist will listen to him or whether she will harm him as he may have been harmed in the past. By slowing down the process it reinforces the therapeutic tone of safety and offers a piece of education, namely, that psychotherapy cannot be hurried. By directing the patient's attention to what is happening in the moment we hope to increase his mindfulness and to sharpen his skill in self-reflection. Ultimately attending to the anxieties at hand will assist in widening the therapeutic conversation, but not necessarily in the direction the patient may have initially expected. Instead it might lead into new and unforeseen directions. Let us turn to an example.

KEITH

Keith, an accountant in his fifties, had been seeing his therapist for close to a year. He was a stout man with a receding hairline who took to intellectual pursuits, at which he was very gifted, as a way of affirming his self-esteem. He had been married for twenty-five years, and the marriage was "a happy one," as he would say now and then. "For health reasons" and at the recommendation of his internist, Keith decided to take a class in ballroom dancing given by the local university's extension division. There he developed a crush on one of the female instructors, a woman in her late thirties. Although Keith stated that he had no intention of straying from his marriage he did find himself flirting with her. At first he was quite elated at her easy positive attitude toward him. But after a time, and as much as he did not want to, he found himself preoccupied with thoughts of her. He was unable to fight fantasies, which were deeply pleasurable, and he became depressed when he did not see her. This was new to him. Distressed by the intensity of his feelings he sought therapy on the advice of a close friend whom he had known since college.

In this particular session Keith has great difficulty talking. There are numerous silences and tentative, frustrated attempts at speaking. At one point Keith says:

> Pt: It's my body. I, I . . . I can't find the words. I feel so . . . inhibited. (*Silence*) She's so lovely. Lovely. (*Silence*) Slender long limbs. So graceful. (*Pause*) This is really hard. I don't know. (*Pause*) I can't think of anything to say. I'm sorry.

Th: You mentioned feeling inhibited.

Pt: Well, yes. Yes. Boy [note that the word "boy" comes almost immediately after the therapist's use of the word "inhibited." It is perhaps a statement of how Keith views himself], I usually have a lot to say, don't I? I don't like to talk about my body. But I guess I have to, don't I? Okay, well . . . (*Silence*)

Th: It does seem awfully hard for you to talk about this. Perhaps we can start by your saying something about what makes it so difficult to speak to me about your body. Let's start there.

Pt: Okay. Well, I'm embarrassed even to use certain words to describe parts of me.

Th: Why is that?

Pt: Well, because . . . That's a good question. (*Silence*) Um, well, I think it's . . . because . . . well, I think it's like this. If I say certain words then it's like you'd be looking right at that part of my body. It would become visible. You would see it. I mean that's what it would be like. Not that you would actually see it. Not that I would be naked. I would never be able to bear that. I would cringe and roll up. It would be the same thing with her. Even though I fantasize about her, I couldn't ever have her see me—well, you know, naked. That's never going to happen. I'd die. She's so lovely. Long limbed, firm, in good shape. Beautiful green eyes. And of course I'm married.

Th: You long for her. (*Picks up on Keith's using the word "long" twice now.*)

Pt: Yes. Yes, I do. (*He nods slowly, pensively.*) And I feel so guilty to boot. I'm a married man. And I have principles. So, I'm ashamed of me physically and guilty for . . . wanting . . . her . . . sex . . . with her. (*Here Keith is speaking deliberately, even somewhat intellectually. Then there ensues a silence. Then a short burst of affect.*) Oh, god! How did I get here? (*Silence, during which he breathes heavily and regains some control.*)

Th: What just happened? (*Encourages his staying in the moment with his feelings.*)

Pt: Um. I was overcome.

Th: Indeed.

Pt: I became aware . . . I mean very . . . deeply . . . so . . . of always feeling self-conscious of my body . . . Since middle school I think. Perhaps even before then . . .

This illustration points out Keith's hesitation approaching difficult feelings, his resistance. These feelings are connected to deeply fixed experiences of shame about his physical self and guilt for wanting sexual pleasure with his dance instructor. As his therapist gets to know him better, and as their alliance strengthens she will try to be more specific in her observations of what he does and when he does it. For example, and this is purely hypothetical at this stage, she might say: "I notice that you are being very intellectual just now. And only a few moments ago you were speaking about the nape of your dancing instructor's long neck. Maybe the two are connected?" Or perhaps, "At the end of last session you were talking about the 'staleness,' to use your word, of your marriage, and today you are discussing the pros and cons of the death penalty. I wonder if you are feeling guilty about your sexual dissatisfactions and desires."

The therapist's interventions were geared to helping Keith get at what was preventing him from speaking about difficult issues regarding his body and sexual feelings, namely, his shame and guilt. As the therapy progresses, we can expect Keith to become more aware of possible erotic feelings toward his therapist. Such feelings, and for now we can only speculate on their nature, are aspects of the patient's transference, which we will take up in the next chapter.

23

Transference

Who's there?

—William Shakespeare, *Hamlet*, act 1, scene 1, line 1

I seem to have loved you in numberless forms, numberless times.

—From a poem by Rabindranath Tagore, "Unending Love"

THE TRANSFERENCE AS CARRYOVER

The patient's descriptions of his difficulties, his hopes for therapy, and of his anxious concerns dominate the story he tells. Sooner or later there will come a time when something changes in the atmosphere. The relationship between the patient and therapist feels different. The patient may experience an immediacy in the relationship that at first feels puzzling. He may experience an increase in tension, a greater alertness to the person of the therapist: her appearance, way of speaking, discernible habits, what he sees in her office. The patient may become curious about her, afraid of her, attracted to her, begin to admire her, or start being obstinate, even antagonistic. Perhaps he finds himself contending with some combination of experiences. Although some patients try very hard to keep these feelings to themselves the therapist usually picks up something of this change emanating from the patient. She senses he is concerned with her, thinks about her in various ways, and develops feelings in relation to her. Some of the things he says about other people, past or present, make her feel strangely addressed in an indefinable way as though he is speaking indirectly about her. Some may appear to be doing research on her; look her up in the directory, try to find out where she lives, perhaps even drive by her house. Even her office building can take on a charge! Patients can go to considerable lengths to construct an image of their therapists, try to form conclusions about them, and develop theories about their personalities and how they conduct their lives. Positive feelings for her may go as far as idealizing her. Negative feelings, anticipations of being criticized, humiliated, and rejected can appear as well. In either case the therapist recognizes stirrings of the transference. If there is one area of psychotherapeutic work in which both therapist and patient are made aware of the power of internal forces it is in the transference.

The word *transference* literally means "carryover" and refers to the person's "carrying over" aspects of earlier experiences with other people into his present relationship with the therapist. The therapist's restraint, which prevents the patient from knowing her in the more detailed manner in which he knows people in social contexts, mobilizes him to fill his picture of her with meanings borrowed from elsewhere in his life. Transferences thus become means by which the patient remembers, relives, and communicates qualities of relationships that he has, often for long periods of time, kept out of awareness and remembrance. However lively they may become transferences must not be read as fully accurate communications of past, objective realities. They are subjective creations composed of memories of earlier relationships with essential and influential people and significant events, all in terms of how the person experienced and understood them. They are suffused with and colored by the affects and feelings that they stirred and are enriched by fantasies of all sorts.

Whatever their appearance, it is striking to observe how emotions experienced in the transference can sometimes feel so real: dependence, erotic feelings and temptations, fear, jealousy, competition, love, idealization, admiration, all directed at the therapist with a sense of immediacy. These are bona fide emotional reactions *carried over* from other situations and connections. The intensity of transference phenomena can be dramatic or minimal. It tends to vary greatly from one person to another and usually fluctuates within any given person's therapy. Transferences can seem to be absent, or appear obscurely or delicately in short-term treatment as well, sometimes even within a single hour.

Transferences occur not only in therapy but also in life at large. At times one notices that a person's reactions either in words or in behavior do not properly fit the situation at hand. It may seem as if the person reacts to somebody else who, however, is not present. In our day-to-day lives, though, transferences are allowed to stand without comment. They are not usually articulated between people, especially if they seem to fit the situation sufficiently. Therapy, however, is a special situation. The patient adapts to the relatively unspecific therapeutic situation by giving it and the therapist meanings drawn from other relationships in his life, and they come to be explored as such.

Take, for instance, the patient's very expectation that help may be found by entering therapy. Very likely it will derive in part from transferences from earlier experiences that other people could be and were helpful. Transferences of all sorts, at first unconscious, can come to be recognized as part of the person's relations; their meanings can be explored and newly understood within the patient's current reality.

Because transference feelings can become mixed and intense, the therapist can feel pulled in a number of different directions. At times she may find her realism and therapeutic skepticism challenged, perhaps even the experience of her professional identity. In cases where transferences are benevolent they may be gratifying to the therapist. If they are negative she may experience them as unsettling and frightening. The work can be stressful. Sometimes the therapist will find that she has to cope with resistances of her own in the job of keeping track of the patient's unrealistic feelings and their interpretation. Observing, understanding, and sometimes interpreting the meaning and purpose of such carryovers are tasks the psychotherapist faces frequently.

TRANSFERENCE AND RESISTANCE

While transference reactions derive from earlier phases of the patient's life he experiences them as current and realistic responses to the therapist. As the circumstances and contexts of certain parts of the patient's experience are explored the origins of what is now manifested in the transference can become clearer. Patients tend to resist such explorations with the same forcefulness that they applied originally to keeping certain experiences, conflicts, and feelings out of awareness, sometimes for a long time. Thus resistances in themselves can be transferences, carryovers. Here is an example.

A middle-aged woman, already in therapy for some time, one day turned her attention to the therapist's office, judging it rather old and used. The arms of the chairs were worn and the walls needed new paint. She liked the therapist from the start but hated herself for liking him. She scanned the room, then looked at the therapist, and said with a sarcastic tone, "You must be a very good therapist." The therapist asked her why she thought so. "Because you rely so little on external props," she responded. As a positive transference response on the manifest level, she mocked him and perhaps the therapy as if it was nothing but theater. The patient's comment expressed her resistance to a more unequivocal expression of her positive feelings for the therapist. Also she was a woman who always liked the best of everything. It was an offense, a thorn in her flesh, that the office was rundown. Perhaps she also found it disconcerting that she could like a person who cared so differently from her about his material surroundings.

As they become recognizable in the therapy, transference elements may often have to be lived with quietly by both partners while the exploration of other and earlier issues in the patient's life yields a context that helps explain them. And practically speaking, especially in most time-limited therapies, many transferences will have to remain without interpretation.

MANIFESTATIONS OF THE TRANSFERENCE

Transference in some form is most likely present from the start of the therapeutic relationship or even before. Patients can fantasize about the therapist before they see her, or even make phone contact, and may or may not be consciously aware of doing so. Remember Patient C who in chapter 17, while waiting for her first session, wondered whether Therapist C was "as fine as his furnishings." Thus a patient's choice of therapist may partly be affected by his fantasies or by what he may know about her. If he knows nothing he may still start forming some kind of picture of her in anticipation. Her name, for example, can be the nucleus around which a fantasy forms.

Some patients express their interest in the therapist early in the therapy. They ask questions about her age, her family, her origins, her interests, and so on. Patients may be curious about a therapist who has an accent or is from a different ethnic group. The therapist may feel besieged, invaded, and annoyed by such inquiries while she is trying to preserve a certain degree of anonymity. Times may be stressful when she has to bear up under the patient's inquisitively close and detailed observation of her body, her personality, her ways, and her things. Tactfully, avoiding a caricature of the totally unresponsive "analyst," she will find a way to convey to the patient that what he experiences is the center of interest. Carefully she will try to explore with the patient what motivates his interests and which anxieties he hopes to assuage by knowing answers to his questions. The patient may resist her efforts and take offense that his inquiries are not responded to in a conventional manner. At best he experiences them as puzzling; at worst as an insult, a rebuff. There are different ways of responding to such inquiries. Therapists have to find their own methods of dealing with them. One therapist might resort to dispensing some consumer information and say: "You know, the idea of therapy is for you to tell me about your thoughts, feelings, and concerns, even about me. I may be fairly quiet at least for a while, the point being to hear from you." Another might make a compromise and say that she might answer a particular question, but not until both parties have explored the patient's ideas and fantasies about her and his reasons for wanting to know. In any case she would want to preserve her privacy and her patient-centered therapeutic attitude. The less the patient knows about the therapist the more likely it is that his fantasies about her derive primarily from his own inner life.

Patients can drop clues about the nature of the transference in all manner of ways. Early on in the therapy one patient, a young man named Steven, told his therapist of roughly the same age that she surely must have a cat—named Fluffy. Another patient, John, a man in his mid-forties, took great issue with the placement of his therapist's clock, insisting that it be repositioned so that he could track time more easily. One can infer much from these comments. What was Steven's experience of cats? Did Steven perceive his therapist to be full of fluff? Maybe the "touchy feely" type? Or silent perhaps like cats can be? Did he view her as a potential pet? Was this a comment about nurturance, how much he wants, what he can expect? And how to understand John's relation to the clock? Were his comments veiled references to the therapist herself as an unknown quantity? Did he not want to be surprised by the end of the session? Was he afraid of losing himself, of getting out of control? And what would it all mean if he wore a watch himself? What if the watches were not exactly synchronized?

Even in a therapy conducted from a psychodynamic point of view, it can happen that transference manifestations appear completely absent. Absence of any comment or sign of curiosity about the therapist should not right away be taken as an indication that the therapy is wanting for transference. In some cases a therapy might just be too brief for recognizable transferences to develop. At any rate, from a psychodynamic perspective you really can't have a therapy without transference.

It is not unusal to find the patient too sensitive to tolerate feelings about the therapist that he discovers in himself, thereby resisting their communications stoutly. In other words the patient may be inhibited in his thoughts and feelings or in expressing them. Transference reactions may, nonetheless, develop in the patient's inner world and be recognized by the therapist in the patient's behavior, utterances, attitude, and in the atmosphere he creates. And so the transference simmers for what could be a long period before heating up and showing itself more openly.

Alice, for example, a college junior, was seen for more than a year. The therapist eventually observed that in all their time together Alice never mentioned anything about her. Alice backed away from the comment. Interestingly, a few sessions later she stated in response to some questions by the therapist that she did not know the color of her father's eyes. The therapist understood the comment to reflect Alice's difficulty getting close. Alice seemed to have no expectation that anyone else would come close enough for her to know the color of their eyes, and for herself to be seen and known. She also wondered if there was something Alice did not want to see or if she did not want to be seen in some way—or both.

On grounds of her observations, the therapist may well form ideas of what kinds of transferences might operate in the patient's mind but elect to remain silent about them and not bring them into the conversation. At any given time she will have to rely on her judgment of the patient's tolerance for transference interpretations. Her ideas, nevertheless, will reflect her understanding of the interactions between her and her patient and guide what she will or will not do. How important this might be can be seen in the case of Patient C in chapter 17. Had that patient continued in therapy, Therapist C would have needed to be especially aware of her erotic feelings and fantasies. Silently understanding the intensity of her reactions, he would have had to exercise careful reserve in order not to stimulate further what was presently so difficult for her to bear; in such encounters even an empathic comment could set off deep longings.

THE VARIETY OF TRANSFERENCES

Transferences are highly individual phenomena. Nevertheless, certain typical kinds are frequently encountered. In other contexts we have already referred to positive and negative transferences. When favorable and benign feelings toward the therapist assume a somewhat more personal quality, such as attachment to and admiration of the therapist, we speak of *positive transference*. Occasionally such transferences can grow to exaggerated degrees, such as when the patient has come to see her as all wonderful, beautiful, omniscient, and wise. Some positive transferences, for a while, provide the patient with a special sense of safety (the therapist is experienced as a protector), and they support his willingness to tolerate anxiety and explore his resistances concerning other matters.

Negative transferences contain very different feelings and expectations. They have an aggressive quality, appear as instant distrust, suspiciousness, criticism, resentment, expectations of being abused, hated, persecuted. Past disappointments in the patient's life have impaired his ability to trust but need not realistically characterize his actual earlier relationships. Like other transferences they can be understood as possible products of primitive, early desires embedded in fantasies, conflicts, and misunderstandings. In negative transferences the patient may feel endangered and react aggressively in fantasy, speech, even some sort of direct or displaced action. Aggression can be a defensive reaction against positive, loving, or admiring feelings toward the therapist that will never be reciprocated as wished. Negative transferences often heighten the patient's resistances in all areas. A therapist's insensitivity can stir negative transferences as well.

More specifically positive transferences may appear in the form of increased dependency, sometimes accompanied by greater apparent helplessness. The patient may feel or behave in a childlike way. In other cases transference desires for offerings of love and intimacy may be joined by erotic feelings and wishes. In Patient C, for example, we likely saw what was an intense and immediate erotic transference. In her case the feelings were so overwhelming that she decided to discontinue the work. When such intense feelings appear at short notice a thoughtful exploration of their source may be strongly resisted or altogether blocked. When dealing with very zealous, ongoing erotic transferences, the therapist needs to sturdily hold on to the frame, insist on its maintenance, and communicate this, perhaps repeatedly, to the patient. In extreme cases the therapist, herself, may need to end the therapeutic relationship. Idealizing transferences are often met as well. They express admiration of the therapist, are often the attribution to the therapist of the patient's own high standards and conscientiousness, which he finds himself unable to meet in the present but might yet hope to reach.

Patients don't come in with just one predominant set of feelings. Transferences are complex; they develop and change. What was a set of idealizing and dependent feelings may give way to more erotic ones as time goes by. What was initially maternal may become more erotic. There are combinations of feelings. A person who finds himself becoming dependent on the therapist reacts with hostility and starts pushing her away. Some patients find it difficult or impossible to experience mixed, ambivalent, or conflicted feelings. They will see the therapist in black-and-white terms: love then hate, admire then detest her, alternately. They present difficult therapeutic challenges.

TRANSFERENCE ENACTMENTS: SHOWING RATHER THAN TELLING
When patients are unaware of their transferences they are likely to express them through action. That is, they will show rather than speak them. These dramatizations are important unconscious communications and are called *transference enactments*. Generally speaking enactments amount to a kind of psychological theater. As such they give form to invisible internal states, make them tangible.

Although we tend to discuss enactments when they give us grief they really are happening all the time in many contexts. We are always showing and revealing, articulating and communicating something in action rather than words simply because it is impossible to be conscious of all that is occurring inside us. Unconscious elements are always at play.

In therapy enactments are often found occurring vis-à-vis the frame. Unaware the patient will capitalize on the concrete aspects of psychotherapy—money, space, time—to play out his issues. He may come late, leave late, bolt out of the room at the end of the hour, leave early. He may not pay his bills on time or at all. Or he may, because he is overly compliant, pay his bills on the dot or even early. Visible and concrete relative to less tangible internal states, components of the frame are easy targets for enactments.

Because enactments involve aspects of transference the therapist herself is sometimes drawn into the drama, whose meaning may be understood only slowly as the dynamics become clear. Some comment from her acknowledging that something is occurring between them is often enough to give the patient pause and engage his curiosity without prematurely interpreting or imposing meaning. This takes sensitivity and discipline on the therapist's part. When sufficiently confident of the meaning of this interplay one can then bring it to the patient's attention. Occasionally at lucky moments the patient comes to the understanding on his own. Emphatic statements may have to be made where there is some threat to the integrity of the therapy, such as the patient's becoming violent, or threatening to leave altogether.

The case of Mary provides an example of a simple enactment. Mary came to therapy because of depression. Each time the therapist ended a session she would consistently dawdle, taking her time putting on her coat, picking up her various bags, and walking to the door. She would often talk throughout this process. Eventually it became clear to the therapist that Mary's behavior was a way of extending the time she had with her, something she would do around her mother. The mother traveled a great deal on business, and Mary could never be with her enough.

Notably, although Mary's therapist was male, she still transferred maternal feelings to him much as a female patient can transfer paternal feelings to a female therapist. Actual gender can influence the formation of a piece of the transference, but fantasy is its most fertile soil.

Another kind of transference enactment occurs when a patient *turns a passive stand into an active one*, that is, he does to the therapist what a significant person, say a parent or a spouse, has done to him. A transformation takes place in this sort of situation, which involves the patient's identifying with the aggressor. The patient takes on the significant person's role and shows the therapist what it is like to receive such treatment from him or her. The therapist then feels what the patient must have felt.

ANDREW: THE DOOR OPENS

As an example let us return to Andrew from chapter 21, the twenty-year-old tall, lanky man with pale blue eyes who is profoundly withdrawn. Recall his long periods of silence and tendency to fall asleep in session as forms of passive resistance. Recall that he also began to resist actively by being late to sessions or missing them altogether. In the following session, roughly two-and-a-half months into the work, Andrew arrives twenty minutes late.

His therapist, having grown increasingly frustrated and irritated by Andrew's lateness, feels a need to address the issue. She feels she has a handle on what is going on. Andrew walks in to the office . . .

Pt: Sorry I'm late.

Th: Yes. (*Pause*) What are your thoughts about that? (*She says this in a relaxed, nonthreatening manner, and by doing so gives Andrew a chance to reflect on his behavior.*)

Pt: I don't know.

(*The two sit in silence for a long while.*)

Th: Where did your thoughts turn?

Pt: I don't know. I guess I just spaced out.

Th: Hm. You know, I actually have some thoughts about your lateness.

(*Andrew looks up.*)

Pt: What?

Th: Well, let me tell you. I think that by coming late you are conveying to me something important. I think that coming late in your case is your way of showing me what it was like for you growing up in a home where people were inconsistent and unpredictable. The great frustration you felt when you didn't know what you could expect. I think it is very important to you that I *really* know this.

(*Silence*)

Pt: I remember coming home from school and never knowing if mom would be drunk or if dad would be coming home. I'd try to stay away as long as I could, but I had to come back . . . if only to sleep . . . It was frustrating. I'd get so angry . . .

Andrew's lateness illustrates his resistance but also represents a transference enactment. The therapist provides Andrew with a strongly stated interpretation of his behavior. Her impression that he seems to understand the interpretation at least to some degree seems supported by his responding with further confirmatory ideas and the expression of affect. He communicates something about early conflicts with his parents, about loneliness and anger, and his reactions to these. He seems to identify with his parents' unreliability and inflicts this unreliability on the therapist. At the same time (and this was articulated only later in the therapy), Andrew makes himself feel like a victim by expecting a punitive response from his therapist. And so he shows both sides of his relationship to his parents. Before he had received the interpretation he tried hard to avoid looking at and speaking about any and all of these things. Unconsciously he attempted to accomplish several things at the same time. This is an example of *multiple function* at work.

Regular transferences and passive-into-active displays can also be thought of as *transference tests*. By dint of a test the patient unconsciously checks out whether the therapist will react to him in accordance with his expectations. The therapist can either pass or fail. In Mary's case one could think of her behavior as constituting a test of whether the therapist would listen to her need for more time. After some discussion the therapist asked Mary if she would like to come in twice a week. Mary agreed and her dawdling decreased. In Andrew's case if the therapist passes she will have shown him that, contrary to his experience, people can be reasonable, committed, and reliable. If she fails then she will have fulfilled the expectation that people are not. Mary and Andrew are in effect dipping their emotional toes into the therapeutic water to test its temperature. If it is too uncomfortable they will retreat, their resistances will deepen; if not, then they may continue and open up more.

The therapeutic work takes an important step forward once transferences are encountered and explored. While the patient has so far primarily talked about his story he now begins to live it to some extent. The therapist now serves as a presence in relation to whom the patient lives out his efforts at clarifying his situation and forming new adaptations. At first he is not fully aware that he is doing more than merely responding to the therapist in terms appropriate to the immediate situation at hand. The therapist's relative anonymity, which she established right from the moment the therapeutic understanding was formed, allows, even forces, the patient to live the situation in his own terms. These terms, then, become apparent and available to further therapeutic observation and interpretation.

24

Countertransference

A certain symmetry exists in the clinical encounter. As the patient develops impressions of and feelings toward the therapist so does the therapist develop the same toward the patient. As the patient lives his story so does the therapist hers. Although it is expected that the therapist will gradually learn more about this new patient it is also true that her picture of him is never purely objective. Every so often she will become aware of certain emotional reactions that may be surprising by their strength, persistence, and despite her attempts to maintain an unprejudiced and open attitude, their seeming irrationality.

Together with the patient's feelings her feelings influence the development of the relationship as well. Once the patient consciously or unconsciously begins to communicate his transference views and emotions to the therapist, such as we saw in Andrew's case, she may find herself being stimulated to respond emotionally to them. She is dislodged to some extent from her position as the objective observer.

As it happens with the patient the therapist's reactions may begin right from the start and with very little information, sometimes in response to the first telephone contact. She may have reactions to the sound of the patient's voice, his anxiety or apparent lack thereof. She may muse about how sweet he seems. She may wonder at that hint of entitlement, have ideas and associated feelings about what he will look like. A wish or a fear may be stimulated. Or both. She injects her own expectations and anticipatory feelings into her image of the prospective patient whom she has not yet seen. She develops a transference toward this image that, obviously, derives from hopes, wishes, and particular memories of her own. In other words, as she encounters the patient's transferences once things develop she will bring a *countertransference* to meet them. Awareness of one's countertransference is important to understanding the patient's development and the origins of his difficulties. Significant countertransferences may lead to the therapist's being preoccupied by her own emotional responses and interfere with her ability to stand back sufficiently from the onslaught of the patient's transference demands. Let us revisit Andrew and the aforementioned pivotal moment in his therapy. Andrew's therapist had grown increasingly frustrated and irritated by Andrew's lateness and felt a need to address the issue. In fact she had begun to be annoyed with him earlier in the work by his silences, his falling asleep, then his lateness.

But she was also able to recognize that these reactions were clinically significant. She understood Andrew's behaviors as communications that relied for their impact on producing feeling in the therapist. In order for the therapist to really get it she had to really feel it. She had to feel the anger that Andrew felt. That is how good literature, theater, or a good movie make their impact. They produce feeling in their audience. Andrew's therapist also understood that her reactions, although real and difficult, were inevitably and expectably provoked, and that they could be used in clinically appropriate and useful ways. Consequently her intervention was deeply empathic, neither judgmental nor punitive. It conveyed to Andrew that behavior, his behavior, was communicative, that it had meaning, and that it was tolerable. In so doing she reinforced the therapeutic situation as a safe one. Altogether this resulted in the emergence of warded-off memories and feelings and laid a piece of the groundwork for Andrew's eventually understanding his transference, his resistance, and defenses.

As we stated earlier transference enactments are rarely one-man shows. In Andrew's case one could also speculate about hypothetical events in which a therapist's countertransference reactions mesh with the patient's transference in such a way as to produce a *countertransference enactment*. This could have happened if, for instance, she had emotionally withdrawn from Andrew at that juncture. In Mary's case, for another example, a small countertransference enactment would be seen if Mary's therapist had responded to her childlike desires for time and affection by prolonging the hour or spending a lot of time on the phone with her. Of note therapists will commonly find themselves costarring in these shows before they know what is happening. If continued without examination these actions would take the therapist beyond the careful conduct of therapeutic investigation.

Let's now look at a hypothetical event involving Andrew's therapist. Let's just say that without reflecting on what she is doing she asks him why he is late, commenting on the irritating effect it has on people. She is unable to stand back from her feelings at this moment and cannot see them as clinically informative. Perhaps she is fixated on frame issues or engaged in an educational agenda aimed at modifying Andrew's behavior. Whatever the case she is unaware of her countertransference reaction to Andrew's unconscious expectation of her as a punitive and noncaring parental figure who has now turned on him. She asks him to explain his lateness, which of course he cannot. At most he might be able to offer some rationalizations. Her observations about his lateness, although accurate at face value, come out of the blue and essentially validate Andrew's perception of people as unpredictable and of himself as bad. Unlike a more empathic therapist she provides no context for Andrew to understand his behavior. It is likely then that, true to form, he might express his disappointment and anger by doing one or more of the following: withdraw by either continuing to have nothing to say, spacing out, falling asleep, coming late next time or not at all, thereby feeling defeated and uncomfortable. It is also likely that Andrew will begin to experience increased depression and hopelessness. The door is once again being bolted.

The therapist could also act out by choosing not to wait but to leave the session if Andrew was late, producing a more concrete rendition of the abandonment he experienced early in life. Suppose Andrew is forty minutes late, only to find his therapist gone. Consciously Andrew would likely experience this as deeply disappointing. He would probably rationalize the therapist's behavior saying to himself something like, "Well, she had other things to do. Why should she wait forty minutes?" Probably he would feel angry, guilty, punish himself by apologizing, shut down, and become more depressed. Unconsciously Andrew may read the situation as confirmation that people are unreliable, that they leave when you need them, and that probably he's just too hot to handle. Although Andrew's behavior pushes against the frame it is still within its bounds. This suggests that he holds some faith in the therapy and does not want to lose it. This patient needs to know that his therapist, unlike

his parents, will be there. Only in this way, assured of the safety of the therapeutic situation, will he eventually be able to see how he actively contributes
to the quality of his relationships and his life.

It is important to note here that, unlike Andrew's case, there are times when
enactments become extreme: not paying at all, excessive verbal aggression,
physical-sexual boundary violations. The last of these violations is also a vio-
lation of the law. If extreme violations are allowed they reveal something seriously off kilter not only in the patient's but in the therapist's own psychology
as well.

What these imaginary situations show us is that we all have the potential to
fall prey to our emotions and, because we are human, we will do so in our career. They show us the clinical and ethical importance of self-awareness,
gained by individual psychological work and personal psychotherapy, and by
consultation and collegial exchange of experience. The disruption of the therapeutic relation caused by enactments can often be corrected if the therapist
has looked back at what happened, owns up to her part in it, and provides an
opportunity for retrospective exploration of the event jointly with the patient.
Some action on her part may well be required to repair the break. Take the
imaginary therapist: What can she do? If Andrew does not show up giving him
a call may help. Given his past experience the mere fact of her contacting him
may do more than anything else to build him a bridge on which to return.
When she sees him again she could first ask him about his reactions to the last
session. She also has the choice of taking the initiative: "You know I think I
made a mistake last week when I said such and such. As I thought about it
I realized that my words must have sounded much like something your parents might have said—rejecting and punishing—and I think that you react to
that kind of thing by withdrawing. Perhaps we can talk more about that and
understand better what went on between us. What are your ideas?" From there
the two may be able to disentangle the various strands of thought and reen-
gage in a working mode. The therapist would have demonstrated that she can
be flexible, that she can bear to look at her own behavior, that she can speak
the truth and not distort or avoid it at another's psychological expense. She
would have demonstrated that things are potentially reparable and that rup-
tured trust may be mended. In this way she increases her chances of passing a
transference test by admitting fallibility and protecting the patient's sense of
his reality. If a therapist cannot look at herself then how can she expect that of

her patients? It is hard to admit an error, especially in circumstances in which one is expected to be the wiser partner. But it is clinically and ethically the sound thing to do. If you have that gnawing, uncomfortable feeling that something you did may be amiss but are unable on your own to see your way through it then consultation is in order. If such discomfort never arises then something is amiss. It's one thing not to know; it's quite another not to know that you don't know. Continued exploration of our biases and blind spots cannot be legislated, but it is a requirement in our profession. And ultimately a therapist practices and lives on her honor.

25

Clinical Neutrality

The idea of *clinical neutrality* is central to the conduct of psychodynamic work and affects how we listen to and comment on what the patient brings; it is particularly relevant when we deal with conflictual material.

A neutral stance refers to the therapist's remaining impartial to all sides of a conflict rather than supporting one side or another. In doing so she must have sufficient inner freedom to consider all the various feelings and thoughts that arise in her in response to the patient's situation. Such a stance gives every side of the patient's conflicts an equal hearing. Chances that the patient will arrive at a deeper understanding of what is involved for him are greater if we resist throwing our personal suggestive weight in any particular direction. Salient issues can then be more fully explored and worked through. The response to Andrew's being late by his hypothetical therapist reflected a momentary lapse in her ability to maintain clinical neutrality. For reasons of her own she was unable to consider possible conflicts Andrew was experiencing as they expressed themselves in his behavior. She allowed her emotional reactions to shape her intervention in a way that was not helpful to him. Her reaction inhibited further exploration because implicit in her comments was her view of what he should or shouldn't do.

Conflict means that there are no easy answers at first. A worthwhile exploration of the issues at hand takes time. If we can lend patients our ability to withstand the feelings generated by the deepening and zig-zagging conversation and accept the fact that a solution will inevitably entail losses as well as gains we will have done good. Neutrality does not mean aloofness, indifference, or remote silence by the therapist. A therapist can feel free to make observations and inquiries and enter into conversation with the patient as long as equal respect is given to all the patient's varying concerns.

Nor does the idea of neutrality mean that the therapist must abandon her personality. Psychotherapy is not a social event to be sure, but it is a mistake to assume that in order to be objective and even-handed we must mold ourselves to some caricature of what a therapist should be. This rings of falseness, and patients will pick it up. We saw something of this with Therapist F in chapter 17, whose approach to his patient was rather rigid: he wanted to "facilitate a process by which he could understand himself better." Clearly Patient F needed more than this. In our ongoing assessments of any particular patient we must be sensitive to how much he can tolerate. And we engage different parts of our personalities, often quite intuitively, in response to this.

In certain situations, such as when a patient is struggling to make a decision, the therapist's neutral stance results in the patient's not feeling helped or satisfied for the time being. He is then likely to push for advice: "Okay, I still don't know what to do. So what do I do?" Here we can find ourselves in a dilemma. On one hand we hope to assist the patient to find his own way on his own terms by exploring the various issues involved, which takes time; on the other we find ourselves faced with pressure for immediate action and a demand for definite response.

These moments are the confluence of many rivers: the river of transference, the river of countertransference, the river of reality, the river of societal expectations for what psychotherapy is, the river of hope, the river of disillusionment, even despair. A good deal of resentment, even rage, may emerge from the patient, and this can be very difficult for us to bear. Indeed it may rekindle our own doubts, perhaps about aspects of our education, our own psychotherapy. None of this is inconsequential. The way such situations are handled can make or break the therapy, especially early on when we don't yet know very much about the patient, when things are still tentative. It may feel as though the patient is saying, "Prove to me this works." At later stages of the therapy the therapist has the benefit of a longer and stronger connection, times of positive feeling and movement, and a sense of the patient's dynamics as well as her own reactions. In other words she has been down some of these rivers. But in the opening stages of a therapy the territory is as yet mostly uncharted; the therapist does not have as good a lay of the land as she needs. Nonetheless how she proceeds will contribute to the tone of the rest of the journey, indeed if there is to be a rest of the journey. Much hinges on how these moments are handled. There is great suspense here and no certain outcome. For some these can feel like moments of crisis.

Whatever the stage of the therapy and however the two will proceed both parties in our view must face, perhaps more than once, the river of reality, the real fact that no ready solution may be available for now. This is a hard fact. It is not just a fact of therapy; it is a fact of life. Patients may react to this in various ways. Some may fight it and rant and rail; others may withdraw. Some patients may play with the thought of stopping the therapy or even do so. This would amount to premature foreclosure and to relinquishing further development. We know that continued exploration of the patient's thoughts, feelings, and memories is in order. Not rarely material relevant to making a decision appears in contexts that at first glance seem to have nothing to do with the ways in which the dilemma is posed. Different perspectives may develop, making solutions and further progress possible.

It has been our experience, however, that whatever the initial reaction, most patients, such as Ann from chapter 15, generally come to feel steadied knowing that arriving at solutions takes time. It tends to ground them. It is as though there ensues a pause followed by the words "Okay, now we can begin the work." Similar moments may occur throughout the therapy, perhaps many times. For now let us stay with these moments as they appear at the beginning of therapy.

At such a crossroads the therapist, with all this knowledge somewhere in her mental library, might say, "I think that we have at this point come up against a very important reality, that being that there aren't any easy answers apparent for now. But that does not mean that our explorations must cease. It may mean that we have to, like good detectives, expand our sights and look under different rocks." It would be good to have a "rock" or two in mind to offer the patient as an example. At such points the therapist may also introduce the concept of conflict. She could say, "I think that what makes deciding so hard for you are your very mixed feelings about . . . (such and such). Perhaps we can spell these out more . . . "

In a very practical way comments such as these amount to giving the patient some consumer education. They also function as a means of either introducing or reinforcing a piece of the therapeutic understanding. There are other ways of responding. At a later point in the therapy the therapist might say something like, "Well, it is not as if we haven't encountered this place and these feelings before. Usually when this happens it has something to do with . . . "

We might, of course, indicate to the patient that he seems not yet ready to make a decision, that he may wish to put a moratorium on choosing for a while, but in a manner that invites and aids deeper exploration: "Perhaps you are not ready to make a decision for now. There seems to be more to think about." The patient may respond in a difficult way: "But I need to decide now. I don't have all the time in the world."

Here we may do a number of different things. We might feel free to remind him of certain relevant realities and point out objective facts he may have overlooked up to now. "Well, it seems that what is so difficult now is coming to terms with some very upsetting realities," or "But, if I understood correctly, weren't you told you could apply next year, even the year after? Perhaps you have some mixed feelings about these alternatives."

A detailed exploration of the patient's fantasies about the consequences of his deciding on each one of the existing possibilities may be helpful. One can, for example, say, "Well, what do you think of the idea of accepting the offer?" or "Let's think about the impact of telling your son he can't come back home."

As much as we would like a patient to be able to take things more into his own hands, occasionally our presumably greater maturity, experience, and judgment might have to fill in where his resources are insufficient: when the patient's reality testing is impaired, sense of agency is suffering from a developmental lapse, or dependence on the therapist has become too great. Further, if the therapist feels it necessary to give some advice it would be important to explore how the patient experiences this before he acts on it: "You heard me say that it might be better to do . . . (such and such). How do you feel about that?"

It is good to have some handy responses for times such as those described, although it should be remembered that different patients may require some variation on them, some difference in nuance that cannot necessarily be predicted. At such times therapy is improvisational. And there will always be those times when we are truly stumped, able to comprehend what may have happened only in retrospect. In whatever way we choose to proceed, however, we are guided by a concern for protecting our connection with the patient and strengthening any developing alliance.

The bottom line here is that as therapists we often have to deal with these kinds of moments. It takes time and continued experience, perhaps looking afresh at our own incertitude, perhaps even losing certain patients, to sort things out for ourselves, to develop our own orienting stance. This kind of thing is learned and relearned over and over again, and may result in a certain degree of ease and comfort with edginess, or at least some ability to tolerate it. An example comes to mind. A patient was nearing the end of his first year of psychotherapy. He had been feeling stuck for a time and one day spoke angrily to his therapist. "I have so many doubts about this whole therapy business!" he exclaimed. "Where is it taking me? Tell me, damn it!" Feeling the patient's distress, the therapist, nonetheless, remained calmly thoughtful, eventually and in a careful way, saying, "How could therapy proceed without doubt?" This patient quieted down and the work continued and deepened.

Let us turn to the example of Dennis, a premed psychology undergraduate, who comes to therapy at the end of his junior year. To some, Dennis's concerns may not seem very dramatic, no one is dying or divorcing, but they are extremely important to him.

Dennis must choose whether he will go on to graduate school in psychology or medical school. In Dennis's initial version he outlines this dilemma. He is very frustrated and wants the therapist to help him decide what to do. He has been tormented by this stuckness for some time, and he hopes to make a decision soon, certainly by the end of summer. The therapist encourages him to speak of his concerns. Whenever he asks her what he should do she responds with some version of, "Well, let's look at it. Imagine now that you are in graduate school, describe thoughts and feelings you might have, all that is involved for you." A similar example may be made with medical school. As Dennis continues he begins to speak of his mixed feelings. He spontaneously brings up other pressures in his life, such as with his parents; he widens the conversation. But he always comes back, often with great frustration, to his initial dilemma, usually with the refrain, "but I still don't know what to do after graduation."

One day, about six weeks into the therapy, Dennis comes to the session particularly despondent. He speaks of feeling depressed at not having yet found a solution. He also brings up an incident in which he got angry with another student. The therapist remarks that this is the first time she has heard him speak of his anger. At a later point in the session, when Dennis continues to bemoan his continuing dilemma and stalemate, the therapist remarks that the two of them are at a crossroads in the treatment: she says that he is indeed correct about the continuing stalemate, but he has also begun to introduce new thoughts, topics, and feelings into the hour. He has brought in feelings of anger and depression, as well as his relationship with his parents. Dennis and the therapist have some choices of their own to discuss. They can continue to discuss the pros and cons of graduate as opposed to medical school; or Dennis can stop therapy altogether; or they can recognize that the issues at hand are more broadly connected to other aspects of his life, which is probably why a decision is so hard to make. At this point Dennis, quite on his own, begins to address his resistance, namely, his very real concerns about discussing matters more deeply. He speaks of not wanting to have deeper issues, not wanting to be diagnosed à la DSM-IV; he was called a lot of names growing up and is very spooked by any kind of labeling. At a later point the therapist asked Dennis if there was a part of him that liked coming to therapy. He said yes, that he felt listened to. Dennis elected to continue with therapy, and gradually emphasis shifted away from school choice to relevant aspects of his relations with his parents and peers.

Even though Dennis elected to stay in therapy, and even though the conversation deepened and widened, he still insisted on advice, a solution, and will likely continue to do so. In some cases it turns out that the patient's paralysis has less to do with the nature of the conflicting issues than with the process of deciding itself. The mere idea of change of any kind may feel very threatening. The patient may, for instance, want to avoid commitment or dealing with the loss of certain possibilities when he settles on any one in particular. This was interpreted to Dennis at a later time. More information about his parents came forth then, about their intimidating attitude, pressure to mold him in their image. Feeling any pressure to decide on anything reminded him of this and felt like a defeat.

The idea of the therapist's neutrality does not refer to an existential stand. It is a useful piece of therapeutic practice for obtaining the widest knowledge possible, under the circumstances, of the patient's inner world. Dennis's therapist did what she could to help him think through his choices and broaden their conversation without alienating him. Her approach was effective because she demonstrated flexibility, even at times some playfulness. We are often in the position of having to straddle a delicate balance between staying neutral on one hand and yet being flexible enough to understand the patient's needs and relevant realities on the other. Dogmatically not giving advice is just as naive as wantonly giving it. Dennis's therapist did not eschew advice. She might have given some in a more direct way than some other therapists, but she did not embrace doing so either naively or impulsively, driven perhaps by fear of losing a patient, of incurring his anger, or even by antagonism toward the concept of neutrality. She observed tact as well as respect for where Dennis was, for his level of psychological-mindedness, and for the fact that therapy was a new experience for him. Later she will induce Dennis to do more work on his own. There are situations in which the patient's transference and character are such that he will put the kibosh on any suggestion or invitation to explore. And it may take the therapist a bit of time to catch on to this. When she does she might turn this recognition over to the patient, saying something like, "It's hard not to notice that you are unhappy with all the options or their explorations. What do you make of that?"

We will touch upon the issue of neutrality also in the context of later case examples.

26

The Therapeutic Alliance

The *therapeutic alliance* refers to a special sense of companionship that may develop between patient and therapist in the course of their work together. It manifests itself in their jointly looking at material, puzzling about it, turning it over and over, recognizing problems, questioning meanings, and in being concerned with exploring them. It is an implicit, wordlessly agreed to alliance usually instigated by the therapist at times when she offers an observation or interpretation as an object for joint examination, for joint thinking and feeling through. Positive transference feelings on the patient's part facilitate his accepting such offers.

The therapeutic alliance is different from the therapeutic understanding, which we have discussed earlier. The therapeutic understanding involves a general agreement between therapist and patient-to-be that they think they will be able to work together and wish to do it. It is understood that the patient knows something of the nature and implications of the work, and that the frame has been more or less defined, negotiated, and settled. The therapeutic alliance evolves from it as the work develops and depends upon it. One really can't experience the alliance without some understanding of what one is going to be doing. What would there be to ally around?

The alliance comes about with increasing trust. Evidence of it is usually found in increasing freedom of expression on the patient's part and receptive listening on the therapist's. In some therapies the alliance is built more quickly than in others, some patients experiencing a positive transference sooner than others. It is important to distinguish the alliance from (1) an initial good connection and (2) the transference. A good connection is important but does not mean that the patient is working jointly or in a committed way with the therapist. Also, although the alliance is easily apparent during periods of positive transference, it is not merely a fair-weather product. If genuine, it endures through difficult periods of resistance, stagnation, negative transference, and discouragement and keeps the treatment going. *They are in it together.*

The alliance can manifest itself in various ways, always referring to an endeavor done in partnership. Take, for example, this excerpt from Madelyn's therapy.

Th: Last week you spoke of feeling like a burden to your friends when talking about yourself. (*Madelyn nods.*) I wonder what it's like for you to talk here.

Pt: Well. (*Pause*) It's strange. It's not something I'm used to. It's not that I don't want to speak about me with my friends. I'm on my mind, and I want to. But I don't because of the burden thing. Here, though, I feel I can speak. At home at night, for instance, I'll often think about separate things like my job, what happened with a friend etc. . . . but not so much about my feelings. Here I think more about my feelings, and I think maybe I can put the whole together. (*Pause*) And . . . you listen. You are impartial. You don't give advice. But you listen. I don't usually listen to other people's advice anyway. My parents know me, and they often give me advice. And there are times—sometimes—when I get disappointed in them.

Th: Disappointed?

Pt: No. Not really. I don't mean to say that. I mean I don't particularly want to do what others want me to do or advise me to do. I want to come to it myself. Does that make sense?

Th: I think what you are telling me is that you prefer not to be beholden to the advice of others, that you prefer to do what comes to make sense to you and in your own time.

Pt: Yes, sort of. Yes. That's right. (*Pause*) But I think there's more to it . . . What I'm really saying I think is that I'm hoping something new can happen here between what you know and what I know.

Th: Oh! That's different. Say more.

Pt: That we can combine forces somehow. (*Pause*)

Th: (*Smiles*) It sounds like you are hoping that something can be created between the two of us.

Pt: Yes. Created. Maybe *we* can help *me* find a different way to be. I'm in a rut. I'd like something new.

Here Madelyn is differentiating the therapeutic relationship from others in her life, from family and friends. And she is actively struggling to find the right words. Furthermore the therapist's comments are not experienced as gospel. They are used as fodder and built upon ("Yes, sort of . . . But I think there's more to it . . . What I'm really saying . . .") The therapist encourages Madelyn ("Oh! . . . Say more"). And then Madelyn puts words to what she would like the two to do, that is "combine forces." Note how she uses the word *we*. And, not incidentally, combining forces is exactly what they are doing: in this vignette both Madelyn and her therapist are stimulating ideas in each other. To all this the therapist smiles as she introduces the idea of a joint creation. She is also likely smiling because of the vividness of the budding alliance and the perhaps only temporary release in pressure, knowing that the patient understands her own active role in the work and seems to be making good progress.

Alliances are not always manifested as clearly or in an equally well-articulated manner. They can be expressed in many different ways, through a smile, a nod, even a silence. One patient, after once again complaining in her usual fashion about her usual peeve, sighed, then looked at her therapist and said, "You know me!" She and the therapist then smiled warmly at each other, in a kind of gratified way. The comment not only showed that the patient could stand back and look at herself, it showed that a joint understanding was present, a result of joint work.

In order to facilitate the alliance the therapist can choose to use words and phrases that underscore the collaborative nature of the work. She may, for example, refer to "our work"; talk about "us" ("Let *us* come back to that"); or use the pronoun "we" ("We don't know," "Why don't *we* continue to explore that," "So far *we* haven't really understood how you came to feel this way"). She may also resort to words such as *together* ("Why don't we think about that *together*"). The alliance is also furthered if the therapist formulates her ideas and interpretations as invitations to further pursue lines of thought and exploration rather than as dogmatic conclusions that cast her as the authority: "What do you make of . . .?" or "I've been wondering about . . ." or "Have you considered . . .?" or "How does this resonate with you?" or "Perhaps an interesting way to look at this is . . . ." are some examples. Tact and sensitivity are required of the therapist to avoid unduly strong efforts to force development of the alliance on the patient. Too much "we" at any time but especially when used too early may make the patient draw back, feel intruded upon, and it may jeopardize the alliance rather than further it.

V

The Nitty Gritty

27

What Does a Therapist Actually *Do*? A Starter Kit

"What does a therapist actually *do* in the hour?" Here we will focus on the nitty gritty of psychotherapeutic work: on what to listen for and observe, what to comment on and how, when to be silent. The nitty gritty is endless. Every therapist has to cope with the potentially unlimited number of things to attend and respond to as the therapeutic process moves along. What this means is that for the most part there is no one correct way to proceed in any given place in any given hour. To add to this, what each individual clinician is open to at any one time is limited and changes. Some things we see; some things we don't. Given the enormity of the clinical bounty it stands to reason that we cannot encompass it all. So what we propose to do is present you with a "starter kit." This kit will contain samples of clinical material collected with the purpose of demonstrating what we feel to be important and relatively frequent scenarios and pieces of technique. We hope that with this kit you will start to build your own personal library of clinical possibilities.

Before addressing what therapists actually do we must recap what we have learned of the essential tasks of psychotherapy. Remember the patient has sought assistance because he has a problem. He may be at his wit's end, unable to control his anger, discipline his child, stop procrastinating, cope with a loss or even (for some) success or newfound wealth. He enters our office with some statement of his concerns, what we have called the *initial version*. It represents what he is aware of about his problems. It also represents the extent of his capacity to do his own psychological work up to this point and the extent to which his adaptations have been able to serve him. He senses their limits in his stuckness. He does not at the moment know how to help himself. Our immediate aim is to help the patient loosen up and become less blocked. We do this in preparation of helping him "dismantle" existing and troublesome adaptations and reconfigure them in new and more useful ways.

We said that we accomplish this largely by encouraging a *widening of the conversation* between patient and therapist. Through such widening we hope to assist the patient in allowing more material (memories, feelings, fantasies) into his awareness. We try to help him to talk with an openness he is sure to be unaccustomed to in everyday life, to go beyond the limits of the initial version of his troubles. We hope to help the patient experience something new about himself, to put him in touch with unexpected views and ideas, to see them in ever wider contexts. By facilitating and examining his ways of thinking and feeling and of interacting with others, including the therapist, the patient may find new resources within himself.

We see this starter kit as something of a guide to how a therapist facilitates widening a conversation, a process that continues really throughout the course of a psychotherapy, and something of how she might gradually help her patients pull things together through the use of *interpretation*.

28

Listening

Doing all this is not easy, to be sure. But it is useful to remember that we are quite accustomed to listening to other people speak in nonclinical situations. Be they family members or friends or a chatty someone on the train, if we listen long enough some of us are likely to have a few thoughts about what it is we are hearing. We may notice certain recurrent themes: "He always talks about people leaving him." We could even develop a hypothesis or two about how this person is put together: "I think something must have happened to her in childhood" or "He was never the same after she died." Sometimes we are tempted to offer an opinion: "I think you should leave him. He's a no good you-know-what"; a consolation: "It's really not so bad. Men are like buses, you know. Another one is bound to come along sooner or later"; or perhaps even a reprimand: "Serves you right, you fool! You always get yourself into these situations! How many times have we gone through this?" We may attempt to explain the situation as we see it: "I think she's behaving that way because she's having an affair." And we may also say to ourselves or to another in puzzlement, even frustration: "This is beyond me. Normal people don't act like this" or "Why can't this person see this?" As therapists our comments to the patient are sure to be more constrained than in these examples. By checking our reactions and maintaining our neutral, even-handed stance we allow the patient the wide sweeping freedom to bring up all sorts of thoughts and feelings. This makes it possible for him, by gradually and increasingly looking at himself, to make observations, expand ideas, find *his own way* through his dilemmas as well as his own solutions.

As you will recall, a psychodynamic perspective puts forth that people are unable to take something in or let something be known because by doing so they are likely to feel endangered in some way and experience anxiety. We have mentioned the existing tension between the patient's wish to know and be known and his need to foil just this endeavor. We know how his resistances, anxieties, and defenses all interfere with the conscious illumination of painful or conflictual material; how defenses work to keep memories, thoughts, and feelings separate and disconnected. So when we scratch our heads over a patient's behavior and say to ourselves, "People typically don't act like this" or "Why can't this person see this?" we refer to our partly intuitive experience of the foibles of human beings, on which, with further training, our clinical knowledge rests.

And so we approach the task of widening the conversation. But that which is beyond awareness, unconscious, does not, of course, give itself up easily. It is contacted in special ways. When we encounter a patient in a session we do not begin the work by providing opinions, explanations, or interpretations. Nor do we engage in debate or persuasion. These will not help even though we have already begun to feel that we understand important things about the patient's situation. Therapists, especially beginners, often want to speed things up. They deliver their as yet unconfirmed ideas like a sword into the heart of the matter, before the patient is ready to hear them. Beginners may want to see "therapy in action," perhaps to show their supervisors that they are on the ball. This is understandable. But it is a common misstep. As we have discussed vis-à-vis the resistance it is incumbent upon the therapist to use her technical knowledge and experience to prepare the patient *gradually* to hear her developing observations and impressions. More like peeling back layers of the proverbial onion. The pace and timing of one's thoughts and observations, then, becomes very important. Why go to the trouble of saying something to the patient if he can't hear it, if he receives it as just a dry piece of someone else's thought with no felt relevance, or if it leads him to attack or defensively retreat?

A course of psychotherapy, once it has found its footing, goes through stages and phases of all sorts. The continuing relationship between patient and therapist holds them all together. Its intensity and quality may undergo many changes at different times. Particularly important are the degrees to which our patients become involved in the exploration of their inner lives. At times they will widen their attention and free themselves of some of their need to be rational. They will permit themselves to recognize strange, apparently useless, puzzling, or repugnant fantasies or ideas and allow themselves to feel in unaccustomed ways.

To reinvoke Loren Eiseley's images we are there in the ooze of the swamps and the tide flats. The waters have receded for the moment, leaving exposed all sorts of creatures and debris. At other times it is as if the waters have risen again; the ooze and the things in it have been covered over once more. Less is seen. These are periods of heightened resistance perhaps. Even then we may be able to work with whatever was recovered when the water was low. For our purposes Eiseley's swampy, tidal images serve to spotlight a liminal region in which advancing or receding waters illustrate expansions and constrictions of consciousness, of fluctuations of awareness. We agree with Eiseley when he writes of "things on the tide flats and what they mean, and why . . . they ought to be watched," that it is there on these flats "that strange compromises are made and new senses are born." Much of psychotherapeutic work occurs on these oozy margins, the range of preconscious activity.

Psychotherapy is predominantly transacted through words. Unspoken and intuitive parts of the therapeutic relationship are importantly involved. But it is the words that give name and form to a patient's experience; words articulate self-awareness, curiosity about self and others, and ways of interacting. They are an essential vehicle for examining and modifying unworkable adaptive patterns. Although we listen to and observe aspects of people every day, in the clinical encounter we are asked to do so in a rather special, somewhat paradoxical way.

On the one hand we allow the material to just wash over us without any strong preconceived notions about what is going on. We try to keep open and receptive to whatever may happen in the hour, including what is happening in our own minds. We allow ourselves to think expansively. We are attentive to what is being said and how, including apparent omissions, holes, or contradictions in the patient's story. We may not yet understand their nature or purpose but find ourselves taking note of them. On the other hand, drawing on the things we already know, quietly there in the background, filed in our personal library, we maintain thoughts, observations, even some tentative expectations.

Thus informed we listen, perhaps becoming cognizant of a gradually emerging pattern of things that are potentially and particularly important in our view of the patient's inner workings. So we remain alert to those things, as a mother is to the sound of her infant's cry, as a hunter to the snap of a twig, or a detective to a converging pattern of clues. We try to be sensitive and thoughtful observers of what goes on, ideally without any desire to exert control.

Once we discover a significant meaning in what the patient says we face a choice between continuing to listen or commenting to the patient on our impression. Proper timing of such comments is important and has to be considered. Oftentimes, however, we sense and perceive things unaware. A detail will emerge that will inhabit our unconscious and from there quietly sculpt our impressions and reactions to a patient, its significance becoming apparent only later. Think of a film in which the camera lingers on an image. Take Alfred Hitchcock's classic *The Birds*. In a scene near the beginning of the film the protagonist is shown looking at a caged songbird. Hitchcock places this image before the viewer without comment. Only later does the importance of this image become apparent when nature, embodied in scores of birds, turns on man. And so it is with listening and observing in therapy. Not all the details will grab and shake you, but that does not mean they have not registered to some extent, as in the Hitchcock film example. Indeed they have been flagged on a different level of consciousness to be highlighted and appreciated at some future time as the drama unfolds. Anna Held Audette writes that Georgia O'Keeffe started to notice bones in 1916, but they only began to appear as subjects in her art in 1930. Admittedly a rather lengthy incubation. But you catch our drift.

Therapy's basic agenda to improve the patient's life situation is one of those things resting backstage in one's internal library. It is important that the therapist be attentive to those things in the patient's communications that are relevant to his current life experience. For example we might notice that a person makes repeated efforts at accomplishing things only to sabotage them, that he felt like saying something but visibly restrained himself, that he unconsciously manages his affairs or relationships in a manner that makes little sense or is counterproductive. These problems and concerns, not just as presented in the initial version but as apparent in the fullness of the material over time, are essentially what we hope to help the patient address. We view them as indicating that he is unable to resolve a crisis in his present state of adaptation. In response to all these matters the therapist must allow her perceptions to sweep over a wide range of issues, including some far away from the immediately presenting complaints or those brought forth in the initial version. The patient has tried to solve his problems in some way or accommodate to them or avoid them but has done so within a self-imposed and limited range and with little success. We try to help the patient understand things in terms of conflicts, wishes, and anxieties that have been kept outside his consciousness. So we listen, observe, and communicate with this in mind.

When we listen to patients we do so on a number of different levels. In this chapter we will talk about the various things one listens for in a session. Initially listening is tedious. Over time, however, it becomes easier to follow our patient's multiple utterances. They may extend from the happenings of their day to descriptions of people or to recalling memories. Because our aim is to expand the therapeutic conversation a criterion for a useful intervention would include signs that the range of the patient's thinking, feeling, and imagining is widening and deepening. Put slightly differently we can consider a session productive if we experience or learn something about the patient that we did not already know. In such cases we can assume with some confidence that we are on track.

As we listen to what a patient says we gradually begin to obtain a clearer picture of his view of things in his life and in himself. We hear his explanations of why things are the way they are and learn what he believes to be the reasons for his situation. Some of the patient's perspectives may not meet the test of common sense. They might be unrealistic or mutually contradictory. As the therapist follows all this she may notice that a portion, if not a good amount, of what the patient tells could be seen in different ways. And she will recognize that the sum of all his views reflects useful and constructive efforts at adaptation as well as some that lead to failure. Their exploration will ultimately become central to the work the therapist and patient will do together.

There can be great variety in what patients tell us, in how they tell us these things, and in the purposes their communications serve. All this is hard to describe, but we will try to consider material from three, by no means mutually exclusive, perspectives: content, manner, and process.

CONTENT

When we speak of *content* we refer to *what* the patient actually says, to what in other words is the outer skin of the onion. The therapist, from the beginning, has encouraged the patient to try to express himself as freely as he can, to talk openly about spontaneously emerging fragments of thought and fantasy, to attempt not always to be logical or systematic. This touches on the concept of *free association*. It refers to the flow of uninhibited speech, saying whatever comes to mind in an uncensored way and seeing where this leads. Free association is something of an ideal that people more or less approximate depending on their level of anxiety and trust. It is a fluid yet coherent expression of one's inner life and is distinct from the less organized tangential or circumstantial communications. *Tangential* means merely touching on subjects but avoiding their essentials. *Circumstantial* refers to speech that veers away from the point, wanders around again and again, and into what may appear unnecessary detail, but finally returns to it. Circumstantial speech can on one hand feel tiresome to the listener at times, while on the other hand it can open creative paths to other matters. Generally the more relaxed and coherent a patient is, the more he is able to express himself by associating freely. In the following we discuss the ways in which the therapist listens for content.

One very basic aspect of listening involves the therapist's paying attention to *themes.* By theme we refer to the subject of a conversation. Recall the cases of Madelyn, Jeffrey, and Vincent (chapter 16). Madelyn's session contained themes of difficulty connecting with men and fear of graduation. Jeffrey brought up themes concerning dating and what it means to come to therapy. And Vincent was struggling with feeling uncared for, possibility being cheated on by his girlfriend, and the threat of having to live alone.

The patient's thoughts and feelings form the themes. The therapist will try to listen for what these thoughts and feelings might be. Let's consider the following account.

Greta was in therapy for depression and a tendency to get involved with violent men. Several weeks into the therapy the therapist-in-training asked if she could tape-record the sessions. Greta, quite abruptly, said no and continued to speak about a man in whom she was interested. As the session went on Greta began to speak of how the men she has dated have all wanted things from her and how she gets used. Her voice became strained. The trainee felt Greta's anger. She even became rather intimidated by her. Nearing the end of the session she wondered if asking to tape the hour had something to do with the direction it was taking.

Th: As you were talking about being used by men I began to wonder if you felt as though you were being used by me when I asked whether I could tape our meetings.

Pt: Well, yes. I came in here to get away from all of this bullshit, and wouldn't you know it, I have to deal with what someone else wants—again.

Th: I see. (*Pause*) Your voice seemed . . . well, strained to me.

Pt: I was pissed at you.

Th: Oh. Tell me about that.

This is an example of a therapist following the patient's thoughts and especially her feelings *within the hour*. She tracked Greta's anger and connected it to her thoughts. (This is also an example of something like a minor interpretation, relating to a transference matter. The therapist was wondering whether Greta's thinking went in part toward demanding men because the therapist had made a demand of sorts as well. We consider interpretations later.)

Thoughts and feelings can also be followed *across hours*, that is, over the course of a number of sessions. Take this example of a young man, Hal, who in the midst of a deep depression unfortunately had to wait three weeks to see a therapist at a community clinic. These excerpts are taken from two consecutive sessions, A and B, about six months into the therapy.

Session A

Pt: I went to the emergency room today. I couldn't quite believe it. I told you I get these terrible headaches. They're not migraines, but they're bad. I had to wait a long time to be seen. It was frustrating, and I got irritated at the nurse. Everyone was rushing about. I almost left, but I really needed some help. I wouldn't have gone unless I really needed some medication.

Th: Your mentioning the ER reminds me of when you first came to the clinic to see me. (*The therapist is picking up on a theme that emerged when the two first met, as well as on Hal's affect.*)

Pt: You remember what I said about it taking a lot for me to come here?

Th: (*Nods.*)

Pt: You know that I keep things inside. Finally, after a lot of thought, I decided to come and then I had to wait for a therapist.

Th: In fact you began today's session with the words, "I was sick. I thought I was going to die." Do you have to be at death's door before you allow yourself to ask for help?

Pt: I'm a strong man. I do a lot for myself. So when I come for help it's because I really, really need it. I don't ask people for help normally. Rarely in fact. I get as much done by myself. And then, of course, people get the idea that I don't ever need help. And they're surprised when I do. Because I keep things to myself.

Th: You're the man who never cries wolf, but this time you really made your needs known.

Session B

Hal begins the next session with two stories both characterized by the theme of his being angry at another person. In both stories Hal stated that there wasn't much use in arguing. It just didn't seem worth it.

Th: The theme of having angry feelings seems to be very much alive for you right now, especially the idea of anger being a useless feeling at best.

Pt: Well, what is the use? I express it, and there is no response. Anger is not useful. Nothing is done. Nothing comes of it. All of it is a waste of time. A waste of energy.

(*Silence*)

Th: What are you thinking?

Pt: Just how useless anger is. You say something. Nothing happens, and it just sits there inside you.

(*Silence*)

Th: Last week you began to tell me about our first session and how you keep things inside. (*Therapist picks up on a related theme.*)

Pt: I was angry at you. I told you that then. When you asked how I felt about not being able to start right away. I was upset for most of the day. A friend said that you have to be falling apart to be seen anywhere these days. Feeling depressed won't cut it. Well, I wasn't falling apart. I don't do that. But I feel pain. And I don't show it. So people think that I'm strong always. I was crying the morning before I came here. But I didn't cry here. I should have known not to expect too much.

Th: So you kept yourself from showing me the extent of your feelings.

Pt: In my family anger meant people going out of control, losing it. Nothing good ever came of it. Maybe a slap across the face or someone getting drunk and yelling. So I don't do anger. At least not publicly. So when people ask me, "Why don't you get help?" I get angry. I can't answer. I go blank.

Th: You may have just answered the question, in part at least. It seems that you have come to expect that no one will hear or see your feelings, that people won't meet you where you are.

Pt: Most of the time I mope when I'm sad or angry. That's not good, I know. But then it turns to putting on a smiley face and going about my business. Then the smiley face takes over.

Th: It's safer for you to show nice feelings rather than not so nice ones I think. (*Therapist refers to a defense.*)

Pt: Well . . . I do have friends that I can show things to. John can hear it if I'm sad or anxious . . . and . . . I can get angry with you.

(*Silence*)

Th: You mentioned being angry with me and then fell silent.

Pt: I didn't want to think of you as a bad therapist. I mean then . . . when I first came. (*This may be some hint of a persistent concern over the therapist's "goodness." Given how much is happening in the hour she decides to let the process unfold of its own accord.*)

Th: Hm.

Pt: I wanted to keep seeing you. I hoped that I would get to continue with you. And I'm glad it turned out that way. You seemed to understand. I couldn't think of you as not understanding what was very deep inside. I was confused.

Th: You've experienced the world as not having responded to the depths of you, and how awful if it should happen again . . .

In this account we encounter, from Session A to Session B, the development of a number of different things: recurrent themes, the emergence of new themes, strong feelings. We also see some beginning indications of Hal's view of himself and the world, and his expectations of therapy, including references to the therapist. Note that these references began with Hal's description of the ER and the ER nurse. The therapist hears in the story allusions to crisis, seeking help, and the responsiveness of helpers, and she picks up on them. This opens a way for the patient to express his anger at her and to voice his bitter expectations of therapy and people in general; it doesn't do much good to expect anything from anyone! This emerges as part of Hal's troubles. His relations to other people are generally quite conflicted. His experience of these same troubles in his relation with the therapist is an example of *transference*. Note that the therapist's freedom to refer back to a difficult moment in the first session and Hal's freedom to consider the therapist as "bad" imply something about a more fully established *therapeutic alliance*.

In the following we see another example of how a patient views herself. We also see how this view comes into *conflict* with unrealized parts of herself. It is extremely important that we listen for and be able to recognize conflict since it is fundamental to a psychodynamic understanding of how people are put together.

Tammy, a woman in her late twenties, entered treatment because she abruptly left her fiancé, Kevin, to have an affair with a man named Seth. Tammy presented with an agitated depression. She seemed flighty and a little disoriented. She portrayed Seth as a ne'er-do-well: unemployed and continually borrowing money. To her dismay, but not necessarily surprise, Tammy discovered a history of petty theft and drug use. The therapist inquired into the attraction Seth held for Tammy. "His body," she replied with a laugh, "I'm not going to deny it." She was sexually drawn to him as she was never drawn to Kevin. It was clear to her, however, that Seth was irresponsible and a potential philanderer. It soon emerged that Tammy maintained an identity as the sweetie pie in her family, a reputation that brought with it a set of expectations, which she found stultifying. Several sessions were spent discussing Seth's liabilities, and Tammy seemed adamant about leaving him: "I know it. I deserve better. He's bad news. I'm definitely drawing the line." Very soon after this series of sessions Tammy left treatment without warning.

It occurred to the therapist, unfortunately after the fact, that perhaps she had not listened carefully enough to the clues. Just as she had left her fiancé, Kevin, Tammy had left therapy without warning. And just as he was an upstanding citizen so might the therapist have seemed to Tammy. Tammy had been telling her all along that she had had it with being a sweetie pie. She was likely drawn to Seth not only because of his sexy body, but because of the forbidden erotic fruit that was his bad behavior. In retrospect then the therapist began to notice many possible sources of conflict, the most salient being Tammy's feeling torn between the pull of her "bad" erotic fantasies and the stultifying pressure to be sweet. There was something to be gained and something to be lost in both these positions as she currently experienced them. The therapist thought that she had sided too much with Tammy, the sweetie pie. Tammy likely needed to explore her own "bad" side and may have felt pressured. She had lived much of her life according to other people's agendas. Not yet willing to give up this man Tammy could have left because she found the therapy limiting in this way. Also, she possibly did not wish to disappoint her therapist: afraid of criticism and rejection, she may have wanted to avoid all this by quitting. This account illustrates the centrality of conflict and keeping a neutral stance, as well as the transference. It also underscores the importance of listening for information about significant people in a person's life: family members, friends, lovers, and colleagues.

In addition to knowing about the important other people in the patient's life, the therapist's listening is enriched if she is interested in knowing something about *the goings on of the world* in which her patient lives and which to some degree she shares with him. Many of these things are learned from what patients describe of their daily activities, interests, environments, routines, obligations, and concerns. Gradually the therapist will also come to understand something of the cultural backgrounds of her patients, their ways of family living, their religious views, even superstitions. Therapists should also be reasonably aware of current social and cultural events, politics, and sports. What's happening in the news, and entertainment, both classical and popular? What are the current colloquialisms, fads in the arts? What are the popular talk shows, movies? What's big in the theater, literature, music? Of course it is impossible to know everything. But it can be argued that knowing who Britney Spears is would not be such a bad idea if one were treating an adolescent today. Any of these people and events can touch upon and express a patient's concerns, fears, fantasies. A patient's stories or jokes may serve the same function of indirectly expressing personal concerns. People often find it easier to speak about something indirectly or by just hinting at it. They may do this consciously or not.

How about this example taken from an opening session? Frederick, a man in his late forties, comes to therapy complaining of panic attacks. The session contains a reference to an extremely popular television series that has apparently entered many a therapeutic conversation.

> Pt: Do you watch *The Sopranos*?
>
> Th: It's a popular show. What makes you mention it?
>
> Pt: Well, the lead, Tony, Tony Soprano, gets these panic attacks. Which is what I get. I didn't think it would take a TV show to get me to call someone. My wife has been pushing me for a long time. I never would listen to her . . . until I saw Tony Soprano.
>
> Th: What is it about Tony Soprano?
>
> Pt: Well, if he can do it, then maybe I can.
>
> Th: I see.
>
> Pt: Yeah. You see he's a tough guy. I'm in the construction business. And it's a tough business. I can't have my crew lose respect for me. I can't be feeling nervous and panicky. I got to keep on the ball. What if it shows? Maybe if I had a little Prozac. What do you think?
>
> Th: I think we can keep that door open, but first let's talk a little more before we decide what to do. I'd like to know more about your panic attacks. When do you feel the panic coming on?

This reference to the well-known TV show is determined by its main character being quite involved in therapy himself and with a female therapist. With transference possibilities in mind, the therapist responds to Frederick's question by acknowledging the show's social impact without divulging her interest, thus preserving her anonymity. It is likely that the show has already stimulated transference fantasies.

Now let's turn to this excerpt taken from the middle portion of a therapy. Hannah has concerns with her body image.

> Pt: I just don't want anyone to see me in a bathing suit or, God forbid, naked. I don't like my body . . . I'm thinking about *The Phantom of the Opera.* I saw it last week when I went to New York.
>
> Th: What about it? (*Therapist follows up on this reference.*)
>
> Pt: Well, the idea of this man so horribly disfigured, hiding himself from the world. God forbid anyone to see this face. I imagined someone pulling off his mask, what would then happen, and if it would be bearable—for him or the other person. The idea of hiding away from the world forever and ever is so awful to me.

One may also wish to listen for interesting uses of words, ways of putting things, or slips of the tongue. Let's continue with Hannah and the previous example, noting that the therapist stays with the topic but focuses the conversation. The therapist could have chosen to go with any number of things. She could have asked about Hannah's body image, the image of hiding, details of the disfigurement, further details of the play, or who that "someone" might be who pulled off the mask. Instead she decided on the following:

> Th: You used the term "pulling off." That's an interesting way of putting things. Why that term?
>
> Pt: Well, because I don't think he would ever take anything off himself or allow anyone else to. For anyone to see behind the mask would require something forceful, a very forceful measure.
>
> Th: You began by referring to not wanting anyone to see *you* in a bathing suit.
>
> (*Silence*)
>
> Pt: It would feel as though someone had yanked off all my protection. I would feel so exposed. I would die. Sometimes I ask myself what it would be like to let go, to uncover myself and enjoy the feel

of the sun on my body at the beach . . . But I can't. I'm too self-conscious. I would quake.

The example of Hannah serves as a good example of someone speaking about herself while initially appearing to speak about someone else. In response to the therapist's comment she proceeds to speak directly of her yearning to feel uninhibited. The therapist wonders to herself about possible exhibitionistic fantasies but will keep these thoughts silent for the time being. Bearing in mind the image of yanking off protection the therapist will, for now, stay with Hannah's anxieties about her body, her feelings of shame and anger that she keeps bottled up, and her concerns about letting go. She also silently considers the idea that "unmasking" may refer to Hannah's curiosity about the therapist or a concern over being psychologically unmasked herself.

Then there is Carl, who comes to therapy with a history of trauma and who makes the following *slip of the tongue*:

Pt: The history of our family is punctuated with a number of fires, if you can imagine that. In one instance my sister poured water on a grease fire. Water on a grease fire! Can you imagine that! How utterly stupid! *The fire became enraged.* It began to spread and engulf things. Oh god, no. Not another one. How many times does this have to go on? Must I always put out fires?

Th: You said the fire became enraged.

Pt: I did?

Th: Uhm. What do you make of that?

Pt.: Don't know.

Th: Could it be that you were enraged?

Pt: I was angry. I can definitely say that.

Partly by the patient's noticing what he is doing and partly by the therapist's pointing to what the patient has just said the train of the conversation can branch out into new, unanticipated directions. In the course of such happenings the patient's range of consciousness can widen. Connections of which he was not aware before may rise into his awareness. This may result in some enrichment of his adaptive resources.

Metaphors

As we have discussed patients will often allude to their personal experiences indirectly because it feels safer. Some personal meaning of which he is not aware at the moment may be expressed through the material of daily things that serve a symbolic purpose. Individually or in their combination they may be metaphors signaling other concerns. Thus therapists have good reason to pay attention to the use of metaphors in the patient's speech. All sorts of things can be used as metaphors: food, sex, weather, sports, entertainment, geography, religion. In this vignette Betsy comes to her session irritated and flustered. She has just returned from a trip cross-country to see her mother.

> Pt: My mother just insists on my doing things just like her. I have to hang up my clothes just like her. Or she goes in and adjusts them. She gives me perfume but it's always the same as what she's just bought. And she insists on doing my laundry. (*Betsy shudders.*)
>
> Th: What was that just now?
>
> Pt: A shudder.
>
> Th: Why?
>
> Pt: I don't know. She can't let me do what I want.
>
> Th: I hear that, but a shudder. I think there's more going on here.
>
> Pt: Yeah. I know. It makes me feel yucky. I want to tell her to wash her own stuff and leave mine alone. Go away!

Here Betsy is conveying her reactions to her mother's closeness using clothes as a metaphor. Manifestly she speaks about mother hanging up her clothes and doing her laundry and her reactions to it. But there is potentially more that lies beneath the surface, out of the patient's awareness. The therapist senses this when she comments on Betsy's shudder. As Betsy continues the therapist begins to form some hypotheses about what this could mean. One thought has to do with the possibility that Betsy dislikes her mother touching her. The therapist could choose to let this go for now and get more information; she could follow up on the affect by saying something like, "What does 'yucky' mean?" or if it felt right she could say something more direct such as, "You don't want your mother near you." Perhaps even, "You don't want your mother touching you." The point is that Betsy is giving a lot of information in her allusions to clothes, touching, laundry, perfume, all things that have to do closely with the body. Also, the therapist thinks of a shudder almost like trying to shake something off from the skin or shrinking from a touch. If she were to go deeper she might even begin thinking of dirt, smells, covering up dirt with nice fragrances. The word *yucky*, being rather childish, suggests that these feelings may go quite a way back. If there is merit to these speculations, and as the therapy progresses further, we might expect to hear themes having to do with shame, soiling, exposure, and covering up. Let's look at a few more examples of the use of metaphor.

The following example is taken from a therapy well underway. We see that the therapist has said very little. He has let the session unfold and followed what happened. The patient, Nora, a woman in her thirties, is mostly quiet. Normally articulate words do not come easily to her this hour. When she does speak it is forced and difficult. Thoughts seem to dry up quickly. There are many silences. Although the therapist doesn't comment specifically on this he keeps it well in mind and they inform what he does. About halfway through the session and after a fairly lengthy silence he asks:

Th: Where did your thoughts turn?

Pt: I'm not thinking very much of anything. Not feeling much either. I don't even feel much toward you. Funny, I did once. Remember? Months ago. I felt a lot. I think maybe I even loved you. But now, nothing.

Th: I think maybe you are protecting yourself from those feelings. They were very difficult for you.

(*Silence*)

Pt: I'm thinking of a film. I can't remember the name of it. It has to do with this starving artist who is taken to a restaurant where he can order anything he wants, but he asks the waiter only for, I don't know, cabbage and lemon I think. He was poor and used to that. He didn't want to eat something wonderful because then he would miss it terribly the next day. So he stuck to what he was used to even if it wasn't all that terrific. So his life would be bearable.

Th: I think you also sour things up so that you can bear your long-ings. (*The therapist picks up on associations to the word lemon. He could have also picked up on the boring nature of a steady diet of cabbage and lemon but did not. Perhaps because souring is more immediate, more visceral, more evocative.*)

Pt: No! Well, maybe. I'm just scared. I'm scared of the moments I feel close to you. I don't want them to end. And they do. They always do. I don't want to miss them. I don't want to taste something and then not have it again. It's too painful. I'd rather not have it at all. (*Long silence*) I guess I do mean to sour things. If souring things means staying away from feelings. (*Pause*) I can't not come back. But I can't leave either.

How about:

Pt: It's so dreary outside. It's been raining for six days now. And it's cold. I get so depressed. It was like this when I came to Seattle five years ago. I was used to warmth. The rain just wouldn't quit. I hate the rain.
Th: Perhaps you can eventually get to a place where the weather both inside and out don't always have to mirror each other.

By using the patient's own language the therapist tries to direct the patient's attention toward his own inner life. Let's return to Carl and an excerpt from another one of his sessions.

Pt: When I came here I thought you were cold. I said to myself, I'm really going to have to watch it. But now I really like you.

Th: What was it about me?

Pt: Your features were cold to me. Then. Not now.

(*Silence*)

Th: Yes?

Pt: When I first came here and heard your accent I thought that I was going to take it on like I have other accents. But I haven't. It's an English accent, isn't it? I'm interested in England and their conquering different countries. (*Carl continued to talk about this for a while, making references to the various countries that were colonized by England.*)

Th: By keeping your own accent you keep from being colonized by me.

In this next example a sports metaphor appears:

Pt: My husband completed the New York marathon Sunday. It was a happy occasion. He trained so hard. He's also talented.

Th: You don't sound too happy.

Pt: Well, I am for him. But . . .

Th: But . . .

Pt: I'm not so accomplished. I get discouraged easily. Last week I didn't even want to come back to therapy.

Th: You are wondering if you can go the distance, I think. In therapy as in other things.

Pt: Therapy's hard. I don't think I have it in me.

Th: Go on.

In this vignette the therapist chooses to direct the patient's attention to how she was feeling ("You don't sound too happy"). She does this by developing a nascent sports metaphor with the words "go the distance." It is interesting to note that the comment "Go on" implicitly encourages the patient not only to develop her immediate thoughts but also to continue in therapy.

Sometimes the therapist's introduction of a metaphor of her own can be very productive. It can give the patient a new way of looking at something. But on the whole it is preferable for the therapist to depend on the patient's own metaphors and not to impose less related metaphors stirred from within her internal world. If she does introduce a metaphor it is important that she intuitively maintain a very careful balance between what the patient has actually said and what it evoked in her.

Fantasy

According to Sigmund Freud fantasies are pleasurable and wishful and are not subject to the constraints of reality. One should listen for patients' fantasies.

Here the patient is a twenty-nine-year-old named Daniel in therapy for about two years. This fantasy emerged when his therapist came back from vacation.

Pt: Where did you go on vacation?

Th: (*Smiles.*) Where do you think?

Pt: I don't know.

Th: Well, what do you imagine?

Pt: Okay. I think you went to the Caribbean. You spent your time floating in the warm water. It was very sunny and warm. You have a bit of a tan.

Th: Why do you suppose I went there?

Pt: Don't know. Just did. Where did you go?

Th: You imagine me floating in a sunny and warm place.

Pt: Better than being here in the snow. You take a lot of vacations. My last therapist never took time off. Well, very little. You must be quite rich, I think. To be able to afford so much time away.

(*Silence*)

Th: Tell me more.

Daniel's fantasy contains various images of his therapist's body, in a bathing suit, or bikini, or nothing, tanned, amidst the elements. He also alludes to her leaving him, which his previous therapist did not. It seems as though Daniel has erotic wishes for her although as yet not fully articulated or explored. Not sure which track to follow, that of her body or her absence, the therapist simply asks him to tell her more, and she will listen for these themes as they arise in subsequent material. Daniel may wonder if she is married or has a boyfriend. He may experience frustrated longings and feelings of jealousy. These are potential elements of Daniel's fantasies as they arise in the transference. As more material accumulates about these themes, and the therapist begins to feel more secure in her formulations and in Daniel's readiness to hear them, she will begin to think of presenting these issues to him. And she will do so in a way that helps Daniel understand better the ways he relates to the people around him.

Dreams

Dreams are important clinically because they are understood to be an important means to access aspects of a person's inner world that are beyond his conscious awareness. Dreams can serve both defensive and synthetic functions. Their defensive properties show in their often cryptic, puzzlelike quality, which makes them difficult to understand at the outset. We must talk our way into them in order to know their significance. Their synthetic properties emerge, for instance, in the remarkably economical and succinct way that a single image or vignette can bring together many themes, a phenomenon known as *condensation*. The dreamer is working on all of these themes. Like waking phenomena dreams also have multiple functions. Freud asserted that one important purpose of dreams is the expression of images that represent the person's wishes, often very indirectly, as fulfilled.

Dreams are infinitely varied. They can be vivid or vague; clear or confusing; coherent or fragmented. They may proceed slowly, a single event unfolding in detail, or quickly, a series of images one following the other in rapid fire. They can be frightening or pleasurable. They can be dreamt but once or recur over time. Dreams are made of many things. They can incorporate the previous day's events (known as *daytime residues*), as well as pieces of distant memories.

Our approach to dreams is to engage them as we would any clinical material. That is, we explore the patient's associations to various parts of the dream and the dream as a whole. Dream images, although sometimes suggestive, should never be assumed to have a general and fixed meaning. A popular misconception still exists that dreams can be understood by referring to some dictionary of dream symbols that will unlock their meaning. No one piece of dream content has a general or universal meaning. The meanings of a dream are specific and unique to the dreamer. Its content, when and how it is dreamt and communicated, can only be understood in the context of the patient's own feelings, associations, and the quality of his relationship with the therapist. We ask the patient for his thoughts and feelings regarding the dream in order to get at its meaning in terms of his own life and issues. Sometimes the meaning of dream material will reveal itself only over time. Sometimes not at all. When musing over a dream it is helpful to keep in mind when it occurred: in the course of an issue under scrutiny, in relation to a life event, in the aftermath of an interpretation, and so on. The following example demonstrates some of the above points.

PERCIVAL

Halfway through the session Percival, a man in his mid-twenties, reports a dream of the previous night.

> Pt: I had a dream last night. I have no idea what it means but it was so real. So I thought I would tell you about it. I dreamed that I received a letter from my doctor. The print was so blurry that I couldn't make out the message. I remember feeling really scared because I knew it contained important medical information, some test results. That's it. That's the dream.
>
> Th: What comes to mind?

Percival has difficulty associating to the dream, to its various images—"my doctor", "the blurry message," "some test results"—or to the dream as a whole. During a period of silence the therapist reflected back over the hour. Percival had opened the hour referring to last week's session, which he missed without notice. He reported having tried to reach her to cancel but that there was something wrong with her voice mail so he gave up. He also spoke of blemishes that appeared on his skin, which he continued to worry about despite his physician's assurances that they were not cancerous. The therapist thought to herself, "Hm, there is something here about thwarted attempts at communication; a concern about something growing on/in him; and increasing anxiety." Given his difficulty associating to the dream she thought she might say something, but what? She decided on something interpretive and would see where things went:

> Th: I wonder if you may be worried about something not being communicated well. It's interesting how the dream with its blurry letter follows your telling me how you couldn't reach me.
>
> Pt: You know, my neighbor, Jerome, the one I'm friends with, always says that I'm always afraid of the worst. He says that it doesn't surprise him that I am convinced that I have skin cancer even though the doctor said I was fine.
>
> Th: Tell me more.
>
> Pt: I think Jerome is impatient with me. I think he's pushy. He's staying with me right now because he's having trouble with his girlfriend. But it's been over a week and he doesn't leave. And sometimes he's

not respectful, like in the morning he'll use the bathroom for a long time and I have to get ready for work. Also I think he thinks he can stay as long as he wants. I'm getting pretty upset. I don't know what to do. I can see why his girlfriend kicked him out.

Th: Sounds like you'd like to kick him out too.

Pt: Yeah. I get more angry each day. More frustrated, you know, the longer he stays. It's getting to where it's like something is eating away at me.

Th: Like a cancer?

Pt: Yeah. (*Pause*) It's killing me. (*Pause*)

Th: This difficulty setting a limit is a theme that's come up before in our work.

Pt: Yeah, I know. (*Pause*)

Th: What do you imagine Jerome would do? (*Pause*)

Pt: I get a little scared. He won't become violent. That's not what I mean. But I don't think he'll be nice about it. He'll give me a guilt trip and I'll forget what I wanted to say and maybe I'll say that he can stay longer or something. It's happened before like that. (*Percival goes on to talk more about his inability to tell Jerome what he wants from him, namely to leave soon, that basically enough is enough.*)

Th: As you were talking I was thinking about your unsuccessful call to cancel last week's session. Today you opened the session by saying, in essence, that you couldn't get through to me. I wonder if, as with your neighbor, you are afraid to tell me certain things.

(*Silence*)

Pt: Yeah, you're right.

(*Silence*)

Th: Yes?

Pt: I wanted to tell you that I wanted to stop counseling. I'm going to be starting evening classes and I'm going to be pressed for time and money.

Th: But something stopped you from making sure I got the message. You gave up, so you said. What did you imagine I would do?

The therapist rightly thought that there was much more to Percival's reluctance to continue therapy than he was letting on even to himself. She brings the conversation into the here and now and addresses his resistance. Based on what she already knew of Percival, it likely had something to do with his fears of just how troubled and stuck he actually felt and of what she might think of him or do, perhaps as retaliation. Percival decided to stay in therapy. Although he would continue at times to enact his considerable ambivalence to being in therapy he was increasingly able to stand back and talk about what happened. In the sessions to come he would elaborate on his self-perceptions, which included the dread that he was so disturbed as to be "diagnosable," his thoughts about the therapist, and his chronic hypochondriasis.

MANNER

Attending to the manner in which a patient carries himself or speaks can be just as important as following content. People communicate things in ways other than through words. When we speak of *manner* we refer to *how* something is conveyed. This can be obvious or very subtle. Does the patient laugh, pause, remain silent, edit himself, withhold? Is he blocked, pressured, passive, apologetic, tentative? Is he mired in detail, vague, confusing, hard to follow? Sometimes commenting on manner includes a reference to feelings. Does the patient, for example, come across as whiny, paranoid, sad, ashamed, angry?

How is a person groomed: Does he smell bad—remember Lenny? What kind of smell is it? Body odor, cigarettes, alcohol, incense, perfume, fish (yes, it has been known to happen)? Is his hair neat, clean, long, short, stylish? How is he dressed? Sloppy, smart, impeccably even? Seductively? Appropriately? Is he decked out in jewelry? Is a certain item or color always worn? A locket, a scarf? Black, red?

What about posture? Does the person sit up rigidly? Is he closed up with arms folded? Does he hold onto his seat? Is he relaxed, open? Someone may slouch. Put his feet up. Does this change over the course of the hour? Another sits at the edge of his seat clutching a bag or jacket. At some point he may relax and ease into the chair, allowing it to hold him. After a while he may let go.

Or not. There are times when a person will look as though he is ready to run out of the room if you so much as blink.

Does he lisp? Stutter? Have a facial tick? Tap his foot? His finger? Laugh or cry easily? Or at certain times? Does he blush or become flushed? Sneer? Frown? Look serious, worried, contemptuous, sad, anguished, despairing?

Where does he look? Into space, out of the room? At you? How? Where? Does he avoid contact? Turn away at times?

Does the patient bring you things? Photos? Food? Gifts? Once in a while? Or habitually? Does he leave things in the office?

Is he early? Late? Perpetually? Never?

Is he polite? Does he express gratitude?

Does he pay on time? With a check? Cash? One patient would pay at the beginning of the hour, casually placing the check on the desk *en route* to the chair. Another patient would laboriously write out a check at the end of the hour, extending the session, thereby getting more for his money. Another would place a check in a sealed envelope with the therapist's name written on it. Yet another would mail her payment. Is a copay paid each session, monthly, perhaps with no discernible pattern?

Such are some of the things to keep in mind when observing patients. There is no obvious need to try to understand each single instance. But one or the other of these happenings could provide a sample of a continuity that may be a significant feature of the person's life pattern. Again, when we comment on manner we are not forcing ourselves to understand. We go on listening and follow our perceptions closely.

Vagueness

In this example Simon, a rather hysterical man, speaks in a vague and diffuse way. He approaches his feelings but goes no further.

Pt: I always feel so bad. I get so anxious. My heart beats fast. I even sweat. No one knows how I'm feeling. I hide things very well.

Th: (*Pushing for specifics.*) When did you last do that?

Pt: Oh, yesterday. Or maybe the day before. I don't know. But it was scary. The whole world felt like it was going to cave in. Did you ever feel this way?

Th: (*Smiles.*) Why do you ask?

Pt: Oh, I don't know.

Th: I wonder if you're concerned that nobody can understand what you feel.

Pt: Maybe.

In response to the patient's vagueness we see the therapist pushing for specifics in order to pin him down a little. In this regard you may recall the vignettes of Harriette (chapter 5) and Valerie (chapter 21).

Confusion

In this example Rosie begins the session in quite a muddle.

Pt: I just got back from a meeting with my professor. Before that I had to go to the bank. The meeting was terrible. I was thinking about all sorts of things—the bank, my grades. The professor was digging in his drawer for something. I wanted to tell him why I was doing so badly. He tried to say something to me as he was looking around. Then after the meeting I was so upset. I felt that I had acted liked an ass. I tried to talk to him but the phone kept ringing. Eventually he turned the ringer off. But then I had to go. So much is going on. I'll have to go back to the bank to finish up there after I end here . . .

Th: I'm really quite confused. You seem very pressured. Why don't you slow down and tell me again about the meeting with your professor?

By expressing her own confusion, the therapist reflects Rosie's confusion back to her. Sometimes patients have the expectation that the therapist knows what is happening and can automatically connect the dots. At such times a comment such as "I'm confused" or "I'm having trouble following" conveys to the patient in a nice way that the therapist is listening but cannot read minds.

Self-Editing

Patients will often edit themselves. One can infer a self-edit in many ways. A therapist can, for example, feel that the patient is withholding something; notice an expression, a gesture, a change in emphasis; or catch a comment such as in the following example in which Harold is struggling to come to terms with his wife's infidelity.

> Pt: I can't forgive her for what she did to me. She expects me to have gotten over the affair, but I haven't. I can't. When she saw how much devastation it caused she bought me things, as if that would make up for things. She was surprised when I was not as appreciative as she, I guess, wanted me to be. I know how this must sound to you. But sometimes I feel that there is nothing she can do to make up for what she took from me. My trust. She half expects that the whole thing should be over and done. But these things are never over and done with. I'm sorry. I can't be different. I'm so hurt.
>
> Th: You edited yourself just then, I think. You were speaking with conviction and then commented that you knew how this might sound, that you're sorry.
>
> Pt: Yeah. I'm not sure why. I doubt myself. I always have. Now it's worse though. I don't know if I love her anymore, if I can ever trust her again. But, you know, I can't imagine life without her . . . Maybe that's why I said I was sorry. Sorry that I can't get myself to leave her even though I'm so disappointed in her and so angry.

Expressions of Affect

It is also important to register communications of affect, such as laughter. Take the example of Oscar, who does not feel comfortable dating. Oscar is an intelligent, outgoing young man who is making a career as a comedy writer.

> Pt: Why is it that I can't get a date? I don't feel I have any control in the matter. I'm intelligent. I'm a nice-looking man. At least according to my mother. Well. Okay. So I'm not Mel Gibson, whatever she might think. She actually thinks I look like Mel Gibson. Seriously, she's convinced. Guess where I get my solid sense of reality from. But clearly you don't have to be Mel Gibson to get a date. Just look at my friend, George. No hunk that George. Let me tell you. But he has this cute girlfriend. Why? What's it about me? There's no rhyme or reason to any of this. There are these nothing-special-looking guys getting, I don't know, Crepes

Suzettes. I can't even find me a few crumbs from a lousy pound cake. (*Joint laughter*)

Th: You know, we laugh, but it's really not so funny how you feel so out of control, that there is no rhyme or reason when it comes to women.

Pt: Well, if I didn't laugh then I think I'd cry.

Th: Hm. Tell me.

Or how about Eugene, a very staid elderly man, who begins by discussing his retirement.

Pt: I retired several years ago. It was quite a transition. I would categorize it as, as . . . a loss. Yes. All those years.

Th: A loss. What else falls into that category?

Pt: (*Silence*) Well, moving from Atlanta to San Francisco when I was twelve. It was just after my mother died. (*Tears well up in his eyes.*) Oh, my! Excuse me.

Th: That took you by surprise.

Pt: Yes. I thought I had cried all there was to cry a long time ago. My word! These things are still with you after so many years.

Th: You were not anticipating that the impact of your mother's death could reach you after all this time.

Pt: No. Well. It was an awful, awful thing. Her dying. And, well, me so young. Oh, here I go again . . . I'm going to take one of your tissues.

Th: Take two.

Pt: I think I may need even more than that. Oh dear!

The following concerns Lynnette, a woman of thirty-two, who comes to therapy because of depression. As the weeks go by her therapist becomes increasingly angry with her. She feels Lynnette's rage and both subtle and not so subtle jabs. For example, Lynnette might comment on the therapist's clothes being out of style, how she phrases a comment, or her choice of upholstery material. After one such remark, the therapist finally said, "I felt that punch."

This took Lynnette by surprise. She became flustered, at which point the therapist said, "I think something important just happened here. Let's both stay with it and see what we can learn."

In this illustration, the therapist comments on what Lynnette has been evoking in her for some time. Here you may recall Greta, who was very angry at her therapist-in-training for asking to tape the session. The therapist followed Greta's affect throughout the session, in large part by monitoring its impact on her, namely, her feeling increasingly intimidated.

Pauses, Choice of Words, and Extra Careful Speech

Let us return to Betsy, meticulous in her physical and verbal presentation.

Pt: Mom never lets anyone see her cry (*pause*). The rest of her family is not like that (*pause*). They show emotion (*pause*). My mother is very careful when it comes to showing emotion (*pause*).

Th: How so?

Pt: She keeps things inside (*pause*). It kind of keeps you guessing at what she's thinking and feeling (*pause*).

Th: You seem very tentative to me today.

Pt: That's my mother too. Tentative. I guess she (*pause*) infused me with her caution.

Th: Infused. What an interesting use of the word.

Pt: It's important that I find the right word. I don't want to misrepresent myself or show people what I don't want them to see. I don't like talking all that much. I feel unsafe very quickly. I'm very careful how I dress as well. I need to be in control of how I come across. Keep the outside nice. Don't let people see what I don't want them to see.

Clearly Betsy expresses a general defensiveness that spreads through much of what she says as well as her behavior; it may actually be a broader feature of her character.

Behavior

As we use the term, manner also refers to behavior. Here is an example of a therapist commenting on a patient's behavior: Miles is a young man of twenty-two. He comes to therapy because he is extremely anxious and this is affecting what he hopes to do after graduating from college this year. Miles has been in therapy for about two months. During this session he speaks of painful feelings connected to being criticized by his father. At a number of points in the session he begins to tear. He will blink away his tears, even wipe them away quickly with his hand. Eventually the therapist says, "I notice that you have been crying on and off this session and that you have not taken a tissue. Why do you suppose you haven't?"

This observation not only points out a behavior pattern to Miles it also asks him to consider its meaning. In making such observations and posing such questions the therapist can also gauge how psychologically minded a patient might be.

PROCESS

As the therapist listens to the patient's tales of everyday life she is mindful of what he selects, of the manner and tone of his expression, how he groups his topics. When we speak of *process*, we refer to this grouping or *sequence* of themes, thoughts, feelings, mannerisms, and other things over some period of time. This time frame could mean a little piece of a session, a large piece of a session, or what transpires across sessions. Patients are frequently unaware of their train of associations, let alone that something could be organizing what they are saying. Remember that the unconscious is not governed by our everyday notion of space and time. So when attending to process note the different topics or themes that appear in proximity to each other—shifts in the session, great and small, such as disparities of affect, abrupt changes in content, even contradictions, or silence. Keep in mind that seemingly disparate topics may be unified by a stream of common feeling, an underlying theme, an attitude. Sequences may reflect an unconscious connection. Over time one hopes that patients will grow more self-aware both of the contents and the processes in what they are saying. Let us consider what such sequences can reveal.

In this account Alistair struggles with anxiety and guilt feelings over separation from his mother:

Pt: I'm not sure what to say here. I feel anxious. I'm no longer in crisis. Where do I go now? I don't know what to say. I haven't really thought about what I was going to say. So I'm not prepared. (*Pause*)

Th: Can you say more about *that*?

Pt: Well, maybe I'm not being a good patient. I don't have a direction or a goal. I feel that I should be using my time productively, that I should come with something planned to say. So . . . I feel very self-indulgent. Very guilty.

Th: What comes to mind around self-indulgence?

Pt: My girlfriend, Kim. She always, always says that I don't pay enough attention to her. She's very critical of me. In that way she's just like my mother. She's often said that I am very self-engrossed. The other night . . . Tuesday. Or was it Monday? It was Monday. We were talking about the previous Friday. I had a very hard week. And I was very tired. So I fell asleep, and she was very angry at me for doing so. She felt ignored. That reminds me. (*Smiles.*) I had a dream last night. It had to do with someone who came to the gym where I work out. I was very attracted to her. In the dream we were attracted to each other. And she kissed me. And I wasn't sure what to do. Kim's criticalness—is that a word?—reminds me of my mother. I can do nothing right. Kim said that I can be obnoxious in public. And aggressive. When we were Christmas shopping I said something to the salesman about the jackets that were on sale, that they weren't that terrific. I said it as a joke. We both knew it. Kim said that I insulted him, that I had no business saying things like that. They weren't his jackets. We're not connecting like we used to.

Th: I understand that the week was long, but I wonder if falling asleep was a way of not being with Kim. I wonder if you were tired of her as well as the week in general.

Pt: Yes. Definitely. That's exactly right. I am tired of her. I was bored. She's like her mother. Her mother is critical of her. And she's critical of me. And my mother's critical of everyone. And I'm tired of it all. All we do it seems is argue these days. The other day she asked me about my anxiety. I spoke to her about it, and then she said that all I did was talk all about me.

Th: So you are not a good boyfriend, son, or patient.

Pt: (*Laughs.*) That's right. Critical relationships are what I'm used to. They define me. They tell me what to do. I want to get away from them. So many shoulds. So much frowning and guilt-tripping if I do something my mother, and now Kim, don't like. I guess I'm also afraid of doing something you wouldn't approve of.

Th: I'll think you are self-indulgent.

Pt: (*Nods.*)

Th: You get anxious I think when you wish to be free of shoulds—boyfriend shoulds, mother shoulds, therapy shoulds. At such times you are not sure where to go, and you don't want to do the "bad" thing. I think that you can only allow yourself to dream about what you want.

Pt: I feel Kim is burdensome now. My mother never approved of her. But to leave her is to admit that she was right. And I'll hear it from her. I don't know what to do . . .

In this hour Alistair begins by describing his anxiety at not being defined by crisis, then he shifts to his girlfriend, Kim, and her dissatisfaction with their relationship. He is saying that he is anxious and guilty about doing what he wants, which is to be free of obligations. The therapist follows Alistair and links his associations together in her comment, "So you are not a good boyfriend, son, or patient." She then ties in the dream ("I think you can only allow yourself to dream about what you want"), thereby alluding to conflict. Alistair picks up on this: to leave Kim is to prove his critical mother right. Alistair's view of relating is one of obligation that he doesn't want to fill, feels guilty about, and absents himself from. It seems that both he and Kim avoid having pleasure in their lives.

In this next vignette, Freda also talks about guilt, albeit over asserting herself:

Pt: Well, it's holiday time. I always get sad during the holidays. You're supposed to be happy. Families getting together and all.

(*Silence*)

Th: Go on.

Pt: I don't know what to say. I've been thinking about my father and my brother. I've been sad that they're both not around. And yet this is a happy time. I'll be spending time with my son and his wife and new baby. And I'm happy about that. But my father and brother are dead and that makes me sad.

Th: You're both happy and sad.

Pt: I guess I am. I guess you can be both. I'm happy that things have changed between me and my son. I feel that he loves me. I have good friends. There are these older ladies at the club I go out with sometimes. They're always giving me hugs. There are a lot of people who love me. I had them over to my apartment a few weeks ago. One of them wanted to know if she could see another unit. I thought of my friend Ann who lives two doors down, but there was no way I was going to bring this lady over there. It's a pigsty. Absolutely filthy. She has these dogs, and she never cleans up after them. There's shit or something all over the place. Ann always asks things of me. So does her sister. Can I drop her off here, pick up this for her, do that? And I, like a fool, do them.

Th: You struggle with helping her.

Pt: Yeah. I have to set limits. I get guilt-tripped by her and her sister. Sounds like my father, doesn't it?

Th: Tell me.

Pt: My father was filthy. He would never take care of himself and his place. It was a pigsty like Ann's. One day I took him home from some place. And he was walking up the stairs in front of me. And there was this horrible thing coming down his leg. It was piss. He couldn't take care of himself. It was so gross. So awful. There is this grown man who can't even see that there's urine coming down his leg. I don't want to be like that. I had to go. I couldn't stand to see it anymore. None of us could.

Th: What happened?

Pt: Well, I saw him into the house, told him to wash up, and then I left. I couldn't take it. Then I felt guilty.

Th: You began the session by referring to your father being dead. You then spoke about difficulty setting limits with Ann, and how Ann is like your father—both filthy. I think that saying no to Ann is so hard because it is like you are killing your father and you feel so guilty. (*Therapist is referring to the process and linking Freda's associations.*)

(*Silence*)

Pt: Yes. Father was a hypochondriac. Anything to get our attention. Most of the time nothing was wrong. But I could have done more. I could have cleaned up his leg at least. He sucked us dry. He was a vampire. He took and took from us.

(*Silence*)

Th: What are you thinking?

Pt: He wanted nothing from life. Football. He'd watch games on TV and that's it. Baseball too. But not basketball for some reason. He was so passive. Never would go to the doctor unless we urged him. He died of prostate cancer. A preventable thing. He'd want so much from us, and yet he seemed to care nothing for life. I could never figure that out. (*Silence*) I don't want to be like that. I don't want to do that to my own son.

Th: What do you mean?

Pt: I don't want to be passive like my father. I don't want to burden my son. My son will ask me if I need something. Like for my apartment. But I don't ask. I'm very careful. It wasn't always that way. But I'm different now. And he can lean on me.

Th: As you've come to better understand your relationship with your father things have changed between you and your son.

Pt: I'm more ambitious than my father . . .

Let us consider the sequence of things that Freda is talking about, the flow of her associations. Freda opens the session with a statement of her ambivalent feelings about the holidays, namely, her happiness that it is a family time and her sadness at the deaths of her father and brother. She then associates to the ladies at the club, who give love to her and are maternal figures. She then brings up Ann, her dirty, sorry, and dependent neighbor to whom she has difficulty saying no and who reminds her of her father. Putting these associations together the therapist then comments that saying no is so hard for Freda because it is connected to killing her father by neglect. Freda can hear this because she has been hinting at it up to that point. From here she goes on to talk about her father's hypochondria, passivity, and vampirelike dependency, then how she is different from him. She seems to want to prevent identifying with her father in certain respects. It is likely that the theme of guilt will come around again as she continues to discuss her ambition and independent pursuits.

Note here that the reason why many dynamically-oriented therapists choose to say little, especially at the start of a session, is to allow material to emerge and build on itself. The therapist then can draw upon the various associations and begin to pull them together as these therapists have done.

Dreams are also important to attend to in terms of process. In the following, although the content is relevant, the more immediate concern appears to be linked to process.

Walter, a man in his twenties, presents the following dream: He is alone on a beach being attacked by prehistoric beasts, pterodactyls, with very large beaks with teeth. When asked what comes to mind, Walter states that the dream is a recurrent one dating back more than ten years. He then refers to his previous therapist's comment that teeth were symbols of power. Later in the session Walter's mood shifts.

Pt: I want you to tell me what my dream means. My previous therapist would tell me things about my dreams.

Th: Well, what was it like for you when he'd say such things?

Pt: Like he cared. You just sit there. You give me nothing. He was interested.

Th: Did you agree with him?

Pt: Yeah, I did. He made a lot of sense. Why don't you give me your thoughts?

Th: Give you my thoughts! Wow!

(Silence)

Th: Let me tell you. I am careful not to push my thoughts on you. You have told me many times how easily influenced you are by the opinions of others, and my aim is to give you as much room as you need to form your own interpretations. But this clearly makes you angry with me.

Power did subsequently emerge as an important theme over the next few sessions. This issue, rooted in his relationship with an authoritarian father, had its manifestations in the therapeutic work. Specifically, it appeared in Walter's struggle for power in therapy sessions with scary, larger-than-life therapists. Indeed in this context Walter was able to say on his own, and with something of an "aha!" experience: "My God! Pterodactyl! Ptero-dactyl! Terror doctor!"

Listening to Oneself

As we mentioned at the outset listening goes two ways. In addition to the patient a therapist must also direct a portion of her attention inward. She will try to pick up on much the same categories of things that go on in her as she does with the patient: thoughts, feelings, images, memories, fantasies, behaviors. Does she identify with the patient? Think of him in inordinate ways? Forget things about him? In our discussion of transference and countertransference we discussed such matters. Let us look at the following case.

Edward is a divorced thirty-five-year-old airline steward. As usual he came to the session on time and took his seat. He began by reminding the therapist that he had gone on a first date with someone from work. The evening had gone "so-so." When asked to expand Edward recounted the events of the date beginning with where they met, what they decided to do, and how the evening ended. This was not the first time the therapist had listened to Edward tell of a "so-so" date. He was angry and, in characteristic fashion, expressed this in contempt for the appalling state of public restrooms, the physical ugliness of the general public, and the environment. He was not an uninteresting man at all, but this session found the therapist alternately thinking of her chores for the day and scanning Edward's attire and her bookcase, which needed tidying up. She was also listening and following, but with no real pressure to say anything. She was, as it were, half in and half out of the session—at times maybe only a quarter in. It had been a long and tiring day, and she was kind of on "rest mode," which felt comfortable.

After about twenty minutes had passed, Edward stopped talking. Quite a sizeable silence ensued, which the therapist broke with the standard, "Where did your thoughts turn?" Edward replied, "Where is this all going?" The therapist perked up. She was taken aback. At the same time she thought to herself, "Oh no, I'm not in the mood for this." She didn't know where it was going. It was late and to have to attend "en pointe" was feeling just too much. But . . . she had rallied many a time before and gotten through. "Tell me more," she responded with a mixture of alertness, trepidation, and resentment.

> Pt: I don't know if I want to come here anymore. All I do is talk and you say nothing.
>
> Th: Go on. (*She shifts in her seat and recrosses her legs.*)
>
> Pt: I don't think I'm getting any better. I feel just as depressed as I've always felt.
>
> *The therapist wonders what has happened. She feels guilty for having spaced out. For not knowing, for charging, for not being a better therapist. Her last session with him was very productive. Now this. Further she feels as though she has been struck dumb yet needs to say something quickly. She does the best she can.*
>
> Th: Well, let's look at what happened.

She goes over the contents of the session in great detail. Despite her seeming inattention she had surprisingly taken in much of what he said and hoped to convey that she was present, for whatever that was worth at this point. For Edward clearly it wasn't worth very much.

> Pt: You sound just like a textbook. I don't need to hear that. This is therapy by numbers. I don't need to pay for this. This quackery! This, this . . . I don't know what! Where on earth did you get your credentials? On some island somewhere?

Edward proceeded to ball out his therapist. The therapist listened attentively. The two were definitely engaged but in an upsetting way. Eventually she said that something important happened in the session. He was obviously very angry with her, and it had to do with her being silent. Beyond that she wasn't sure what it was, what all had transpired, but if she let go of what just happened, he would be right to wonder about her and feel as he did. She asked if what she had just said stirred up any ideas for him.

> Pt: I felt like I was talking to the wall. You were listening, I could tell. But you weren't saying anything. And I was getting angrier and angrier.

> Th: (*He was losing contact with her, she thought, and that's what was so upsetting, enraging, and frightening for him. It may not have mattered how this disconnection was kicked off. Why would that come to her as something of a revelation? It was such a basic concept.*) You felt a loss of connection between us, I think. God forbid this should be a so-so therapy.

> Pt: (*Edward is still. He then nods.*) Yes. I didn't know where you were.

> Th: Off on some island somewhere?

They proceeded to discuss the various emotions he had been through. Every now and then for the following week the therapist pondered the session, specifically the beginning, the contents of his talking, and the strange fluctuations of her attention. She began to pull together some ideas about Edward and what might have been going on in the hour. On the most evident level, which was addressed in the session, Edward felt a loss of connection. He was angry because he felt she had rejected and abandoned him. But what lay deeper, she thought, was how Edward's angry and embittered affect pushed her away, spaced her out. He feared connection as well as craved it. As scary as aloneness was it was also scary, perhaps scarier, for him to be connected. She felt that nothing she could have said that session would have made a difference to him. Perhaps that's why she had remained silent and distant. In a way that she had been unaware of at the time she was disconnected as well, perhaps even pushed away, by Edward; this, combined with her already feeling tired, had made her all the more vulnerable. She would bring this up to Edward next time. That is, suggest that he also feared closeness and that his angry feelings were easier to bear than his needful feelings. Perhaps "so-so" was safer than "wow-wee!"

This example brings up other issues. For one thing, silence here was not used deliberately but was an aspect of the therapist's reactions to the patient. It was part of an interpersonal dynamic that had been set in motion. For another thing, it shows the importance of keeping a neutral therapeutic stance, of not reacting defensively, but staying levelheaded. And this requires attending to what is being evoked internally.

Also, it demonstrates the idea of *relearning*. We learn things a first time, whether in a classroom or with a patient, but we also learn them again and again, in *experiential* ways, each time a little differently. In this instance the therapist was surprised that Edward's need for connection should have escaped her. She was reminded here of its force, but also of the fears connected with it; of what it is to sit with a patient's defenses; and of the power of human interaction. She felt as if she were learning things, already familiar, for the first time. "Aha!" she felt. Although a concept may be familiar it will not materialize with different patients in exactly the same way. Such is learning through actual experience. Undoubtedly this therapist will again be surprised and awestruck when concepts once more leap from a page and into the real life of the clinical encounter.

Beginning and
Ending Sessions

The beginning and ending of sessions mark important transitions from day-to-day life to the more fluid world of psychotherapy and back again. We introduced this idea in the context of the frame, contrasting Lewis Carroll's description of Alice falling down a hole into Wonderland with C. S. Lewis's description of four children entering Narnia upright through soft fur coats. In this chapter we return to beginning and ending sessions in greater clinical detail.

BEGINNING

How patients and therapists act at the beginning of one of their appointed sessions depends, among other things, upon the stage of their work, whether the hour is one of initial assessment, the first actual therapy session, or a later hour in an already ongoing process. Here we are concerned with hours spent in already continuing therapeutic work.

The way a session is begun depends on the inner states and expectations of both patient and therapist. Under the best of circumstances the therapist would feel open-minded and curious about what the patient might bring. She would be aware of her recollection of previous sessions and, to some extent, of where in the work both of them find themselves. The patient, on the other hand, may feel eager and hopeful, anxious or doubtful, in conflict of some kind or other, willing or hesitant to talk.

Generally it is preferable to wait for the patient to open the hour in any fashion he might. This imparts to him that the hour is his to do with as he pleases and that he is expected to initiate and be active. Of course this expectation may be met with a variety of reactions. Depending on the patient's level of anxiety, his psychological-mindedness, this stance may have to be modified.

Patients can open the hour in multiple ways. Many will typically greet their therapist with "Hi, how are you?" A simple and benign response such as "Good" or "I'm well, thank you" might be appropriate. These inquiries are generally on the order of social niceties. Although not without meaning they are mannerly, a way of acknowledging the therapist as another human being. They may express a wish that the generally reticent therapist show more of herself and help the patient to deal with his anxiety. Such introductory comments sometimes come to be a kind of entry ritual and, in that sense, part of the frame. With very anxious patients who are not sure how to begin a simple "Well, tell me how you are," or "How are things?" may be in order. Another response to a "Hi, how are you?" could be, "Fine, thank you. Tell me about yourself." As more of a bond and an alliance come to be, one might begin to explore the thoughts and feelings connected to these various openings. They are possible therapeutic material in themselves. One might observe, "I've noticed that it is very difficult for you to begin talking on your own," or "It seems easier for you to wait for me to open the hour. Is that so?" You might ask what the patient thinks of this or whether he experiences similar difficulties in other situations, looking for common elements in what might be making him anxious.

Some patients will begin by asking the therapist, "What were we talking about last time?" This is an interesting opener, laden with meaning. Is the patient testing the therapist to see whether she remembers? Had she paid attention? Is he saying that he does not know how to begin? Is it that he truly does not recall? If so then why? Does he experience the hours as discontinuous? Could he be wishing to meet more often? To his inquiry you may ask whether anything of the previous session comes to mind, why he supposes he can't remember. You can also simply say, "Say more." One particular patient who could never recall the previous session came to understand that her experience of the hours as discrete and separate entities was a way she protected herself from feeling connected to her therapist. Closeness, as it turned out, especially with her mother, gave her a queasy feeling from which she needed to back away and which she had trouble further articulating. This is also a good example of the defense of isolation of affect.

It can happen that a patient comes late. It is usually worth commenting on events such as this one. One can observe the straight fact: "You are late today," or more ambiguously: "Trouble getting here today?" or more directly: "Did you find it hard to come here today?" keeping in mind anxiety and resistance. It can also happen that the therapist is late. This piece of behavior will generally not be jointly explored in a similar way, even though it may reflect anxiety and resistance on the therapist's part. But the therapist, partly because she is being paid by the patient, may feel obliged to give some compensation for lost time. She could make an offer: "We are late starting today. How are you for time? Can you stay an extra five minutes?" Most patients will be able to do so. Some cannot or will not. You can offer to make up the lost time at some later date. It is useful to listen for themes alluding to lateness as the hour and subsequent hours unfold: being stood up or cheated; feeling rejected, abandoned, angry, bereft. If they occur, then you could say, "I notice that you've been talking about rejection. I wonder if that comes up today because it has something to do with my being late."

ENDING

Ending a session stirs up all manner of feelings and can be difficult for both patient and therapist. The beginning of a session ushers a person into a space apart from ordinary life. Here he can think and feel and speak deeply, even fancifully. The ending of a session returns him to the pressures of reality. Be it soothing or troubling it asks him to come to the "surface" again. There is a separation that can be felt as an abandonment, as a mini-termination. It reminds him, as do the requirement of a fee and other things, of the boundaries of the relationship. The patient may wish that the hour could have gone on forever. He may feel sadness, anger, resignation, or even shame at being sent away. On the other hand he may feel relief and be glad to get back out into the air. The ending of an hour can be also experienced as an interruption or unwelcome pause in the course of ongoing work, perhaps as frustration at not being able to get on to the next chapter. At times patients will state that they feel overwhelmed when leaving the session, that they must somehow cope with continuing strong feelings at work or at home. Some patients may feel a need for greater continuity, to step up the frequency of the sessions. These all can become intensified if a break in the work is at hand. You may recall the vignette of Doreen in chapter 5.

Either therapist or patient may happen to initiate the ending of a session. Most often it seems to be the therapist who indicates that the hour is up. She can do this in a number of ways: "We'll need to stop here," or "We have to stop for now," or "Let's stop here" are examples. Ending hours brings up many and mixed feelings in both patient and therapist. The therapist may feel regret (perhaps even guilt if she is glad that a difficult hour is over). In reaction she finds herself extending the hour, or she softens her language, as in "Let's pause for now," or "We'll continue next week." If she feels tempted to end the hour early, not wanting to hear anymore, she will have to examine herself and try to recognize what in the therapeutic material or in herself may have caused her to feel and react like this. How both parties experience ending a session deserves attention.

Sometimes patients push the limit. They bring up seemingly important topics in the last few minutes. They touch upon a difficult matter but flee before it can be further explored. Others want to extend their time. One way to deal with such situations may require tactfully cutting in, saying something like: "You know, we need to stop and time is up!" If the hint is not received you may have to cut in again. Some patients keep on talking even as they walk to the door. If this persists it will pay to point to it: "I've noticed how you have difficulty leaving the hour." And then there are the "doorknob" comments, made just as the patient is at the door. Here you may recall Neil, whom you met in chapter 5. To these you might say something like, "It's interesting that you should bring this up just as you are leaving. Let's take it up next time." (Sessions can be extended also by doing the converse, the patient arriving early and sitting in the waiting room.) Still other patients, without meaning to push limits, are in the thick of something as the hour ends. They may be crying or in the middle of an important story. In such cases some flexibility is in order. Here you might say, "You know we will need to end in a moment, but please do finish your thought." Again, if this turns out to be a regular occurrence, bring it up.

One other thing. Sometimes we may feel a need to summarize or wrap up the session. Such a temptation may be a response to feeling guilty for ending the hour. Doing this gives the wrong idea to the patient that sessions are blocks or units of lessons rather than phases of continued work and a progressing relationship.

30

Making Comments

"Do not arrange stones in too abrupt or sophisticated a manner but rather tentatively."

—Yoshitsune Gokyohoko (twelfth century), The Sakuteiki, *the Secret Book of Japanese Gardens*

Up to now we have examined in detail how a therapist listens. In what follows we hear the therapist speak.

As therapists we are fundamentally aiming to tell the patient new things about himself. We don't, however, advocate any specific rules about how to do this. We rather prefer to speak of a *manner* of commenting. Comments generally are best couched in *open* and *flexible* terms—not from on high, as dogma. It is, after all, the patient who is the author of his inner world, not the therapist. It is the patient with whom our words must resonate.

Our suggested manner of commenting observes the concept of *clinical neutrality*, already discussed at length. It also observes *timing*. We referred to timing in chapter 20 but feel it is important enough to repeat here. A good sense of timing can be quite an ineffable thing, similar to a comedian's knowing when to deliver a punch line, or an actor's sense of dramatic pause. Good timing not only increases the odds that the patient will hear your comment, but it can deliver the comment with greater impact. Timing also influences the use of silence, which we will take up by and by.

When making comments, it is generally advisable to start at the surface and make our way down; to start with what is known or near to being known, on the assumption that what is conscious or preconscious is easier for the patient to apprehend than what is more fully hidden or unconscious. A surface comment is based on material that has "come ashore," that is, it is heard in the patient's associations. Seasoned clinicians know never to underestimate the power of a "surface comment" in helping the patient open up. What may be obvious to the trained observer is not necessarily so to the patient. As we get to know the patient we find ourselves in a better position to offer the timely fruits of our efforts at understanding and drawing connections.

It should be kept in mind here that all the following recommendations are general ones and that there are exceptions to every rule. We hope that through the therapist's repeated example the patient will eventually learn to do his own reconnaissance, his own uncovering. A session can be thought of as productive if something more about the patient becomes known.

PHRASING

In our comments it is preferable to use the patient's own idiom: his language, terminology, and metaphor. In this way we want to underscore, give credence and value to the patient's own experience, and not risk putting words into his mouth. Ideally you may wish to think twice about comments such as "You look angry" or "You look sad," because they sound definitive and you could be wrong. If you are wrong such comments may confuse those patients who tend to doubt their own perceptions. Instead you could ask the patient if he is angry. Better yet you could observe something about his expression in a more general way: "Something seems to have come over you," or "You're crying," or "Your brow is furrowed." Or in Dennis's case (chapter 25) the therapist might have used his experimental psychology idiom at their crossroads, saying, "Well, look, *you* explore things. You see something interesting and introduce an independent variable and see what happens. If nothing interesting happens then you introduce another, maybe more than one. Isn't that how investigation proceeds? We tried something that seemed most indicated. Now we can try something else. Or we can stop the investigation."

FACILITATING COMMENTS

These comments convey that you are listening and are interested and encourage the patient to say more. They will include all manner of things such as:

Prompts: For example, "Go on," "Tell me," "Say whatever comes to mind," "Any thoughts?" "How so?" and interested noises like "Hmm!" or "Aha!"

Empathic statements: These comments as well demonstrate that you are listening and understanding what the patient is saying. In that sense they facilitate further communication. Examples of empathic comments are "You are telling me that you felt extremely betrayed by her," or "I think that maybe it was very difficult for you to tell me that."

SEEKING CLARIFICATION

When we seek clarification, we ask the patient to explain or describe something further in hopes of throwing more light on the matter at hand. We may want factual or emotional clarification. To these ends we can ask *questions*; keep in mind that questions to the exclusion of other kinds of comments may feel like an interrogation for some people. For others they may feel structuring, comforting, and familiar: "Can you say more about that?" "How did it happen?" "What are you thinking about?" "What were you feeling just now?" "Can you spell that out for me?" Or we can make *statements*: "I don't quite follow. Run that by me again, please."

PUSHING FOR VIVIDNESS

We want to awaken in the patient some feeling he experiences in response to a past or current event. Urging the patient to report more sensory detail often facilitates this. We speak of material as *evocative* when it stimulates thoughts and images and associated feelings. So a therapist does well to attune herself to openings in what the patient says that have such potential. At these points she may want to push for vividness. Comments geared toward *detail* or *specifics* are helpful here. One can ask: "Are you thinking of anything specific?" "Can you think of an example?" "Can you describe her for me?" or "That's an interesting word. What about that?" We push for vividness when we have a definite sense that there is more to what the patient says not only in terms of memory fragments but also feeling. Let's revisit Betsy from chapter 28, who is now in her fourth month of psychotherapy.

Th: You know, you seem very tentative to me again today.

Pt: I guess I'm trying to piece things together. I haven't much of a memory of childhood. It's not clear to me at all what was going on. And I don't have much to say.

Th: Yet you remember an incident where your mother was crying.

Pt: Well, yes, when I was five. My mother was crying and kicking and screaming in the middle of the kitchen. This must have happened in the kitchen because there was this very old stove, an old white stove. I think she was by the stove. I'm not sure why she was screaming and crying as she was. (*Pause*) My father was there, standing behind me and my sister. One hand on each of our shoulders. My mother seemed really big. I can even remember what she was wearing. (*Elizabeth pays enormous attention to detail. We saw this even in her manner of dress. Her consciousness is directed to detail.*)

Th: What was she wearing? (*The therapist capitalizes on this. She asks a question geared to eliciting a more vivid response. She hopes that the details will trigger more associations.*)

Pt: She was in this 60s outfit. She had on a pant suit. I'm thinking it was beige or a light coffee color. Her top had a scoop neckline. And she wore a scarf, a dark blue scarf. I see it blowing. I don't know why. It may have been because of her movements. Do you remember those 60s styles? The pants were bell bottoms. And I think she had white boots on. Her hair was down. She was wearing it pulled back with a band. She looked like Sharon Stone in the film *Casino*. Did you see that film? Actually my mother was near the back door. There was a screen door I remember. And she was crying. And my father was saying something to her.

Th: What do you imagine he said?

Pt: I was afraid. Maybe he was saying sorry. My father may have hit her. My mother was actually at the door. At the screen door. Half in and half out. I can see her crying.

Th: Each time you return to your mother's image she is further away. (*Therapist focuses on detail.*)

Pt: Before this began she was in the bedroom in the back. She was on the bed kicking at my father, also punching him with her fists. She was lying on her back on the bed. He was trying to say something to her. He was by the bed over her, trying to evade the kicks. My mother was saying, "Leave me alone! Don't touch me." The next thing I remember was them in the kitchen. When I was at the door looking into the bedroom I remember wanting to say, "Take notice of me. Pay attention to me."

Th: What about me?

By asking Elizabeth to describe what her mother was wearing, the therapist opens the door to more detail: Sharon Stone; mother near the back door; some memory of violence in the bedroom; no one noticing her. Interestingly it is possible Elizabeth was recalling a primal scene memory. Also the triangular configuration may allude to oedipal dynamics.

One may also ask patients to focus on an image that they bring up quite nonchalantly. In this vignette, LeAnne is discussing her social withdrawal:

Pt: I hole myself up. I protect myself. I've built a wall around me, a wall of blocks of ice, I've always said, an igloo but with no opening. I'm not willing to take a chance anymore. Alan hurt me. I never ever expected him to hurt me the way he did. And since then I've closed up. I thought that I would never get involved with anyone again. And then Joe came along. Before Joe left he said that I needed to talk about my bitterness with someone. So I took his advice and called you. Although not for the purpose of getting back with him.

Th: You used the image of ice blocks. This may not be so far off track since we have spoken of your being stuck, blocked if you will.

Pt: Hmm. (*Smiles and pauses.*) I've always used the image of ice because I so often feel cold toward men. Like I'm frozen inside. I have no warmth for them. Ice is also heavy. And I feel heavy inside. I don't feel depressed. I work fine. I mostly like being alone. Ice is strong as long as it's cold. After Alan left my heart froze over.

ALLIANCE-BUILDING COMMENTS

As we have discussed alliance-building comments are geared to reinforce the joint nature of the psychotherapeutic enterprise. They ask the patient to take an active role in the work, to wonder with the therapist, and not to assume that she has all the answers. For example "I wonder what all was happening here? What do you think about it?" "Well, can you help me out here?" "Am I in the ballpark?" "Let's think about that together." "I don't know. Do you have any ideas?"

HERE-AND-NOW COMMENTS

Hear-and-now comments try to bring observations and references to thoughts and feelings into the here and now of the therapy hour. They are ways of bringing a powerful immediacy to feelings to an unfolding process, as well as pointing to the transference, whether or not it will be taken up. Here is Madelyn somewhere in the second session:

> Pt: I have a lot of friends I talk to about problems, and they can talk to me as well. But, well, I can't help but feel like a burden to them. They have never let on that this is so, but it's something I feel nonetheless. I've always been dogged by it.
>
> Th: Is that some of how you feel coming here? (*The therapist brings Madelyn's feelings into the moment.*)
>
> Pt: A little. I really didn't know if my problems were serious enough. There are so many people who have very terrible situations. I think maybe I'm taking up valuable time. Maybe I'm just indulging in talking about myself . . .
>
> Th: Go on.

Other examples include "You're very silent today"; "I have a feeling you don't like to talk about him"; "That's a cheerful idea"; "You are showing me another part of yourself"; "You stopped talking very suddenly"; "You got away from this"; "You seem reluctant . . ."; "This makes you quite uncomfortable I think"; "That took you by surprise." These observations verbalize what you notice about the patient's manner and what he does in or around the hour. They convey that you are listening and aim most often at his resistance and defenses, either operative at the moment or in more characterological attitudes.

SUGGESTING CONNECTIONS

Here we speak about suggesting links between thoughts and feelings without yet offering some explanation of them, thus leaving the patient himself with the challenge of synthesis. For example one may point out simple consistencies: "This is similar to what you said earlier"; "I think this may be a variation on a theme"; "I have a feeling that what you say now relates to . . ."; "You felt it was so embarrassing to tell me this . . . I did notice you were late today"; "You feel uneasy about this and also that." These comments do not say how things may be related. While pointing out synthetic connections they, nonetheless, leave things open thereby inviting the patient to do his own work. Let us look at this example:

Cindy is a twenty-two-year-old grocery clerk who begins the hour saying that she has just been admitted to a junior college, something she has wanted for several years. After informing her therapist of her success she goes on to discuss a number of unrelated issues. Eventually her therapist says, "I wonder if there is more we can know about your not talking about getting into college. You mentioned it at the outset but seemed to drop the subject."

The therapist here suggests a possible connection between Cindy's talking about unrelated topics and her feelings around the ostensibly happy occasion of getting into college. And, as you may have already noticed, her words are a comment on process as well. Cindy responds by talking about her fear of embarking on something new.

Because comments such as these imply linkages but do not make them explicit, they technically do not qualify as interpretations, which we will discuss at length in the following chapter.

Sometimes in life we sense that words are forced or that they fail, that we can be present in silence more than in sound. Silence can be full of meaning. It is to quietness that we will now turn.

31

Being Silent

There is the caricature of the silent therapist. The caricature portrays, but also exaggerates, the striking difference between social and therapeutic conversation. It is a reflection of the actual and purposeful restraint that the therapist imposes on herself. She assumes a silent stance in order to move the patient to a less conventional, and more wide-ranging, intimate, and personal mode of looking at and recording the events of his inner life.

Silence is a tool. It is not a requirement. Nor is it a screen behind which a therapist hides because she has not a clue what she is doing. By the way, when you feel clueless it is always a good idea to acknowledge this to yourself. You would definitely not be the only therapist to whom this happens, and it is generally a good place from which to start thinking about what could be going on. There are no rules when or when not to be silent. But there is that ineffable sense of timing. There is the *feel* that words will only muffle what is there or in the process of forming, deepening. If something blurry is moving about in the depths (the Snout perhaps?) silence can offer it a way to come ashore. Silence, especially at the start of a session, allows material to unfold of its own accord and without interference so the therapist can begin to pull contents together.

Silence can be used to emphasize, indicate great respect, feelings shared, resonances. Silence can be used in place of words when all words fall short, such as during intense grief. The fullness of the therapist's person speaks then and does so more eloquently than any word. On certain occasions, when a patient is struggling with ambivalence, doubt, or unresolved conflict, the therapist's silence may communicate to the patient her neutrality on the issues involved. Not everything should or needs to be spoken all the time.

Silence can provoke anxiety. In ordinary social interaction, on television, radio, the phone, or at a cocktail party, silences are generally avoided for that reason. Of course you should not persist in staying silent if a patient is too anxious. That would be counterproductive and do little to strengthen the alliance. With certain patients and in certain instances talking about the weather is appropriate.

Actually, there is a sort of rule about silence, a rule of thumb: If being silent gets too much in the way, say something.

In general, though, silence shouldn't be avoided because of your *own* anxiety. Tolerating silence is a capacity that can grow as a person matures. This is true for both the therapist and the patient. Just as your ability to talk about difficult issues enables the patient to do so your ability to sit with silence will eventually enable the patient to do so as well. Trouble dealing with silence can be one reason a therapist might elect to reenter her own psychotherapy. Again, the feel for when to be quiet is something that develops over time. The capacity of patient and therapist to bear with and sit together in silence is often a good indication of a sound therapeutic alliance.

When silence continues for a while one might ask the patient where his thoughts have turned. Sometimes this loosens and frees him. He can express a piece of his inner dialogue. At some point you may even ask what it was that kept him from sharing his thoughts more spontaneously. If a patient states that he doesn't know what to say or asks for help you may say something like, "Well, perhaps you can say whatever occurs to you, any flashes of images, or little side thoughts would be fine. And let's see where that takes us. Sometimes we don't know until we get there." This can get the patient going and offer him a bit of psychotherapy education along the way. Let us look at some examples.

Karen is a thirty-five-year-old bank teller. She has been in therapy for six months and is beginning to understand the chaos of her growing up. In this example Karen recounts a time when her older brother, Harry, bit her.

Pt: My mother was telling me not to cry. Harry was just standing there looking innocent. I wasn't permitted to cry. Ever. Or say anything when he hurt me. (*Pause*)

Th: Go on.

Pt: My mother used to scold me if I said anything. Or questioned anything. I was told that I was responsible for people doing crazy things. I couldn't understand why. Why Harry would bite me. Why mom would get so angry with me. If I protested, asked why, I would be yelled at. I couldn't figure out what I was supposed to feel or think. I was so confused. Mom even said if it hurt that much they'd take me to the hospital. Otherwise I was to keep quiet.

(*The therapist remains deliberately silent.*)

Pt: So I apologized. (*Karen is crying.*) So I *apologize*. That's what *I* do. *I keep apologizing.* Over and over again. It's like I need to.

The therapist isn't sure what to say. But she knows enough to be quiet. She feels very connected to Karen, who is crying and looking off into the distance. The air is heavy as if it were a sack of water filled to bursting. Yet there is also a hush. After what seems like a long silence the therapist speaks. The words emerge from her softly, spontaneously, almost without her knowing.

Th: *You* are owed an apology.

Karen looks at the therapist. Then up at the ceiling. Then she closes her eyes. Tears flow freely down her face in the ensuing quiet.

In the next example, taken from a session in the middle of a long-term therapy in which the transference is very much center stage, Sonia challenges the therapist.

Pt: You're not going to just say nothing are you?

Th: Tell me.

Pt: God! That's just another way of saying nothing.

(*Lengthy silence*)

Th: Where did your thoughts turn?

(*Silence*)

Pt: I'm very angry at you.

Th: What about that?

Pt: You should be paying me. I come here and give and give and give you my insides. You give me nothing.

Th: What is it about my silence today? You did not react so strongly last week or the week before.

(*Silence*)

Pt: It's hard for me to . . . talk.

Th: Something's getting in the way.

Pt: Yes.

(*Silence*)

Th: Can you put that into words?

(*Silence*)

Pt: I'm embarrassed.

Th: Uh-huh. (*Silence*) You said that you were embarrassed.

Pt: I'm embarrassed about my feelings. Their strength. How childlike I feel. (*Silence*) I saw you on the street yesterday. You were talking to this woman. You seemed engaged and interested . . . and . . . I was jealous. I wanted to be your friend. I wanted you to talk to me like you were talking to her. And that won't ever be . . .

In this instance silence enabled Sonia's feelings to develop and her resistance to be known. She started out angry, then spoke of feelings of embarrassment, and then addressed yearnings connected to the transference.

32

Interpretations

In previous sections of this book we tried to describe how therapist and patient work together to establish a special mode of conversing with each other. The therapist's function in this is primarily that of a *facilitator* who assists the patient in developing his story as fully as possible. In the course of doing so the therapist will try to get to know more of her patient's life situation and of his inner state. From what he tells her she will develop a picture of him in her mind. This picture will be elaborated by her bringing a second, to some extent independent, view to it. That is, her psychodynamic understanding of the patterns of peoples' inner lives, of the nature of human development, conflict, and adaptation, together with what she has learned from her work with other persons, will enlarge and enrich this picture. Her observations of the patient's behavior within the therapeutic situation and of the ways in which he relates to her will further add to it.

She may soon notice instances in which her views of the patient's story don't always match those held by him. The patient's present understandings appear limited, incomplete, contradictory, uninformed, even biased. Benevolently she finds herself skeptical of some of them. She knows, however, how any person's understanding of himself is motivated and shaped by conscious and unconscious emotional forces that provide reasons for its contents and limitations. On grounds of that understanding she will then aim at exploring, jointly with the patient, those reasons that interfere with his adaptation and comfort.

As we have said before listening in the clinical setting involves the therapist's maintaining a special sort of open-minded, expectant attention. This attitude allows her to construct a notion of who the patient is, what he is like, how he hangs together, and how he leads his life in the way he does. There may be *patterns* in his style of behaving, in how he tends to resist speaking freely, in the troubling issues he describes, in the features of his character, or of his relations with other people. Some of these seem to be clearly related to the patient's difficulties, but he gives no hint of seeing possible connections and meanings in what he brings forth. As the therapist develops her picture of the patient and adds her own impressions and ideas to it she forms a basis for making *interpretations*. She begins to tell the patient new things about himself. This news may be broad or narrow in scope. It can address anything from incidents noticed in the therapist's office to additional, not yet considered meanings of past events, to the purposes of some of the patient's character features, or to the possibility that certain symptoms may serve as disguised forms of communication. Providing such news is, after all, one of the psychotherapist's primary aims. She believes that changed understandings will affect a person's ways of dealing with himself, his circumstances, and his relations with others. Interpreting, then, is a major activity of the therapist, joining and interweaving with other activities such as facilitating the conversation, observing, and collecting information.

Interpreting amounts to a special form of commenting that requires caution, restraint, and tact. Its purpose is to recognize and identify some underlying meanings and reasons in what the patient says and does. The therapist will not jump in and right away try to interpret everything she hears. She will wait until the patient seems ready to hear her. She stays close to what seems to preoccupy him, avoids vague generalizations, and does not try to come up with explanations for everything. Occasionally the therapist may try to meet the patient halfway by merely hinting that something the patient says or does may have particular significance, the aforementioned suggestive comments. At other times she does more than merely hint. She may be more specific, direct, even attempting to explain to the patient what he might be having in mind.

One patient, for instance, has missed his regular appointment two weeks in a row. The therapist now simply points out the fact: "You have missed your appointment twice now without calling. What do you make of it?" She thus points to possible significance in this happening and implicitly calls for an explanation of what this piece of behavior might mean, what purpose it could serve. Under different circumstances she might say: "You had talked about some difficult and painful things last time we met, and then you missed the next two appointments. Were you afraid you might become upset again?" Here she suggests that the patient's staying away had a reason and offers a guess as to what that might be. Interpretations can be made in all sorts of different modes: as pointed observations, hints, suggestive questions, recognizing contradictions, or carefully, perhaps hypothetically stated, guesses at causal explanations involving the use of ". . . *because* . . ."

A brief, theoretical digression: Despite its prominent role in discussions of psychotherapy, the word *interpretation* is complex and in many ways ambiguous. Though Freud opened up our understanding of unconscious processes and their meanings he hardly uses the term "interpretation" in his writings unless he is talking about dreams. His use of the German word *Deutung* does not have the same quality of strictness or sharpness as has *interpretation*, its English cognate. Broadly it suggests the idea of one person giving another a sense of possible meaning of something that is not clearly known. There were times in the development of psychoanalytic technique when analysts strove to formulate crucial and precise interpretations of central meanings in a person's *neurotic* pattern, hoping to bring about its resolution more or less at once. Occasionally it may have been possible to accomplish this. Perhaps more often, intellectual constructions may have been the results rather than truly felt, emotional insight. As psychoanalytic thinking progressed it was understood that good therapeutic outcomes depended not as much on the patient's intellectual convictions. Actually experiencing neurotic problems and to some extent living through and exploring them (in the transference) as they affected the therapeutic relationship turned out to be a much more powerful vehicle of therapeutic change. There they are recognized, reviewed, and understood as they also appear in the patient's wider life contexts. In a process of *working through*, the therapist will point out familiar patterns to the patient when she sees them over and again. Both parties can experience and explore them in order to understand (as far as possible) how they came about and what adaptive aim the patient had been trying to accomplish through them. This all tends to be lengthy and difficult work. Psychotherapy can produce impressive results but does not often do it in the dramatic ways conveyed by novels and movies.

The acquisition of insights does not usually follow a linear path. The patient may begin to understand something of this and something of that within his inner life. Not all of it will have recognizable relevance to his distress or to what he talked about when articulating his "initial version." Single interpretations rarely produce immediate results that dramatically turn a person's life around. It even happens that having arrived at a given understanding, an *insight*, a patient will ask: "So what? What good is it to me to know this?" The therapist may feel quite challenged at such a moment. Even a bit lost. She may, truthfully, not be able to do more than convey an attitude such as that "we don't know yet what good it might be but we will see where it might lead us," thus proposing further exploration. The issue can be left open for the time being. Later, when contexts and circumstances make it relevant, the understanding may reappear in a new and useful light. At any rate it is not unreasonable to assume that any insight contributes, however slightly, to greater coherence within a person's mind and may bring small amounts of relief.

Back to practice: all interpretations involve some observation. Conversely, most, if not all, observations themselves point to possibilities of interpretation. Providing an observation, however modest, implicitly encourages the patient to respond by bringing further ideas. The therapist's comments here do not constitute small talk; they act as stimuli for generative and synthetic processes. For example a therapist could say, "You have on a green shirt today" (which the therapist has not seen before). To this the patient might respond: "This is my favorite one," or "This is my only clean shirt," or "On such a foggy day I needed to wear something cheerful." If the observation is coupled with an explanation of meaning, purpose, or origin it could be called an interpretation as in, for example: "I wonder if you have a green shirt on today because in our last session we talked so much about how your mood was beginning to change." Interpretations can also be incarnated as questions: "Do you think the feelings of disorientation and lack of control resemble how you felt upon your father's death?"

In practice, interpretations are often made first in the exploration of a patient's resistances, as in "You found it hard to tell me about this, perhaps because you thought I would criticize you for it." The patient might agree or not. In any case reference was made to an underlying reason and a challenge for further exploration implied. Aspects of transference may be subjected to interpretation as well. Sometimes this can happen early in the work. In the ex-

ample just given the therapist, referring to other parts of the material, could
have added, "just as you say your husband always does to you."

Connecting seemingly unrelated thoughts, fantasies, or feelings may result
in unexpected understandings. A young, happily married woman had spent
considerable time in therapy to work out her relationship with an apparently
insensitive, forever dissatisfied, and domineering mother. Her self-esteem and
confidence had improved considerably. One day she reported her surprise at
how angry she had been at her husband when she heard him once again mol-
lifying *his* mother, submissively catering to her. The patient could not understand the intensity of her rage. "Could it be," the therapist said, "that since *you*
have taken so much time and trouble to find ways of dealing with *your* mother
you resent that your husband doesn't seem to make a similar effort?" The patient sat up instantly: "That's it! That's exactly it!" she said and seemed relieved.

Patients, of course, reject some interpretations. They may say directly that
the therapist is wrong, that they don't know where she is coming from; or they
leave the matter open and undecided. Other interpretations, such as the one
just mentioned, are enthusiastically received, yet others more quietly. A statement such as "I never thought of it this way" can be a good sign of acceptance
by the patient. Another sign sometimes met with is the patient's saying something like: "I have always known this, but I haven't thought of it." In all instances of interpreting it is important to avoid authoritative or dogmatic
forms of commenting: arrange stones tentatively, as the Japanese master gar-
deners knew centuries ago. Overriding the patient's own views or disregard-
ing his resistances invites the patient to refuse the interpretation and also
causes resentment, temporary alienation, and even perhaps a disruption of
the alliance.

Seemingly quite remote matters may sometimes come to be connected by
interpretation. A woman who for years had endured a disastrous marriage,
until circumstances had ended it, one day reflected on being unable to remember any dreams for more than just a few seconds after she awoke each
day. The therapist said: "Maybe it is that dreams are like flimsy things that
can't hold their own against the hard reality of the morning?" In response the
patient then recalled that for years she had had an often recurring dream that
she remembered well. "In that dream I was crawling and crawling on the floor,
tried, but couldn't ever get up." "But isn't this exactly a picture of your marriage?" the therapist asked. "This is remarkable," the patient said, "you know I

never realized that!" She continued to indicate a sense of really having come to understand something.

In the example that follows the therapist's interpretation shows the patient that there is a connection and unifying meaning to a whole set of separate feelings, attitudes, and behavior.

BEATRICE

Beatrice, a thirty-two-year-old divorced woman, struggles with erotic feelings toward her male therapist. She brings him gifts despite his letting her know that he will not accept them. She cannot accept the boundaries of their professional relationship. She refuses to discuss her feelings around the gift giving except to challenge the therapist's limit setting. Each time he declines Beatrice gets angry, says something rude, and calls him during the week to apologize. The therapist decides to address this repetitive behavior the next hour and feels slightly anxious. During one of Beatrice's protestations the therapist interprets to her:

Th: You know, I think that you feel compelled to continue giving me things because it is a way for you to try to get something, something you were never able to succeed at getting. What that something might be is unclear for the time being.

Pt: What on earth are you talking about?

Beatrice flatly rejects what her therapist says and goes on to talk about wanting a relationship with him. The therapist listens, feeling rather deflated. He thinks back to his feeling anxious prior to the hour. By and by Beatrice says:

Pt: It's not as if I wanted to hurt you by giving you the gift.

Her therapist "instinctively" knows that this is the moment and interprets almost without thinking:

Th: No, but you hurt *yourself.* Can you see? You come with gifts, and when I refuse you feel rejected by me and get angry with me; then you will say something to me for which you feel terribly ashamed and need to apologize. And it happens over and over again. And why this is so needs to be understood.

Later on in the session Beatrice begins to talk about a man who has been interested in her and who has come up in their conversations only now and then. The following week she reports that she has agreed to go to the movies with him.

In this example you may have been aware that the therapist has the benefit of having followed the pattern of Beatrice's behavior and associations brought forth over a number of earlier sessions. In doing so he has prepared the soil for his interpretations. He has begun to perceive that the variety of things she is doing in her relationship with him serves the purpose of inviting rejection. Interestingly his first interpretation is rejected by her but sets the stage for what subsequently unfolds. The therapist's anxiety was likely based on some awareness that Beatrice would reject his comment. He realized that the interpretation would need to be repeated, which is what happened. The right moment came when Beatrice referred to a feeling, specifically one of pain. He could point out to her what she was doing. Then the therapist helped Beatrice see a likely connection between seemingly disparate feelings and behaviors, namely, giving gifts and arranging to be rejected. Interpretations of this sort can result in a greater sense of inner coherence as well as a more defined and purposeful quality to the patient's adaptations. In Beatrice's case the effect was to loosen the grip of the ways she related to the therapist. She could talk about another man and accept his offer of a date. The pattern will surely repeat itself, but important work had been done. It made possible further exploration of the emotions involved, of their tenacity and their power.

Of the therapist's activities interpretations are particularly important and powerful. They are by nature synthetic and provide the patient with new angles on his internal situation. In principle interpretations aim at pulling together and combining a variety of emotionally significant themes or groups of meanings evident in a patient's memories, fantasies, defensive operations, and affects. Because of their contradictory or conflicted relation some themes and meanings had remained unsettled in the person's development. Some became dissociated from one another as a result of the patient's defensive efforts, disconnection being the essential, common activity in all defenses. They separate conflicting thoughts and feelings and thus interfere with the coherence of a person's ego. By now bringing things together interpretations demonstrate and explain something in the patient's life. It could be a particular adaptive pattern, a symptom, an attitude, motive, or intention that influences the patient's experience and conduct. Interpretations aim at demonstrating the continuity of the influence of the patient's unconscious motivations. They also may point out to the patient how he repeatedly acts in certain ways that affect his getting on in life, things he has avoided or has been unable to recognize.

A patient may acquire new understandings in various ways. Outside of therapy a friend's perceptive and empathic observation may lead to a useful insight. Within therapy a patient sometimes makes discoveries all by himself. The safety of the therapeutic situation and the therapist's quiet presence allow him to think, remember, notice, or mull over things more readily than he can do alone or within the constraints of usual social settings. Therapists at times then hear patients spontaneously say things like: "I never noticed that . . ."; "Suddenly it seems to me as if . . ."; "I was not aware of this before . . ." Similar comments can indicate that understandings and insights pointed to by the therapist's interpretations have hit the mark.

On grounds of their experience but also of theoretical convictions therapists sometimes feel convinced that a particular interpretation would be the right one and should be offered. But to reiterate, interpretations should never be phrased in dogmatic terms. Most likely they would be roundly (and with good reason) resisted in such instances. As it is the therapist can never be sure that she is right. She can have ideas, guesses, and hypotheses and should present them in tentative terms. Interpretations then can become topics of joint exploration within the therapeutic alliance, matters to be studied by two equal participants in the work. Even if a particular new insight or understanding seems right and makes sense to both parties the patient may still try to discredit and discard it. The patient may worry that his new understanding has consequences, that it obliges him to make changes in his life, perhaps both internal and external, which he finds too frightening. Although he has come to therapy precisely in order to accomplish changes he is not ready to engage them fully right away. Patients occasionally leave therapy just when it seems to reach some success. Others continue until they can find ways to fit their new understandings comfortably into their way of living. Much of this work is done in the process of working through.

33

Working Through

And time yet for a hundred indecisions,
And for a hundred visions and revisions

—T. S. Eliot, *The Love Song of J. Alfred Prufrock*

The patient may have understood the therapist's interpretation, but this does not at all mean that he has modified his ways of thinking, his adaptations. The interpretation has been accepted but may be understood merely intellectually, not on emotional, even visceral, levels. When we speak of *working through*, we refer to the application of the interpretation in whatever context it becomes relevant. We think of the therapist and patient together trying to muse about its implications. By working through with the therapist's assistance the patient sees more and more how his ways are influenced by issues that he has come to know through interpretation. The patient assimilates, fortifies, and expands existing understandings.

A dynamic view of psychotherapy and working through go hand in hand. You really cannot have one without the other. And this is because a dynamic psychology is a psychology of internal motion and change. Old patterns and the trouble they cause will recur under different sets of circumstances. And they will need to be revisited over and over again as they meet up with new challenges and opportunities for relating. Also, shifts in how we view others and ourselves will require exploration in different situations. The more the patient can work through his issues—now this way, now that way, from this angle, from that angle, in this context, in that context—the more he will know his bungling old ways and the more he can integrate and solidify more adaptive ways of being, though they be nascent and shaky at first. Working through is really always *reworking*.

Working through may well constitute the main work of therapy. While much of it often takes place later in the course of therapy it should not be thought of as a distinct and separate phase in time. One couldn't really say of someone "he hasn't reached the working through phase yet." Working through, like interpreting, can happen at any time in the therapeutic process. Indeed the dovetailing that occurs between interpretive work and working through is a very good example of the nonlinear process of psychotherapy.

Working through is also the tough part of psychotherapy. It is characterized by active confrontation by the therapist of the patient ("It is interesting what you are doing"; "You are retreating"; "You are finding it necessary to . . ."). This confrontation, however, is not to be misconstrued as hostile or as scolding. Rather, the therapist is bringing to the patient's attention in a very direct way his tendency to repeat. Working through, in fact, can be thought of as the counteraction to repetition, as an effort to interfere with the patient's regressive tendency to fall back into older and troublesome forms of adaptation. The therapist puts her weight behind the importance of this recognition. In essence the therapist is saying, "There you go again. These are our understandings. The understandings that we have worked hard at getting. This is not the past now. This is the present. Now that you know this you'd better go and do something about it." This stance may project a dose of suggestion. The therapist is endorsing the patient's acting as an autonomous person who on his own goes and actively does something on his behalf. When recurrences happen the patient and therapist recognize that, because of the varieties of contexts involved, they will not always be totally identical. The more these recurrences or repetitions are worked through, reworked, strengthened, and confirmed the more will be the therapeutic gains the patient has made.

PHILLIP

In outline form the following case illustrates a person's repetitive patterns that required a great deal of working through before they could finally be sufficiently mitigated: Phillip, a teacher in his forties, had an irregular job history of teaching in a number of schools for short periods of a few years, sometimes only months, each. The quality of his work was good and would find recognition. But there was trouble in his relations with colleagues and, in particular, with his superiors. With them, he usually had fallings-out after having worked for a while in any given setting. He would begin to sense them as being deceptive in their friendliness toward him and would suspect that somehow they were scheming against him. Several times in his career he suddenly left a job, sometimes before he even had given notice. More than once he packed up his belongings in the middle of the night and left without having made arrangements for where to go. He came to therapy on his own initiative, driven by a vague feeling that something was very wrong; whether with him or with the people around him he was not sure.

Phillip's mother had died early in his life. During his years in high school, Phillip took care of his slowly dying father, who showed no gratitude for what his son did for him. On the contrary he constantly criticized and demeaned him and was dissatisfied with everything Phillip did or was. There had been no reconciliation before he finally died.

Phillip was quite eager to enter therapy. He paid a modest fee and, for some time, handled this responsibly. Later his payments became irregular, partly because there were phases of his being between jobs. Occasionally he brought gifts, however, and did so again several times even though the therapist gently instructed Phillip that gifts could not be accepted. Phillip took this hard and found it incomprehensible. He saw no problem with not paying his bill on one hand but spending money on presents for the therapist on the other. At one point the therapist ventured to interpret his behavior to Phillip as an effort to obtain the therapist's gratitude and appreciation, even to force him to come forth with it. For many months Phillip resented and resisted this interpretation. At the same time, however, exploration of the dissatisfaction that led him to repeatedly leave jobs showed the same dynamics at work. A great deal of working through had to be accomplished before Phillip could fully recognize them when, once again, he could not find the singular recognition, praise, affection, and gratitude that he intensely, unrealistically, and like a desperate child, hoped to receive from his superiors. The situation repeated itself again and again as always still another effort to reach an impossible goal. In some instances the therapist became able to recognize through hints in the therapeutic relation that tensions in the job situation would soon rise again.

Working through his feelings, wishes, and hopes with Phillip made it possible for him to put his demands into their proper place, to anticipate and prevent further crises, and to gradually develop more balanced and stable relations with the people around him.

34

Termination

Things move into shadows and they vanish; things return in the shape of an echo.

—Lu Chi (261 A.D.), *Wen Fu: The Art of Writing*

The psychotherapeutic work that a patient and a therapist have done together and the relationship they have maintained both have to end some time. In many clinical situations, or under the terms set by sources of insurance, preordained time limits have defined the ending date right at the beginning of the work. Such constraints affect how widely the patient could become involved and how much therapeutic exploration would be possible. If no external constraints require the therapy to be stopped at a specified time its end may come to be approached once an impression has been formed by either or both parties that some useful work has been accomplished. Under these more fortunate circumstances the termination process can emerge on its own power and dynamics. A variety of dynamic issues relating to the ending of treatment can then be explored, worked through, and understood. Motivations, quite unique and specific to an individual case, influence the developing agreement to finish, to postpone, or even to avoid termination as long as possible. *Termination*, then, is not simply an ending; instead it shows itself as a complex and significant process.

Let us look at this process. At the beginning of this book we spoke of psychotherapy as an activity that has many characteristics of a craft. The exercise of a craft results in a product. In the course of psychotherapy the nature and quality of the product become progressively formulated and shaped within the work done jointly by therapist and patient. The product is a changed pattern of the patient's inner experience, one that is less conflicted and more internally coherent. If things go well it paves the way for the modification of some of the patient's adaptations, his ways of living.

Here we review how things can be at the conclusion of a reasonably successful course of psychotherapy. In such cases, especially in the presence of a developed therapeutic alliance, a substantial and cooperative termination process can occur. An end of the therapy comes into view once a patient confidently senses that his situation has improved. The complaint that brought him to the work is gone or much mitigated. Other issues that had come to light have dissipated or come under control. He may be less angry, anxious, depressed, or lonely. His work or studies go better. He finds himself more optimistic about the future, has formed plans, and made preparations. The patient feels he understands himself better, is more content with himself, and perhaps likes himself more than before. He now sees how some of his difficulties had resulted from early painful or traumatic events. He recognizes that some arose from attempts to make adaptations based on hopeful fantasies, efforts to escape anxieties, but also on ignorance and misunderstandings, and frequently on old irrational feelings that have no more basis in his present life. He feels back in the saddle, to use a common saying. He has developed new supports from friends, family, and colleagues or partners that might have been available to him before but that he had been unable to recognize or receive. Closeness and intimacy with some make his existence feel richer and more worthwhile. He can let himself love. He can see others with different eyes. He understands them better, is less afraid, more tolerant, more objective. He recognizes others more clearly as people with their own natures and concerns.

He may feel differently within himself as well. What he thinks or feels appears more vivid, clear, and interesting. He can stand back and observe himself, be perhaps less vulnerable to being carried away by sudden impulses, desires, or affects. Most important he senses himself as more able to sort things out for and by himself. *He can do his own psychological work better.* Even though, as expected, not all his problems and dilemmas have been solved he feels more confident in coping and coming to terms with them. Comprehension deepens of the ongoing continuity of life with its challenges, ambiguities, new conflicts, and possible reawakening of old ones. Greater tolerance within him leads to greater ease and self-assurance. Such are some of the varieties of improvement.

When either patient or therapist, or both, come to feel that they have done good work and that it would make sense to come to an end they do not instantly discontinue the sessions. Instead a desire to explore what ending means to each one begins to arise silently and in time enters their conversation. In this context a sharper focus may develop once a termination date comes to be discussed. Agreeing upon it provides for a clearly and jointly anticipated ending.

Either party's prematurely discontinuing the therapy may, on the other hand, end the treatment too. In this case, however, the patient's unspoken anxieties, his resentments, paralyzing conflicts, overwhelming defenses, or negative transference, just as his hopes, desires, and positive transference feelings, would remain untouched. Disturbing effects on the patient's adaptations could result. Patients at times do provoke early endings to escape an unsatisfying relationship with the therapist that they feel unable to discuss, or to avoid frightening confrontations with their inner lives. Others "flee into health," insisting suddenly that they feel much better. They appear more confident and optimistic, consider themselves cured, and cheerfully disappear. Some return later if their conscious or unconscious disavowal of any difficulty or discomfort fails.

In any case leavings are never without feelings, some of them painful. Regressions may result in the termination phase; some of the patient's conflicts may surface again. This offers another chance to work through existing and even newly awakened issues. Such regressions can be driven by a patient's desire to relive the treatment once more, even to repeat it. Let us take a look at the case of Eva.

EVA

Eva, twenty-three, a nursing student, had been in twice-weekly therapy for about two-and-a-half years. She had been struggling for some time with nightmares, which she came to understand as being tied to her attempts to assert herself and separate from an extremely chaotic and violent family. During the therapy Eva had begun to take important steps toward her independence. She refused, for example, to spend more than half a day with her family on Christmas. Eva also suffered from facial acne. These "flare ups" as she would call them were her life's curse. She was ashamed of her skin, which bore scars. The work of the therapy contributed to her decision to undergo a dermatological treatment that vastly improved her appearance, and a new medication began to reduce her flare ups. She began to feel beautiful for the first time in her life and was able to look at herself in the mirror for more than brief moments at a time. Eva was also able to enjoy shopping and described how she would "put herself together" in ways more colorful and coordinated than she was accustomed to doing.

With termination at hand Eva's acne flared up again. During this phase of the therapy, which lasted four to five months, these flare ups came to be understood as a reaction to the stress and fear of ending. Her nightmares, which had decreased, also intensified once again. In one Eva dreamed that her dermatologist took it upon himself to go ahead with a surgical intervention, during which he lost control of his scalpel. This resulted in a facial cut that bled profusely; from it emerged a devilish monster with sharp teeth. At various times throughout this phase of the therapy Eva would be overcome with anxiety and find it difficult to speak.

In this important phase of the work Eva and her therapist were able to further an understanding of what their ending had activated. In a grand way Eva was wrestling with the question "Can I leave?" They came to know that both the nightmare and the acne expressed Eva's profound fear and conviction that the world was a place in which she could have no control over what happened. Additional meanings of the nightmare appeared in her associations to the dream. Thus Eva wondered if the scalpel slipped accidentally or if the doctor deliberately disfigured her. She reflected on the meanness of her family as she tried to assert herself and their willingness to "cut her down," hurt and shame her. She was able to wonder aloud if her therapist was angry at her leaving. Could she handle Eva's leaving? Eva's growing? Eva's increasing attractiveness? Would she also say or do something mean, open up old wounds, possibly create new ones? With these questions articulated and explored Eva was able to express her own anger at having to lose someone she had grown to trust, and to understand how anger was extremely frightening to her. For Eva to leave in a meaningful way required that she recognize this, the process of separating having been inhibited by a dreaded unconscious identification with her raging and sadistic family members. Related horror and shame asserted themselves in a return of her nightmares, acne, and feelings of confusion and chaos. For Eva anger and chaos went hand in hand. Leaving therapy exposed the question of whether she could express her anger without repeating the sins of her family. Could she do things differently? Indeed could she *be* differently?

A number of processes can be seen at work here serving synthetic and defensive purposes in various combinations. Eva was putting herself together in new ways: she was able to experience and express herself—psyche and soma— as more coordinated and colorful. She also experienced confusion and chaos. It seems that regression here functioned as a resistance to facing difficult feelings around separation. Eva's confusion protected her, for example, from angry feelings, those monsters that caused her debilitating guilt and anxiety. The graphic nature of her dream exposed the intensity of these feelings, how closely connected to the body they were for her, and the violence of their release. The image of the dermatologist in the dream also alluded to feelings in the transference. Was the doctor good or dangerous? In intensely working through the termination together Eva and her therapist witnessed a flare up of the internal drama now within the context of new and greater understanding. Her life had new meaning. She could experience its layers, its complexity, its multifaceted and malleable nature, its continuity, and its vastness.

Amidst therapeutic gains termination involves loss. And there are feelings on both sides. Both the therapist and patient have to realize emotionally that they are parting. For both the interest and involvement with each other will lose its manifest object. So they must delve into the meanings of separation. They must mourn the loss of their relationship. For the patient mourning may involve the relinquishment of fanciful and idealized notions once held; of ways of doing or feeling; of accustomed, even though distressing, existential positions. Therapeutic work can destroy illusions. Termination involves the review and endorsement of new understandings, constructive new adaptive steps, solutions, and accomplishments. The old ways are worn and familiar. The new ways have to be broken in. They feel unfamiliar, even a little chilly.

The patient's transferences to both the therapist and the therapy itself will be present. They may be remembered and recognized, in speech, in unspoken understanding, or in the attitudes that shaped how the two partners related to each other. The unspoken fantasies that influenced the meanings the work had for both patient and therapist are likely to reappear in both partners' feelings about their impending separation. Some patients may experience ending as supportive, nourishing, cleansing, freeing, receiving respect, absolution, defeat, winning. Some may view the ending as a form of relief or loss, abandonment, as a graduation, as having successfully weathered something, gone through a process of revelation, discovery, reconciliation, the reception of a new assignment. Some of the mixture of such feelings will be sensed, articulated, understood, coped with, and then carried away.

As for the therapist she may feel pleased, relieved, and proud of her work. The patient's courage in exposing himself may have impressed her. Or she may be disappointed that she has not done her job thoroughly or well enough. She might think that her patient had not come as far as she had hoped he might. She is frustrated and left in doubt of her competence, all depending on how she thinks of the outcome of the work and of the patient's chances for a better life. She will measure this outcome in relation to the agenda that had guided her work.

Reacting to the impending separation and loss patient and therapist at times feel tempted to modify the stances that they have maintained in relation to each other in the therapeutic sessions. Patients often try to move the therapist away from her restraint and to get to know her in a more conventional way. Long-held curiosity may be expressed through personal questions. They might concern the therapist's story: of her person and way of life, her views of the patient, whether she likes him, might give him a good grade for his conduct and accomplishments in the sessions. Some patients indicate interest in entering a real, personal relationship, of becoming friends with the therapist. Such desires need to be recognized, explored, understood, and reviewed with regard to the continuing value and importance of the therapist's neutrality. The requirements set by professional standards will be part of the background of conversations about these things.

Some patients ask for a diagnosis, prognosis, or grand formulation of their case. Perhaps under the patient's pressure to serve their own sense of closure or to account for themselves to the patient, therapists occasionally do provide summaries of sorts. We think that such summations are best avoided. Things a therapist has come to understand with sufficient confidence should probably have been communicated to the patient at earlier times when they had emerged in the therapeutic process. Patients should not be made to feel that the therapist had secretly collected and withheld important knowledge from them to be revealed in the end. Rather, they should know that, within the therapeutic alliance, the therapist was always *with* them and shared whatever had come to be jointly understood.

No grand summaries, then. But sometimes a last hour brings a naturally arising conversation, a review of how it all was. The therapist might point to gains that both agree have taken place. She may endorse them gently and in this way direct some of the patient's positive feelings toward her upon these gains, perhaps reinforcing them a little by doing so. Discussion may also turn to unfinished issues; material, possibly, for another piece of work at another time.

Some patients make efforts to rise up again from the regression, from the free flowing mode of conversation the therapy had induced; they strive to cover things up again. In the following, we see how Warren, a thirty-four-year-old playwright, struggles with the impulse to do this.

Warren had been in therapy for a little over a year; then he was offered a job out of state and accepted it. He had come to therapy for depression and had been struggling with a block to his creativity and with being single. "Getting off his duff" and looking actively for a girlfriend had been difficult for him. In an emotional session about a month before termination Warren reported a dream. He found himself in his therapist's bedroom. Both were standing, looking at the bed. Warren remarked that the bed was messy. The sheets and blankets were pulled back. In his associations to the dream he reflected on similarities between relationships and the creative process. He explained how shameful expressing his feelings and needs had always been, how messy they were, how so often he didn't know where he was going. Toward the end of the session Warren mentioned the upcoming termination in a direct and forthright way. He told of how messy the prospect of ending was to him, how alone he would feel without his therapist, how frightened he was of all of this, yet how grateful for the experience. Would he ever see his therapist again? And he began to cry. The therapy then began to focus on what it was like for Warren to allow the bed to remain uncovered and messy, for new feelings to emerge even at this late date, feelings he might never be able to put entirely to rest. What it was for him to resist premature and inadequate closure and talk about his feelings.

The temptation to pull away from the regression that reigned through large parts of the work can be strong, even fierce, for some. The patient's defenses tend to be reinstalled; new ones may be added. Warren and Eva could have chosen to turn away from what was being newly uncovered. Impulses to close up wounds, pull up bed covers, to make surfaces appear nice and neat were all experienced at a time in which it was still possible to recognize their operation and bring them into the therapeutic conversation. In the course of extended therapies fluctuations between regressive phases and periods of recovery to more conventional modes will be encountered.

Warren's dream is interesting in that it involved not just any house, but the therapist's house, not just any bed, but the therapist's bed. This suggests his curiosity about his therapist and further transference issues, including sexual fantasies, which had not yet appeared. What is her life like beyond the consulting room? What are *her* dreams, *her* loves? It may also refer to a wish that his therapist not forget him. That she will not cover over her memory of Warren and of their intimate connection, of the room that may have come, in some unspoken way, to be called *their own.*

Some patients experience the *object loss* that comes with termination as leading to emptiness and impoverishment. They look for compensation, for something of the therapist's to take away with them. Something to go with, perhaps a photograph or a prescription of sorts. If she is a psychiatrist she may literally provide a last refill of medicine. Or the patient asks for one of the above-mentioned closing summaries, some last-minute advice on how to cope with anxiety, acting as if anxiety was never explored during the therapeutic process. Little children often need a picture of their therapist or something from the therapy room to take with them when they leave. Always, though, the patient will carry away memories of the therapist. Some of the therapist's ways may enter into his own behavioral repertoire. The patient continues an internal conversation where he plays out both roles, effectively internalizing aspects of his relationship with the therapist. Identifying with the therapist or with some of her characteristics during periods of positive transference may have preceded this. Perhaps he took some of his inner pictures of her into his own sense of identity, becoming like her in some respects. This can particularly be the case if the patient himself is involved in some sort of work with people. *Identification* (as we discussed in chapter 4), a mostly unconscious process, occurs not rarely as a consequence of significant separations in everyone's life. Here it is important to underscore that what is taken in by the patient is not only the therapist but the *relationship* between them, that is, the ways in which the two connected with one another.

Approaching termination both parties may well recognize that no therapy settles all the patient's issues for the rest of his life. Nonetheless, sufficient time should be allotted to the termination process so that neither be left surprised, distressed, or with profoundly unsettled feelings. The covers may be off the bed, but they are not flapping wildly about. The extent of this process can be somewhat proportional to the length of the treatment as a whole. Even in a single-session consultation, for example, the therapist might try to inform the patient that only a few more minutes are available near the end of the hour.

In the following vignette we observe the patient, Madelyn, whom you know by now, during the final hour. Madelyn's was a therapy of about eight months, a therapy that ended because she was leaving the country to pursue a doctorate overseas. Although therapist and patient had extensively discussed termination in the weeks prior to ending, the session shows them still poignantly speaking about unfinished business and Madelyn's feelings toward therapist and therapy. It also shows how old issues can be referred to again, and how new ones can surface right up to the end. The centrality of conflict emerges in Madelyn's talk of "mixed feelings." We see evidence of efforts to put them into coherent contexts and notice how she seems to have understood the difference between what goes on in *her* inner world and what may be the realities of *others*. Of note Madelyn is a patient who is unusually capable of expressing herself. For many who are beginning to learn this craft such a patient may be the exception rather than the rule.

Pt: Hi. This is our last session.

Th: Yes, it is.

Pt: It's very strange. (*Silence*)

Th: What are you thinking?

Pt: It's just so strange. Unnatural. To be stopping now. It seems like we just got started. I've gotten used to coming here. Coming here breaks up my day. (*Smiles.*) At least my day won't be broken up. Seems that I've only just started to explore things. That's why it feels so strange to be ending. Funny I can't even remember what it was I came in with. Hmm. What did I come in with? I can't for the life of me remember. Anyway, I've gotten a lot out of being here.

Th: There is a bittersweet tone to your voice.

Pt: Yes. (*Looks pensive. Silence*) I'm looking forward to going to London, but I'm also a little scared. Will I feel lonely? Will I be able to do the work? Can you come with me? (*Laughs.*)

Th: Tell me about that last bit.

Pt: (*Smiles bashfully.*) I wish that you could come with me. That we didn't have to stop. It feels like we're stopping in the middle of something. I know we discussed this, but it feels really intense today. I feel that you've understood me. (*Pause*) Can you give me some advice?

Th: What do you have in mind?

Pt: Well, London will be new to me. Any advice on what to do if I feel lonely?

Th: (*Hmm. Thinks: We've talked about this. What does this mean?*) You know we've talked about this before. Perhaps its coming up again now has to do with this being our last session.

Pt: (*She is silent for a time, then nods.*) Yes, I think so. I'm just nervous about how I'm going to do without you.

Th: Go on.

Pt: That's it. (*Silence*)

Th: Something tells me there's more. More feeling perhaps.

Pt: Well, maybe I'm still a little angry. About our ending. Angry that I'll have to go it alone. That I'm not all "cured."

Th: You said that you'd gotten a lot out of therapy, but there are also things you didn't get.

Pt: (*Nods.*) What I got was not necessarily what I thought I would get when I came. (*Pause*) I think maybe I did expect a cure. But there was nothing really to cure. There was nothing really wrong. Just these large issues to think about and explore. Like the future and relationships. Oh! Something happened. I asked this man out. He's new to my movie club, and I just took this liking to him. He's really insightful, really nice looking. At least I think so. So, I said to myself, "Well, are you just going to sit there?" So I asked him out. And he said that he'd like that. So we're going for a walk around campus Saturday morning. I know I'll be leaving soon, but I consider this practice. When I asked my friends what to do they said, "Ask him out!" . . . I get scared. I'm concerned about what people will think if it just . . . well, if it's uncomfortable again, and he doesn't want to see me again, even as a friend. But I know my friends. They're good people. They've listened to me before and have been helpful. Oh, that's one of the issues I came here with! Asking for people's advice. (*Pause*) Oh, and you know there's another issue I wanted to bring up. The automobile factory I've been studying is definitely going on strike. I've gotten to know the employees very well and have come to relate to them. I've been thinking about this a lot—going back and forth. My feelings, well, they're mixed. (*Smiles*) I want to join them on the picket line. I think that the management is exploiting the workers. My parents think I'm nuts. Some of my friends do as well. But others don't. They're concerned that this will affect my education, that it will interfere with my getting a Ph.D. I think I can understand this. But I believe that the more experience a person gets the better. No one's going to blacklist me. I think. I guess I'm afraid of that. But I also feel that it's the right thing to do. I want to take what I think is the moral high ground.

Th: You know, you were talking about advice and then moved on to the strike. I think maybe the two are connected. And in this way. You seem to be struggling with the idea of determining for yourself what's in your best interests. Weighing different opinions, and then judging for yourself, even if that's difficult.

Pt: Yes, I think that's right. I asked a lot of people. But when all is said and done I have to do what my conscience tells me to do. What's going on in the factory is wrong. My parents are business owners, and they take a very different position from me. Well, at least I imagine that they would. They don't know of my decision. I mean I imagine they would, based on what I know them to be. By this I mean my internal parents. It's an internal process. I really don't know what they'll say when I tell them. They may actually be proud of me. Oh, I don't know. All this talk of taking the moral high ground. Sometimes I think it's all intellectual gobbledygook. Maybe I should just think in purely practical ways.

Th: Well, intellectually you can think of this as the welfare of the masses as opposed to the privileged few. But in the very real life situation you are telling me about you are asking, "What about me? What do I think? What are my convictions? What do I want to do?" In fact I wonder if the therapy itself can be thought of as having addressed that question "What about me?"

Pt: Yes. I've spent much of the last two years thinking about what was meaningful to me, what I wanted to spend my time doing. This is meaningful to me. This situation at the factory. And I think I have come to a decision. But it's been hard. I'm taking a stand. And I think I can do it without feeling as though I am going to hurt people or burden them with my activism.

Th: You came in to therapy feeling that you were a burden.

Pt: That's right. I did. But I don't feel that way anymore. And I haven't for a long time.

Th: As I think about this what may have been burdensome for you then was struggling with your mixed feelings, being able to sit with them yourself.

Pt: Mixed feelings seem to have been very important for me. And articulating difficult feelings has made them easier to handle. When I have these mixed feelings I tend to ask people for advice, and then I feel burdensome. Whenever I think of asking my parents for advice it's with hesitation. They are not neutral you know. They are emotionally entangled. Even my friends are really not neutral. Better than my parents but not neutral. People all bring their own stuff to any discussion. (*Silence*) In here I can better hear myself think. I guess what I've also gotten from this are connections. There are many issues that all seem connected. I wonder how I'm going to make those connections without therapy.

(*Silence*)

Th: What are you thinking about?

Pt: Well, I guess I could go back to journaling. But a journal doesn't respond to you.

Th: No, it doesn't.

(*Silence*)

Th: A moment ago you brought up the idea of an internal process. What do you think of the idea that there may be aspects of our work that you can carry with you, inside?

Pt: What do you mean?

Th: Well, that you have struggled with doing things for yourself here. You've worked hard at making tough decisions like joining a picket line; making independent moves like asking someone out on a date.

Pt: That's right. Maybe I can do more than I give myself credit for . . . And I can always get therapy at the university in England. It won't be this, but I guess it'll be something else.

Th: (*Nods and smiles.*) You know, in the last few months we've dealt with many issues. One might think of this therapy, being your first, as a kind of overture of themes in your life: your sexuality, relationships, thinking for yourself. I think that all these issues invite further exploration, should you decide to do this again.

Pt: We've really just scratched the surface, haven't we? I'd heard about therapy from friends, and my sister's been in therapy for years. She loves it.

Th: You never mentioned that.

Pt: No, I guess I didn't. Well, I don't see her much. She's in France. I told you that she had problems but I guess talking about that wasn't as important to me as other things. She had a very hard time several years ago, but things are much better for her. (*Madelyn looks at the clock.*) Wow! (*Silence*) I guess we're about out of time. (*Therapist nods and says yes quietly. Silence*) I'm going to miss you, you know. This has been a really good experience.

Th: (*Smiles.*) We've worked closely together and on some very difficult issues.

Pt: Yeah. (*Silence*) I'm really happy I came. (*Awkward pause*) I'll send you a postcard.

Th: (*Smiles.*) I would like that. Thank you. (*Pause*) When exactly are you leaving?

Pt: End of July. I'll be stopping in D.C. for a week to see a friend, then I'm off to London.

Th: You've got a lot ahead of you.

Pt: Yeah. I'm excited. I'm happy that I'll be studying abroad. I feel very good about it. It's an adventure. But we talked about all of that. (*Pause*) So . . . well . . . okay. I guess I'll be taking my leave! (*The therapist looks at the clock and follows her patient's lead. Madelyn collects her things. They slowly get up from their chairs. Madelyn looks directly at her therapist and their gaze meets.*) Thanks again.

Th: (*Nods.*) You're welcome. All the very best to you.

Pt: Okay then. Thanks. (*Smiles, then walks to the door, opens it, and turns back to the therapist.*) Bye.

Th: (*Smiles.*) Bye now. (*Sits down, takes a deep breath, exhales, and is quiet.*)

No therapy then is ever final. It is always just a piece of work because life goes on. New adaptations are required ever again. Unrecognized unconscious issues may be stirred. One hopes that the patient's own psychological work and development will continue with greater ease. A sufficiently positive experience, even though it has had to be brief, might encourage the patient to turn to psychological assistance again if needed. In a way psychotherapy can result in a kind of upheaval in which unrecognized aspects of a person's inner life are given a chance to be known. It can allow the emergence of continually newer versions of the initial story with which the patient began. But not all issues will have been put to rest. Therapy ends because it must. No elusive happiness has been achieved, not all problems are solved. But the patient's understanding of himself has improved. He is better at coping with internal struggles. Perhaps he will pause and choose to handle himself differently where before he would never have considered such. Ideally the patient will find himself able to create more and different versions of his personal tale as life and its vicissitudes continue. The work cannot be expected to have settled the patient's life for eternity. To summon Loren Eiseley once again, there are things still brewing in the oceanic vat, down there still to come ashore.

VI

Ingredients of Change

35

Active Elements in Productive Psychotherapeutic Work

It is time to review and summarize our thoughts about psychodynamic psychotherapy as we have tried to describe them in this book. We began by stressing the importance of a person's inner life and of the individual psychological work he does for his own inner coherence and for his adaptation to the surrounding world. When such work fails him and he finds himself in inner distress and psychological pain he may turn to the psychotherapist for assistance. He becomes a "patient."

We went on to describe the things the psychotherapist can offer in the practice of her craft. There are, to begin with, her theoretical views. They comprise her understanding of how peoples' inner worlds come into being, of their contents, the forces and processes that organize them, and of the forms and expressions of inner conflicts. We introduced the considerations that guide the therapist in creating a setting for joint psychological work with the patient. We discussed the workshop and the tools of her craft. Finally, through various examples, we tried to show the therapist's activities in different but reasonably typical phases of her work. We reviewed how she brings her skills to bear, how mistakes may happen, and how progress may be achieved.

Ideas about the nature of therapeutic progress are implied throughout the book. Although they are sometimes hard to judge we encounter signs of progress in patients' reactions throughout the work, in hearing about changes they have made in their lives and in their overall attitude. They also include the person's sense of relief from burdensome or painful feelings. They appear in evidence of increased self-understanding, of clearer awareness of serious desire, of important aims and purposes, and also of the sources of anxieties, of cumbersome inhibitions, and unnecessary restraints. A sense of greater inner calm and enlarged personal freedom can indicate a useful therapeutic experience.

In the following we summarize some of the active elements we feel contribute to productive psychotherapeutic work.

1. *Basic trust.* The psychotherapeutic process is greatly aided, especially near its beginning, if at some time in his life the patient has had at least some experience of another person's concern, care, or helpfulness. If so this will contribute to the development of a workable therapeutic relationship. As that relationship grows it may itself serve to strengthen the patient's trust. If such was lacking to begin with it may have a chance to develop slowly and painfully in the course of the work.

2. *The therapist's humanity.* Her essential patience, benevolence, honesty, straightforwardness, good faith, inner soundness, and consistency, things that must surround any theoretical knowledge, will not be lost on the patient. His sense of these qualities will persist despite any momentary lapses in the therapist's judgment and emotional control.

3. *Emotional relief.* At any time throughout treatment, perhaps even during just a first or single session, a person in acute distress or overwhelmed by accumulated affects such as intense anxiety, rage, confusion, despair may experience some relief. Being heard by a receptive, respectful, and open-minded listener and not being and feeling all alone may prepare the ground for further therapeutic work.

4. *Stating his case in speech.* Putting his circumstances into words in a tolerant setting may assist the patient in allowing himself to formulate previously unspeakable things. Spoken things can be thought about, organized, kept in mind. This may further his capacity to stand back from pressing concerns.

5. *The frame.* A clearly defined work situation providing consistency and privacy offers the patient the opportunity to speak as openly to the therapist as he might speak to himself, a fact that sets the therapeutic relation apart from other social encounters.

6. *Emphasis on inner life.* Another element is the therapist's committed view of the value and importance of a person's inner life for his adaptation and for the way he goes about living in his world.

7. *Widening awareness.* The therapist's effort in assisting the patient in exploring matters to which he is usually not prepared to pay attention, to go further and into wider contexts than he would ever have done by himself. This involves looking for more detail, encouraging longer pursuits of trends of thought and fantasy, exploration of previously unthinkable ideas, and increased consideration of feelings.

8. *The therapeutic alliance.* An atmosphere of collaboration, facilitated by the secure setting and the therapist's active interest, aids the patient in directing his attention to his inner life and activity. It supports joint efforts to appreciate and understand the patient's situation and his ways of dealing with himself.

9. *Awareness of resistance.* The patient's developing recognition that he consciously and unconsciously censors his thoughts, fantasies, and feelings, and that he does so because of various anxieties, demands of conscience, shame, and many other reasons. Their exploration can open the way to wider insights.

10. *Exploration of basic desires and aims.* Articulation of the patient's driving motives, desires, hopes, and purposes; their reasons and aims in his actions and relations. Such exploration can include their carryover into the therapy and allow examination of how they are lived out in the relationship with the therapist.

11. *Recognition of inner conflict.* The patient's growing understanding that important choices and adaptations are powerfully shaped and driven, sometimes paralyzed, by conflicts between different motivations, that unknowingly and repeatedly he sometimes pursues contradictory and mutually exclusive aims. The therapist's interpretations may assist in clarifying such conflicts and in understanding them in wider contexts.

12. *The therapist's neutrality.* Provides equal and receptive attention to different sides of the patient's conflicts, paired with a "benevolent skepticism."

13. *Complexity of perspectives.* The patient's recognition that the story of his life and development can be understood in multiple ways. Knowing this may contribute to increased awareness of choices and development of his convictions.

14. *Internalization.* The therapist's interest in the patient's inner processes as well as her nonpunitive, objective attitude comes to be taken in by the patient to some degree as is the quality of their relationship.

15. *Working through.* Applying newly gained understandings of conflictual matters, some of them possibly recognized through the relation with the therapist, to the patient's coping with issues in his current life. This involves benevolent but active confrontation of their implications, contexts, and alternatives.

16. *Termination.* A carefully worked-through process entered into once the patient finds himself sufficiently able to do psychological work on his own. And also finally to leave the therapeutic relation with a sense of relative independence and completion.

36

Meditation

Near the end of C. S. Lewis's book the Witch deals the mighty Lion, Aslan, a mortal blow. In the "dead calm" of that terrible night, Susan and Lucy cry till they haven't any more tears. The following morning, however, who should stand before them "shining in the sunrise, larger than they had seen him before" but Aslan himself. Joyful, but taken aback, the girls wonder how this can be.

"Oh, you're real, you're real! Oh, Aslan!" cried Lucy, and both girls flung themselves upon him and covered him with kisses.

"But what does it all mean?" asked Susan when they were somewhat calmer.

"It means," said Aslan, "that though the Witch knew the Deep Magic, there is a magic deeper still which she did not know. Her knowledge goes back only to the dawn of time. But if she could have looked a little further back, into the stillness and the darkness before Time dawned, she would have read there a different incantation...."

"Oh, children," said the Lion, "I feel my strength coming back to me."
—C. S. Lewis, *The Lion, the Witch, and the Wardrobe*

References and Recommended Readings

American Psychiatric Association. *Diagnostic and Statistical Manual of Mental Disorders*, 4th ed. Washington, D.C.: American Psychiatric Association, 1994.

Audette, Anna Held. *The Blank Canvas: Inviting the Muse.* Boston: Shambhala Publications, 1993, pp. 5–6, 44.

Balsam, Rosemary M., and Alan Balsam. *Becoming a Psychotherapist: A Clinical Primer.* Boston: Little, Brown, 1974.

Breuer, Josef, and Sigmund Freud. *Studies on Hysteria.* In ed. and trans. J. Strachey, *The Standard Edition of the Complete Psychological Works of Sigmund Freud*, vol. 2, pp. 21–22, 153, 272. London: Hogarth Press, 1955. First published 1895.

Carroll, Lewis. *Alice's Adventures in Wonderland.* New York: William Morrow and Co., Inc., 1992, pp. 1–2.

Casement, Patrick. *Learning from the Patient.* New York: Guilford Press, 1991.

Danticat, Edwidge. *Krik? Krak!* New York: Soho Press, 1991, p. 220.

Edelson, Marshall. "Telling and Enacting Stories in Psychoanalysis and Psychotherapy: Implications for Teaching Psychotherapy." In ed. Albert J. Solnit, Peter B. Neubauer, Samuel Abrams, and A. Scott Darling, *Psychoanalytic Study of the Child*, vol. 48. New Haven and London: Yale University Press, 1993, pp. 293–325.

Eiseley, Loren. *The Immense Journey.* New York: Vintage Books, 1946, pp. 47–48, 51, 54.

————. *The Night Country.* New York: Scribner, 1947, p. 138.

Eliot, T. S. "The Love Song of J. Alfred Prufrock." In *T. S. Eliot Selected Poems.* New York: Harcourt Brace, 1936, p. 12. First published 1917.

Erikson, Erik H. *Identity, Youth, and Crisis.* New York: Norton, 1968.

Freud, Anna. *The Ego and the Mechanisms of Defense.* New York: International Universities Press, 1966.

Freud, Sigmund. *The Interpretation of Dreams.* In ed. and trans. J. Strachey, *The Standard Edition of the Complete Psychological Works of Sigmund Freud,* vol. 4, p. 122. London: Hogarth Press, 1953. First published 1900.

————. *Two Principles of Mental Functioning.* In ed. and trans. J. Strachey, *The Standard Edition of the Complete Psychological Works of Sigmund Freud,* vol. 12, p. 222. London: Hogarth Press, 1958. First published 1911.

Joyce, James. "The Dead." In *Dubliners.* London: Bantam, 1990, pp. 145–46. First published 1914.

Kluckholn, Clyde, and Henry A. Murray. "Personality Formation: The Determinants." In ed. Clyde Kluckholn and H. A. Murray, with the collaboration of D. M. Schneider, *Personality in Nature, Society, and Culture,* 2nd ed. New York: Alfred A. Knopf, 1953, p. 53.

Kris, Ernst. "On Preconscious Mental Processes." In *Psychoanalytic Explorations in Art.* New York: International Universities Press, 1952, pp. 303–18.

Lewis, C. S. *The Lion, the Witch, and the Wardrobe.* London: Geoffrey Bles, 1950, pp. 10–11, 14, 23, 49–51, 150.

Loewald, Hans W. On the Therapeutic Action of Psycho-analysis. *International Journal of Psychoanalysis,* vol. 41, pp. 16–33, 1960.

Lu Chi. *Wen Fu: The Art of Writing.* Trans. Sam Hamill. Portland, Oregon: Breitenbush Books, 1987, pp. 12, 14, 26, 27. First published 261 A.D.

Mann, Thomas. *Death in Venice.* New York: Vintage International, 1989, pp. 4–5. First published 1936.

Mosley, Walter. "For Authors, Fragile Ideas Need Loving Every Day." In *Writers [On Writing], Collected Essays from the New York Times.* New York: Times Books, Henry Holt, 2001, pp. 161–64.

Nunberg, Herrmann. "The Synthetic Function of the Ego." In *Practice and Theory of Psychoanalysis*, vol. 1, pp. 120–36. New York: International Universities Press, 1948. First published 1931.

Saint-Exupéry, Antoine de. *The Little Prince*. New York: Harcourt, 1943, pp. 60–61.

Sassoon, Siegfried. *Collected Poems 1908–1956*. London: Faber and Faber, 1986.

Schafer, Roy. *The Analytic Attitude*. New York: Basic Books, 1983.

Shakespeare, William. *Hamlet*. In *Shakespeare: Four Great Tragedies*. New York: Signet Classic, 1998, p. 3. First published 1601.

Storr, Anthony. *The Art of Psychotherapy*, 2nd ed. New York: Routledge, 1979.

Suzuki, Shunryu. *Zen Mind, Beginner's Mind*. New York: Weatherhill, 1970, p. 21, 22.

Tagore, Rabindranath. "Unending Love." In *Rabindranath Tagore Selected Poems*. New York: Penguin Books, 1985, p. 49. First published 1890.

Waelder, Robert. "The Principle of Multiple Function: Observations on Over-determination." In *The Psychoanalytic Quarterly* vol. 5, 1 (January 1936): pp. 45–62.

Weiss, Joseph. *How Psychotherapy Works*. New York: Guilford Press, 1993.

Winnicott, Donald W. *Playing and Reality*. New York: Penguin Books, 1971.

Woolf, Virginia. *A Room of One's Own*. New York: Harcourt Brace Jovanovich, 1929, pp. 5, 18, 25, 53, 54, 71.

Yoshitsune Gokyohoko. *The Sakuteiki, The Secret Book of Japanese Gardens*, as cited in Erik Borja, *Zen Gardens*. London: Ward Lock, 1999, p. 60. First published in the twelfth century.

Index

countertransference and, 194, 195;
disappointment and, 128; dreams of,
233, 234, 235; expectations of, 98,
117, 118, 119, 128; expressions of
affect of, 238, 239, 240; fantasy and,
230–31; fees and, 96; first meeting
and, 52; freedom of expression and,
96; hope and, 117, 118, 119; initial
version and, 158, 159, 160, 161, 165;
inner life of, 53, 297; interpretations,
rejection of, 270; language, use of,
229; manner of, 217, 235, 236;
metaphors and symbols, use of, 227;
mindfulness and, 144, 179; painful
material, reaction to, 178; partial
surrender of, 129; physical aggression
and, 96; process and, 217, 241, 242,
243, 244, 245; self-awareness and, 94;
self-editing of, 237, 238; sexual
contact and, 96; termination and,
282, 283, 285; therapeutic match and,
115, 118; therapist, relationship
between, 90; transference and, 117,
118, 182, 183, 184, 185, 186, 187, 193;
treatment, views of, 116; trust and,
119; vagueness of, 236, 237
The Phantom of the Opera (play), 225
private practice: cancellation policies
and, 110, 111; clocks, placement of,
104, 105; fees and, 107, 108, 109, 110;
first appointments and, 110; food
and, 105, 106; furniture and, 103,
104; office space, sharing of, 106;
physical space and, 101, 102, 111;
privacy and, 103; referrals and, 106,
107; safety and, 102, 103; setting up
of, 100, 101; stable environment and,

102; telephones and, 105; transference
and, 103. See also therapists
process, 241; dreams and, 246
projection, 45, 71; projective
identification and, 45; reaction
formation and, 45; regression and, 45
projective identification, 71, 153
psychodynamic therapy, 1, 34, 214; as
active endeavor, 134; adaptation and,
13, 28, 30; aim of, 165, 216; anxiety
and, 37–38, 39; bias against, 15;
character and, 52; clinical neutrality
and, 198; complexity of, 15; conflict
and, 39, 51; constructive regression
and, 167; conversation, widening of,
212, 214; as craft, 11, 12, 14, 16, 17;
creativity and, 47; description of, 35;
development, psychology of, 36;
durability of, 17; ego and, 50;
fundamentals of, 11; history,
personal, importance of, 7; as
improvisational, 201; individual style,
of patient, 52; individual work
during, 29, 30; learning and, 73, 74;
length of, 16; making meaning and,
51; mind, conceptualization of, 7; as
mindful endeavor, 134; motivations
and, 35, 36; past, and memory, 36;
patient and therapist, relationship
between, 7; patients, internal world
of, 7, 8, 9, 21, 30; as process, 51;
professional identity and, 73;
psychoanalysis, roots in, 9;
psychotherapeutic frame and, 12, 13;
regression and, 36; role of, 13;
successful, criteria of, 12; summary
of, 295, 296, 297, 298; terms of, 14;

About the Authors

Angelica Kaner, Ph.D., is clinical psychologist and assistant clinical professor of psychiatry at Yale University School of Medicine. She is also a candidate at the Western New England Institute for Psychoanalysis. Dr. Kaner received her Ph.D. from the University of California, Berkeley. Her interests lie in the areas of migration, creativity, and the teaching and supervision of psychotherapy. She practices in New Haven, Connecticut.

Ernst Prelinger, Ph.D., is clinical psychologist in the private practice of psychodynamic psychotherapy in New Haven, Connecticut. A clinical professor of psychology and psychiatry at Yale University School of Medicine, he is also a member of the faculty at the Western New England Institute for Psychoanalysis. His special interests lie in teaching and supervising psychotherapists in training, the study of processes of identity formation, and the theory of aggression. He lives in rural Connecticut.